CONTESTING LEGITIMACY *in* CHILE

CONTESTING
LEGITIMACY *in* CHILE

Familial Ideals, Citizenship, and Political Struggle, 1970–1990

Gwynn Thomas

THE PENNSYLVANIA STATE UNIVERSITY PRESS
UNIVERSITY PARK, PENNSYLVANIA

Library of Congress Cataloging-in-Publication Data

Thomas, Gwynn, 1972–
Contesting legitimacy in Chile : familial ideals, citizenship,
and political struggle, 1970–1990 / Gwynn Thomas.
p.   cm.
Includes bibliographical references and index.
Summary: "Examines the role in Chilean politics during the
1970s and 1980s of cultural beliefs and values surrounding
the family. Draws on election propaganda, political
speeches, press releases, public service campaigns,
magazines, newspaper articles, and televised political
advertisements"—Provided by publisher.
ISBN 978-0-271-04848-2 (cloth : alk. paper)
ISBN 978-0-271-04849-9 (pbk. : alk. paper)
1. Political culture—Chile—History—20th century.
2. Families—Political aspects—Chile—History—
20th century.
3. Legitimacy of governments—Chile—History—20th century.
4. Chile—Politics and government—1970–1973.
5. Chile—Politics and government—1973–1988.
I. Title.

JL2631.T49 2011
983.06'5—dc22
2010048480

The Pennsylvania State University Press is a member of the
Association of American University Presses.

It is the policy of The Pennsylvania State University Press to
use acid-free paper. Publications on uncoated stock satisfy the
minimum requirements of American National Standard for
Information Sciences—Permanence of Paper for Printed
Library Material, ANSI Z39.48–1992.

FOR *Tim*

CONTENTS

FIGURES

ACKNOWLEDGMENTS

I began this project because I was captivated by how politics is often constituted through a language of family. Thus it seems fitting that my understanding of Chilean politics is intertwined with the personal and professional relationships that developed through researching and writing this book. First, I would like to thank my mentors at the University of Wisconsin, Madison, who gave me initial guidance and support. Florencia Mallon was a generous guide to Chilean history and culture, introducing me to Chile through her classes and giving me my first opportunity to visit Chile when I accompanied her and a group of fellow graduate students to southern Chile. Aili Tripp shared her insights into women's movements and gender politics, including much-appreciated advice on navigating the politics of studying gender in political science. I also benefited from the insightful suggestions and analysis of Gina Sapiro, Michael Schatzberg, and David Leheny. Finally, I was extremely lucky to have had Leigh Payne shepherding me through the initial research and writing. She always provided astute and thought-provoking feedback and has been a generous mentor and friend.

Many of the strengths of this work are based on the invaluable suggestions of a number of excellent Chilean scholars with whom I have had the privilege of working. My understanding of Chilean politics and culture has been shaped by my ongoing conversations with Margaret Power. She has been a generous reader of multiple drafts, and her insightful comments have greatly improved the historical grounding and analytical strengths of the current book. I would also like to thank Julie Monteleone, Claudia Mora, Patricia Richards, Marcela Ríos Tobar, and Susan Franceschet for our ongoing conversations about gender and politics in Chile, which luckily have often taken place over glasses of Chilean wine or coffee at Tavelli. I was also fortunate to have Katherine Hite as a reviewer at Penn State University Press. Her careful and astute suggestions provided guidance for many of the final revisions. My evolving understanding of familial influences on politics and policies was shaped in conversations with Patty Strach, Julie Novkov, Priscilla Yamin, and Kathleen Sullivan.

I have found a welcoming environment at the University at Buffalo, SUNY. I would like to thank a number of colleagues who have read chapters and provided feedback at critical moments, particularly Gail Radford, Patricia Mazón, Claire Schen, Rachel Ablow, and Greg Dimitriadis. Lynn Mather, as the director of the Baldy Center for Law and Social Policy, and Margarita Vargas, as the co-director of the Gender Institute, arranged a wonderful book manuscript workshop where a draft of the manuscript was read and discussed by the Chilean experts Philip Oxhorn and Karin Rosemblatt along with my Buffalo colleagues Elaine Howard Ecklund, Gregg Johnson, Claude Welch, Piya Pangsapa, Hal Langfur, and Sue Mangold. My work benefited greatly from our discussion, especially the perceptive and generous commentary of Philip and Karin. Their suggestions proved invaluable at a critical stage. Karin provided another round of excellent suggestions when she later reviewed the manuscript for Penn State Press. It has been a real pleasure working with Sandy Thatcher, Kendra Boileau, and the team at Penn State Press. I would also like to acknowledge that earlier versions of parts of chapter 2 and chapter 4 will appear in my article "The Legacies of Patrimonial Patriarchalism: Contesting Political Legitimacy in Allende's Chile," in *The Annals of the American Academy of Political and Social Science*, vol. 636 (2011).

My analysis of Chilean culture and discourse also required material support. The initial research was funded by a generous grant from the Social Science Research Council and a University of Wisconsin, Madison, Global Studies Scholarship supported by the John D. and Catherine T. MacArthur Foundation. Teresa Valdés and Mirta Monroy at FLACSO Chile provided a welcoming space in Santiago during my second research trip. At the University at Buffalo, grants provided by the Baldy Center for Law and Social Policy, the Gender Institute, and the College of Arts and Sciences provided continuing support for subsequent research. I received a Nuala McGann Drescher Award from the State University of New York that provided a semester teaching release and allowed me to finish my final revisions.

In Chile, my research depended on the generosity of many everyday Chileans who often went above and beyond their duties to help a "gringa" researcher. I owe a special thanks to the staff at the National Library, the Congressional Library, Isis International in Chile, the newspaper clipping archives at the Pontificia Universidad Católica de Chile, and the media archive in the Moneda. Cristobal Marín, then at Fundación Chile, shared his copies of "Somos Milliones" and insights into Chile's media. The Fundación de Documentación y Archivo de la Vicaría de la Solidaridad has preserved an amazing archive of documents related to their involvement with the social movements against the military government. I thank them for their help in my research and their permission to reproduce the images relating to the AFDD and *Solidaridad*.

Finally, I owe more than I can say to my friends and family. Elaine Howard Ecklund has provided intellectual support, encouragement, and many words of wisdom on how to write, finish, and publish a book. Melinda Adams, Stefanie Nanes, Sarah Peterson, Ruth Mack, Mariella Bacigalupo, and Christine Hentz have provided me with welcome breaks through conversation and good meals. In Chile, Ximena Velasco opened her home to me, helped me to navigate Chilean culture, taught me to make pisco sours, and has participated in endless conversations full of political insights. She is the heart of my Chilean family, which now includes Clemente Velasco, Paolo Hevia, Vivi Hevia, and Magaly Ortiz.

I would not have found the energy and strength for this project without my family. They were a constant source of strength during this process. My sister, Blythe, reminded me to stay healthy and happy as well as productive. My mother and father—Joann and John Thomas—have kept me grounded and provided unwavering support and faith in my abilities. They also made sure I had a supply of Copper River salmon to keep me from missing my family in Alaska when my scholarship took me far from home. Finally, this book could not have been completed without the support of my husband, Tim Dun. His contributions—intellectual, material, and emotional—are too numerous to specify. Suffice it to say that I am blessed to be sharing his life.

ABBREVIATIONS

AFDD	Agrupación de Familiares de Detenidos Desaparecidos (Association of Relatives of the Detained Disappeared)
CEMA-Chile	Mothers' Centers (Centros de Madres–Chile)
CODE	Democratic Confederation (La Confederación de la Democracia)
ENU	National Unified School (Escuela Nacional Unificada)
EPF	Feminine Power (El Poder Femenino)
JAP	Juntas de Abastecimiento y Precio (Price and Supply Control Committees)
MOMUPO	Movimiento de Mujeres Pobladoras (Movement of Popular Women)
PC	Communist Party (Partido Comunista)
PDC	Christian Democratic Party (Partido Demócrata Cristiano)
PN	National Party (Partido Nacional)
PR	Radical Party (Partido Radical)
PS	Socialist Party (Partido Socialista)
SNM	National Secretariat of Women (Secretaría Nacional de la Mujer)
UP	Unidad Popular (Popular Unity)

★ ONE ★

SEEING THE POLITICAL THROUGH THE FAMILIAL

In March 2000, I witnessed one of the most dramatic moments in recent Chilean politics—Augusto Pinochet returned to Chile from London after avoiding extradition to Spain on charges of state terrorism. Pinochet's return reignited deep political divides over competing interpretations of both the presidency of Salvador Allende (1970–73) and Pinochet's subsequent military dictatorship (1973–90). Through the gray fall weather, I watched as rival groups of protestors gathered and clashed outside the Chilean Supreme Court, which was hearing arguments over whether to revoke Pinochet's political immunity and put him on trial for the human rights abuses committed during his regime. Before my eyes, political events that I had been studying as history came to life as Chileans took to the streets to give voice to the deeply held political beliefs that had dominated the last thirty years of the nation's contentious history. Separated by police barricades, ardent demonstrators from opposite sides of the political divide adamantly expressed their radically opposing views about Pinochet, the meaning of his government, and his appropriate place in Chilean society and history.

The Agrupación de Familiares de Detenidos Desaparecidos (Association of Relatives of the Detained Disappeared, AFDD)—a human rights group formed after the 1973 military coup and still one of the most active organizations in Chile—assembled on one side of the Supreme Court's front courtyard. They came carrying the now emblematic black-and-white photos of their missing husbands, sons, brothers, daughters, wives, and sisters. Original members, mostly older women, were joined by a wide cross-section of Chileans, young and old, men and women. The AFDD and its supporters called Pinochet a murderer and argued that he was ultimately responsible for the human rights abuses committed by the military. They demanded justice for the disappearances and deaths perpetrated by Pinochet's government against their families. They hoped that a Supreme Court decision allowing him to be tried for human rights abuses would finally force all sectors of Chilean society to officially recognize Pinochet's crimes.

Pinochetistas gathered on the other side of the courtyard. These committed supporters of Pinochet revered him as the aging patriarch of the Chilean nation, and they condemned Great Britain and Spain for criminalizing the behavior of a man they viewed as Chile's savior. The Pinochetistas believed that Pinochet and his military government had saved their families by restoring order and prosperity to a chaotic and violent situation. These committed supporters called him "their beloved grandfather," claiming that he was a true Chilean patriot and a great leader. For Pinochetistas, Pinochet was not the stern military commander who hid his face behind dark glasses, but—as portrayed by the posters they carried—a benevolent patriarch with kindly blue eyes. As with the AFDD, many of the original Pinochetistas were older women, but the current demonstrations included both men and women covering a wide range of ages. They wanted the Supreme Court to acquit Pinochet, thereby recognizing his role in protecting Chile through what they believe was one of its darkest hours.

For many observers, these protests were simply another example of the stark political differences that have fueled Chile's recent history of intense conflict. I was fascinated, however, not by the expected differences in political beliefs and passions between the two groups but by the surprising number of similarities. As I walked slowly between the two groups, the unexpected parallels in the language and images used by each demanded my attention. To explain their political arguments about why they either supported or abhorred Pinochet, both sides consistently referenced similar beliefs about the importance of family, familial identities, and the relationship of the family to the state.

This personal experience changed the focus of my research as a scholar. I began to ask: Why would both the Pinochetistas and the AFDD claim that threats to their families drove them to mobilize? How do different types of political actors use beliefs about the family as a resource in the pursuit of their political goals? Were similar invocations of familial beliefs dependent on the dominance of women as activists? Why was familial welfare the criterion used by both groups to judge Pinochet? How were appeals to family found in the groups' language and images used to frame and justify political struggle? What did these uses reveal about the cultural beliefs that define the political legitimacy of different governments? How are familial beliefs used to understand the relationship between states and citizens?

My initial fascination with the similarities of familial invocations in the images and rhetoric surrounding Pinochet's return broadened into a much larger inquiry into the importance of familial beliefs within political conflicts, especially around issues of governmental legitimacy and citizen dissent. As I delved deeper, I discovered that appeals to the importance of the family and its welfare were found not only in the clashes over Pinochet's rule but also in the previous political conflicts that had led to the overthrow of President Salvador Allende's Socialist government in 1973. Portraying Allende and his government as threatening the well-being of Chilean families was a common refrain in the arguments of many anti-Allende groups as they sought to convince their fellow citizens of the illegitimacy of Allende's government and to justify his overthrow. During these previous struggles, the use of familial beliefs to explain and defend specific political actions also was not limited to one political faction.

My ongoing research into Chile's contested political history continually revealed that political appeals grounded in beliefs about the importance of family cut across Chile's political divisions. Further, employing familial beliefs to justify political action and to frame political arguments was not limited by the gender of the participants. Challenging conventional notions of how gender influences political action, both men and women who organized for and against Allende and Pinochet incorporated familial language and beliefs in their discursive strategies. Male political elites, particularly state leaders and governmental representatives, called on images of patriarchal fathers, while everyday Chilean men and women framed their demands through a language of family welfare and the importance of familial identities. Thus a language of familial beliefs was used in political struggles by both men and women, by actors associated with the state *and* those that mobilized from civil society to protest the state, as well as those associated with the right, the center, and the left. Finally, I became convinced that these appeals to family should not be seen as only rhetorical flourishes or instrumental invocations designed to appeal to citizens' emotional attachments. Instead, they provided new and important insights into the larger role of gender ideology in understanding and justifying the power relations among states, political leaders, and citizens.

Reframing Chile's Political Struggles: A Familial Lens

This book makes the deceptively simple claim that family permeates politics. My analysis of Chilean politics reveals that normative ideals about what the family is or should be, the roles and responsibilities of members of the family, and the proper relationships between the family and the state, represent a major, though understudied, aspect of politics. Idealized relationships among families and between families and other institutions provide important symbolic and discursive resources for political actors. These familial beliefs are one source of the cultural norms, principles, and ideologies that govern the relationships between states and their citizens, and thus are integral to what George Steinmetz has called the "state/culture" nexus.[1] As Lynne Haney and Lisa Pollard note, familial beliefs are essential to how "power relations are imagined, secured, and reformed" within political communities.[2]

In the chapters that follow, I analyze the political conflicts that surrounded the election and demise of Allende's social democracy (1970–73), the installation and maintenance of Pinochet's military dictatorship (1973–90), and finally the transition back to democratic rule (1988–90), all through the lens of the family. This unique historical sequence provides the opportunity to examine the political uses of the family during political conflicts faced by radically different types of governments and their ideologically diverse civil society opponents. I compare the uses of familial beliefs by an elected socialist-leaning government and a conservative military dictatorship, along with the societal opposition to each. During extensive archival research conducted over sixteen months of fieldwork, I analyzed public political speech, including election propaganda, political speeches, congressional hearings, public service campaigns, magazines, newspapers, and televised political advertisements. My examination reveals that Chile's intense political debates during these years often took place in a common language of shared cultural views about family.

1. Steinmetz argues that scholars across disciplines have promoted a "general assertion of the constitutive role of culture" in the development processes of states, and have turned increasingly to analyzing the state as an entity that is embedded within cultural beliefs and that is shaped and in turns shapes culture. See Steinmetz, "Introduction," 2. This turn has been particularly influential in Latin American history, where scholars have both argued for the continuing need to analyze state development and evidenced a willingness to examine the state/culture nexus, particularly as it relates to gender, race, and nationalism. See Dore and Molyneux, *Hidden Histories*; Joseph and Nugent, *Everyday Forms of State Formation*; Joseph, *Reclaiming the Political*; and Appelbaum, Macpherson, and Rosemblatt, *Race and Nation*.

2. Haney and Pollard, "Introduction," 5. Haney and Pollard develop the term *familialism* to discuss the relationship between state and family. Analogous to the term *maternalism* but with a broader purview, familialism gets at the multiple uses of idealized notions of the family within the development of states and political regimes. Familialism is designed to encompass both discursive and material practices by states and individuals around the family. While I agree with Haney and Pollard's arguments about the importance of familial ideals, I found the term *familialism* too broad to capture the nuanced uses of family that I describe through the four categories of my analytical framework (discussed below).

Based on this research, I argue that political leaders and mobilized citizens turned to familial beliefs to provide the language, metaphors, symbols, and images that framed their political appeals, justified their political actions, and made sense of larger political events. While the myriad invocations of the family by political actors during these struggles are often ignored by scholars, actually paying attention to the discursive uses of familial beliefs by both political actors and ordinary citizens provides a unique lens onto how Chileans sought to frame, interpret, and make sense of these conflicts. Political leaders used specific beliefs about the relationship of the family and the state in their attempts to gain control of the state, to legitimate their political projects, and to criticize their opponents. In turn, citizens relied on familial beliefs and their own familial identities to demand governmental attention, to justify societal mobilization, and to create a public space from which to speak out against political leaders. Actors from across the political spectrum turned to familial beliefs as they struggled over how to assess the legitimacy of their government, explain their political actions, and claim their political voice. Given the strength of Chile's political conflicts, my analysis reveals a surprisingly strong political consensus built around familial beliefs. This consensus was fundamental in shaping Chile's political struggles.

The specifically political uses of family analyzed in this book are embedded within a set of underlying assumptions about what a family is, who its members are, and the roles members play. In Chilean politics, it was the normative ideal of the traditional family—a family grounded in the marriage of a man and a woman, the children that are the product of this union, and the kin relationships produced by the marriage and children—that dominated the *political* uses of family. It was not that Chileans denied the existence of different family forms, such as single-parent households, but that these types of family life were often seen as nonnormative and problematic. Indeed, debates between different political parties in Chile often reflected deep differences over what caused nontraditional families and what the appropriate response from the state should be. These debates, however, rested on a broad consensus that the existence of nontraditional families represented a political and social problem. The dominance of an idealized traditional family in Chile as the form most depicted and lauded in political discourse follows more general trends in Latin America. While recent scholarship has documented the multiplicity of familial relationships in Latin America, both historically as well as currently, the ideal of the traditional family continues to underpin social imaginings of the family and the power of familial beliefs in politics. Even today, the normative power of the idealized traditional family remains strong, although there is more positive recognition of nontraditional family forms.[3]

Certainly, all understandings of the family are situated within broader understandings of gender. The family in any society is one of the central institutions where the socially constructed meaning of gender roles, ideals of femininity and masculinity, and subjective gender identities are formed and contested. In the normative Chilean family, women are seen as wives/mothers who nurture the family and take care of the home, while men are husbands/fathers who provide material sustenance and discipline for the family. When actors incorporate specific familial beliefs as they pursue different political goals, they also both depend on and strengthen related beliefs about men and women.[4] During the time under study, Chilean political leaders sought to uphold the norm of the traditional family. Public adherence to idealized forms of family on the part of political elites could, and often did, exist alongside the failure of individual leaders to fully embody that ideal.[5] Analyzing the specific political uses of familial beliefs provides new insights into broader questions about how gender functions as a "primary way of signifying relationships of power" in Joan Scott's now famous phrase. In Chile, politics takes place not only on a field of gender, but specifically within the arena of family.[6]

Rethinking Chilean Politics Through a Familial Lens

Since the fall of Allende, scholars have tried to answer the following questions: Why did one of the most stable and established democracies in Latin America succumb to military rule? Further, given Chile's strong democratic traditions

3. For an excellent discussion of the dominance of the traditional family in Chile, see Delsing, "La familia," and "Sobre mitos y relatos." For a historical discussion, see Dore, "Holy Family." The investigation of alternative understandings of family held by different groups, while important, is beyond the scope of this study.

4. Dore and Molyneux, "Preface," x.

5. For example, Salvador Allende was widely seen as a "ladies' man," though this did not prevent him from presenting himself publicly as a devoted husband and father. Indeed, male marital infidelity exists within a broader context that sees men's sexual virility as an important part of masculine identity. Among leftist men, a refusal to conform to the norm of familial and marital solidarity was part of the portrayal of a rebellious, subversive masculinity. See Mallon, "*Barbudos*, Warriors, and *Rotos*." See also Rosemblatt, *Gendered Compromises*; Tinsman, *Partners in Conflict*; and Klubock, *Contested Communities*, for additional discussions on how working-class and campesino men both embraced and resisted attempts to promote sexual monogamy within marriage.

6. Scott, "Gender," 1067, 1074. I see paying attention to the familial as another way of getting at larger questions of gender, one that avoids a tendency to treat women and gender as synonymous.

and the growth of large-scale societal resistance, how was Pinochet able to maintain power for seventeen years?[7] Answering these questions has not only dominated the literature on Chile but also influenced larger bodies of work that examine the rise and fall of both democratic and authoritarian regimes during the latter half of the twentieth century.[8] This scholarship has produced important insights into the role of class struggle, stages of economic development, political ideologies, institutional structures, and political elites in the upheavals of Chile. As noted by the historian Steve Stern, however, this literature has not produced many insights into the central cultural beliefs of Chile that supported "the making and unmaking of political and cultural legitimacy" during the dramatic transitions between democratic and authoritarian rule.[9]

Scholarship examining the twenty years under study here (1970–90) is often divided into three discrete areas of investigation: (1) the rise and fall of Allende's democratic government (1970–73); (2) the rise and consolidation of military authoritarian rule (1973–88); and (3) the opposition to military rule and transition back to democracy (1975–90). For all three periods, central questions driving research focus on explaining the causes of Chile's political conflicts and the success or failure of different types of governments and political leaders in managing these conflicts. Across all three areas, more attention has been given to Chile's political differences than its sources of consensus. For example, in explaining the fall of Allende, the role of class divisions has been frequently singled out. During the 1960s and 1970s, the working class increased its political participation and demands, as did the more mobilized campesinos and a growing number of urban shantytown dwellers.[10] In part, these demands were promoted by Chile's political parties of the center (the Christian Democratic

7. Seventeen years greatly exceeds the length of authoritarian rule in Argentina (1976–84) and Uruguay (1973–85). Brazil's military government (1964–85) lasted longer, but the military government reopened spaces—admittedly narrow—for opposition politics through an official opposition party as part of a very lengthy transition process. The military governments of Brazil, Argentina, and Uruguay also ruled through a series of military juntas and bureaucratic institutions that never personalized power to the extent that Pinochet did in Chile.

8. See, for example, Linz and Stepan, *Breakdown of Democratic Regimes*; Valenzuela and Valenzuela, *Military Rule in Chile*; Drake and Jakšić, *Struggle for Democracy*; O'Donnell, Schmitter, and Whitehead, *Transitions from Authoritarian Rule*; and Remmer, *Military Rule in Latin America*, as well as many books cited below.

9. Stern, *Battling for Hearts and Minds*, xx. Stern's trilogy *The Memory Box of Pinochet's Chile* examines how Chileans continue to struggle over how to remember and make sense of the experience of a military dictatorship and the human rights abuses it committed. The three volumes cover the period from the coup in 1973 to Pinochet's death in 2006.

10. For the role of class divisions, see Stallings, *Class Conflict*; for the role of campesinos and agricultural reform, see Loveman, *Struggle in the Countryside*; for the role of urban movements, see Schneider, *Shantytown Protest*, and Oxhorn, *Organizing Civil Society*.

Party) and the left (the Socialist Party and the Communist Party) in their bid to transform this increasing participation into bases of political power.

According to scholars, rising political demands on the part of previously marginalized groups and the growth of the political left threatened Chile's traditional political and economic elite. As conflict mounted, deep ideological divides between political parties in Chile, especially concerning the role of the state in economic development and the proper place of capitalism, became increasingly important.[11] Traditional institutional mechanisms for political compromise failed as Chile's political right and members of the elite became increasingly willing to support military intervention to protect their interests. From this perspective, it was the failure on the part of political leaders—first, to effectively manage the growing societal demands of new groups, and second, to make the necessary political compromises—that eventually led to the breakdown.[12]

If the causes of conflict were often the focus of studies surrounding the fall of Allende, scholarship on the second period has centered on explaining how Pinochet managed to control sources of conflict in such a way as to create a stable and enduring military regime. Given Chile's past political tradition of democratic governance, the stability and durability of Pinochet's rule is especially puzzling for scholars. Pinochet was able to maintain control even during periods of deep economic turmoil and in the face of a wave of massive social mobilization in the early 1980s. Pinochet's ability to weather these crises defied political theories that posited economic success as the reason behind authoritarian stability.[13] Other scholars have focused on Pinochet's consolidation of control over the army and the police and his use of state terror—which included such human rights abuses as mass detention, exile, torture, and the practice of disappearing and killing political opponents—as important explanatory factors. Pinochet's ability to maintain the political support of Chile's upper classes, which was partially based on the implementation of neoliberal economic policies, is also seen as an important part of the stability of his rule.[14]

Finally, when analyzing the reasons for the return of democracy, scholars are divided over where to locate the conflict aimed against military rule and which

---

11. Oppenheim, *Politics in Chile*.
12. For an analysis that focuses specifically on the inability of the political parties and the larger system to forge the necessary compromises, see Valenzuela, *Breakdown of Democratic Regimes*.
13. Przeworski, "Some Problems."
14. See, for example, Arriagada, *Pinochet*; the contributions to "Part I: The Regime's Supporters" in Drake and Jakšić, *Struggle for Democracy*; and Oppenheim, *Politics in Chile*, for a general discussion of these different factors.

groups created the most impetus for societal change. Many point to the importance of the actions of political elites and the opposition to create the political "pacts" that undergirded the transition.[15] Others give more weight to the role of a resurgent civil society, highlighting the role of multiple social movements—women, students, *pobladores*, human rights activists, and unions—in bringing democracy back to Chile.[16]

This literature, while theoretically and empirically rich, has not produced many analytical frameworks that seek to integrate all three periods.[17] The picture of Chile that emerges from these works is that of a political community riven by opposition and disagreement. My book, however, shows how Chile's deep political conflicts were also shaped by *shared* political values and beliefs that were present throughout the entire period. To fully understand the political processes involved in the struggles over Allende's and Pinochet's governments, analyzing the beliefs that opposing political actors hold in common is as important as tracing the sources of division and conflict. Chile's dramatic and contentious politics were often built on shared assumptions about the relationship between the family and the state that helped hold Chile together as a political community even during periods of intense political upheaval.

Paying attention to how familial beliefs were incorporated into Chile's political conflicts reveals that underneath the very real differences among classes, political parties, groups, and individuals, there were also shared beliefs about

15. O'Donnell, Schmitter, and Whitehead's series of edited collections, *Transitions from Authoritarian Rule*, particularly the conclusions reached by O'Donnell and Schmitter in the *Tentative Conclusions* volume, are probably the classic texts that make this argument. See, as well, Di Palma, *To Craft Democracies*. Karl and Schmitter have argued that Chile represents a mixed case; in "Modes of Transition in Southern and Eastern Europe and South and Central America," they claim that when Pinochet lost the 1988 plebiscite he was forced to negotiate with the reemerging political elites, thereby producing a pacted transition. See also Karl, "Dilemmas of Democratization." In "Modes of Transition and Democratization," Munck and Leff argue that Chile represents a case where the impetus for change originated outside the regime, and that Pinochet's lack of willingness to negotiate with oppositional elites meant that the opposition needed a broad-based coalition in order to push for change. Pinochet's ability to shape the transition, however, helped maintain the power of the incumbent elite, and thus Chile developed as a restricted democracy based on elite competition.

16. For a greater focus on the importance of social movements in the transition to democracy, see Schneider, *Shantytown Protest*; Chuchryk, "Feminist Anti-authoritarian Politics"; and the articles on Pinochet's opposition in Drake and Jakšić, *Struggle for Democracy*. *Pobladores* are Chileans from the lower and working classes who live in the urban neighborhoods of Santiago called *poblaciones*.

17. Oppenheim's *Politics in Chile* is an exception, as she traces the political importance of development projects during these periods. But her work maintains its focus on the sources of conflict. In *Why Women Protest*, Baldez also examines similarities, but in the narrower terms of explaining the mobilization and success of women's movements on the right and the left under Allende and Pinochet.

the importance of the family as a social institution, the obligation of the state to protect and promote family welfare, and the importance of familial roles and responsibilities to individual Chileans. These shared beliefs provided a common language for bitter opponents, set the parameters of the debate, served as the basis for a set of criteria used by both sides to judge political claims, and provided an understanding around what might lead to and justify political action. In other words, familial beliefs represented a set of underlying shared assumptions on which both conflict and consensus were built.

Gendering Transitions

Using a familial framework to analyze political conflicts also reveals the larger importance of gender ideology during the shifts between democratic and authoritarian forms of government. The focus on the historical uniqueness of these processes has sometimes prevented the incorporation of recent gender scholarship, mostly in history and sociology, which explores how the cultural and political legitimacy of different forms of government is built on beliefs about the family. In Latin America, scholars have shown how the Spanish system of colonial rule relied on patriarchal understandings of familial authority to justify the larger cultural legitimacy of the hierarchy of colonial rule. While the new Latin American states created after the nineteenth-century wars of independence rejected the rule of the Spanish monarchy, the new ruling elite did not reject cultural connections between familial and political authority.[18] Elite male political leaders continued to rely on familial metaphors and models to help provide cultural legitimacy for the new nation-states they were creating. This pattern continued throughout the twentieth century, as familial beliefs were mobilized to provide political justifications for the creation of modern welfare states.[19]

But these insights into the importance of familial beliefs in justifying different types of state structures have been mostly ignored by scholars seeking

18. I discuss this literature in depth in chapter 2.
19. The literature on gender and the welfare state is quite large and beyond the scope of this introduction. Much of this work, however, focuses on motherhood and maternalist discourses, and does not look at the family in its own right. For an overview and comparative perspective, see Koven and Michel, *Mothers of a New World*. For an in-depth analysis of women's participation in the creation of the U.S. welfare state, see Skocpol, *Protecting Soldiers and Mothers*; Kornbluh, "New Literature on Gender"; and Gordon, *Pitied but Not Entitled*. A recent article that focuses more specifically on the family (as opposed to simply women) and provides an extensive review is Orloff, "Markets Not States?"

to understand the major political shifts between democracy and authoritarianism that dominated the history of many Latin American countries during the late twentieth century. Unlike the case regarding earlier historical periods, analyses of the underlying cultural norms, including gender beliefs, that provide the discursive and ideological resources for the construction of different types of claims about political legitimacy have been few and far between. True, scholarly interest in issues of gender has not been completely absent from the larger discussions about the transitions between democratic and authoritarian governments in Latin America. But the majority of this research focuses specifically on the importance of women as political actors in the social movements that dominated the struggles against authoritarian governments. This literature has greatly expanded our knowledge about why women mobilize, the processes of mobilization for women, and how the relationship between women's movements and the larger political opportunity structures of both authoritarian governments and the transitions back to democratic rule shaped not only women's continued political participation but also the type of democratic institutions that evolved.[20] This research has also highlighted the importance of motherhood as a mobilizing identity for women, as a justification for women's political activism, and as a way to legitimate women's particular political claims.[21]

This focus on women as actors, however, has sometimes obscured how women's movements operate within larger conceptualizations of politics understood through familial beliefs. Certainly, many scholars have shown how women wielded the symbolic power of the image of grieving mothers to stand up to military governments that embraced patriarchal understandings of masculine power. Feminist scholars also explored how military governments partly rested their political power on connections between the familial authority of men and the political power of presidents and generals.[22] But military governments certainly did not create these patriarchal beliefs. Often overlooked in current scholarship is the continuity in the connections between personal and political

20. See Alvarez, *Engineering Democracy*; Baldez, *Why Women Protest*; Franceschet, *Women and Politics in Chile*; and Jaquette, *Women's Movement* (1989/1994).

21. See particularly Alvarez, *Engendering Democracy*, and Bayard de Volo, *Mothers of Heroes and Martyrs*.

22. Taylor has written probably the most developed analysis of the symbolic importance of patriarchal beliefs in justifying military rule in Latin America in her work on Argentina, *Disappearing Acts*. Chilean feminist scholars were particularly insightful in criticizing how patriarchal ideology helped to maintain Pinochet's political rule. See especially Bunster, "Watch Out for the Little Nazi Man," and Valenzuela and Marshall, *La mujer y el gobierno militar*.

patriarchal norms both before and after military rule. Thus existing scholarship more often highlights how the "personal is political" for the women whose activism shaped their countries' politics

By contrast, I am interested in how the "political is personal." Throughout this book, I focus on the mobilization of familial beliefs, rather than either women's mobilization as political actors or the use of maternalism as a political identity. My analysis shows how understandings about the relationship between the familial and the political provide the cultural resources that both men and women use to justify their political actions and to judge the legitimacy of political leaders and governments. This book reveals how familial beliefs formed one of the conceptual frameworks through which the major political shifts between democracy and authoritarianism were debated and understood.

Developing a Familial Framework for Analyzing Politics

In my analysis, I examine the ways in which family was invoked by political leaders and mobilized citizens, and how these uses depended on specific historical understandings of the responsibilities of the state, political leaders, and citizens. I found that the discourses of Chile's political conflicts revealed patterns of consistent and widespread uses of familial beliefs by actors from across the political spectrum. My research into the relationship between the familial and the political became the basis for an innovative conceptual framework consisting of four interrelated analytical categories: *Familial State, Familial Nation, Patriarchal Leader,* and *Militant Families.* These analytic categories capture the four dominant ways that familial beliefs were invoked in political conflicts: (1) how familial beliefs shaped the fundamental responsibilities assigned to the state (Familial State); (2) the role of family in the metaphorical understanding of nation (Familial Nation); (3) how familial beliefs helped define the roles and responsibilities of political leaders, most often the president (Patriarchal Leader); and (4) the role of familial beliefs in shaping citizens' political identities and justifications for political action (Militant Families). In the next chapter, I set the context by examining the historical development of the political and familial beliefs summarized in these four categories. In the following five empirical chapters, I deploy these categories to analyze the patterns of familial uses in defining the political contests and conflicts during the election of Salvador Allende (chap. 3); the conflicts over his presidency, which culminated in the military coup (chap. 4); the attempts by Pinochet to justify the military government (chap. 5); the growth of the opposition (chap. 6); and the transition back to democratic rule (chap. 7).

The Familial State and Nation

My analytical framework is grounded in an interconnected set of widely shared cultural views about family and politics, even though each category seeks to capture one specific use of the family. The Familial State shows the centrality of the political belief that the state, regardless of the government in power, has a responsibility to protect and to provide for the family.[23] Widespread political consensus around this basic understanding of the state can be found in the public statements of both political elites and everyday citizens from across the political spectrum. This political consensus positions the ideals of the Familial State as a central discourse in defining what are seen as the fundamental responsibilities of the state toward society, and therefore what justifies political rule. By drawing on this general understanding of the relationship between the state and the family, political actors can craft claims about the success or

23. For the purposes of this study, I find a common distinction between the state and the government useful for analytical clarity. Drawing from Molyneux's excellent discussion, "States can be defined as a set of coercive and administrative institutions that have as their object the exercise of various forms of power. They claim control over territory and rule through a combination of coercion and consent." States also "generate and disseminate accounts of national interests, seeking to define the boundaries and meanings of nationhood and citizenship." State institutions include armies and police for securing public order and international security, institutions that oversee the welfare apparatus of modern states (education, pensions, health care), the codes of laws and their enforcement, financial and economic structures such as central banks, and the "political apparatus of national and local governments." Molyneux, "Twentieth-Century State Formations," 37.

The state therefore encompasses governments that here refer to the specific leader, party, or coalition of parties currently in charge of the state. Even during the intense political conflicts over the governmental legitimacy of Allende or Pinochet, most Chileans retained an idea of the Chilean state as separate from either of these two governments. Proponents and opponents on both sides routinely judged Allende and Pinochet by how well or poorly their governments were fulfilling larger expectations about the state, regardless of the radical difference in how they had assumed political power. These differences had important political consequences for each government in terms of the types of arguments that each mobilized to justify their control of the political power of the state. Pinochet's government had to take into account that democratic means were considered a more legitimate process for taking power. But if military intervention had been considered always—in all cases, and by all Chileans—illegitimate, then it is unlikely that Pinochet would have received the long-term popular support that he did. In addition, the fact that Allende had been democratically elected did not guarantee his political legitimacy. This book examines the importance of family beliefs in the attempts by both of these governments to craft defenses of their legitimacy based on larger cultural beliefs about the goals and ends of the state.

failure of current political leaders and governments. Chileans of all political persuasions judged their leaders' performance in terms of familial welfare. Both political leaders and citizens turned to the beliefs of the Familial State in crafting arguments about the political legitimacy of governments and political leaders. The Familial State helps us make sense of how claims about the political legitimacy of Allende and Pinochet, as the leaders of two very different governments, were framed and debated by both their supporters and their detractors. Political actors from across Chile's ideological spectrum invoked the beliefs of the Familial State in pursuing their political goals.

Chilean political parties, however, have often differed over the relative importance of protecting versus providing for families, and these differences were a source of political conflict. In general, the Chilean left more often framed familial welfare in terms of economic and material concerns, while the Chilean right often placed more emphasis on issues of protecting both the physical and moral safety of Chileans. The Christian Democrats, who occupied a centrist position, often spoke in a language that combined issues of economic security, traditional values, and physical safety. But these differences of emphasis represent trends rather than absolute positions. Many members of the Chilean left also took a strong moral stand, informed by socialist principles, on the importance of specific forms of families and appropriate behavior within the family.[24] Participants from all political persuasions sometimes defined familial welfare as being about economic, physical, and spiritual provisions.

In this book, I focus on how claims about the Familial State were used by Chileans in contests over political power, such as during elections and in periods of social mobilization. Chileans repeatedly invoked familial welfare as a criterion by which to judge the political legitimacy of their governments and to justify political actions against these governments. I document how the conflicts over Allende and his government were often framed through invocations of the Familial State. As political conflict deepened and Chileans mobilized onto the streets, appeals to the central beliefs of the Familial State intensified. Allende's political opponents claimed that he had not fulfilled the duty of the Chilean government to protect and provide for Chilean families, thus justifying their political actions against his government. Allende and his supporters attempted to counter these positions by promoting their own views of familial welfare and documenting their support for Chile's "proletarian families."

The Familial State was also used to frame political arguments that justified

24. Rosemblatt, "What We Can Reclaim."

military intervention and the establishment of a military government. After the coup, the military and Pinochet drew on the Familial State to legitimize the decision to take and to keep political power. Pinochet and his supporters embraced the idea that familial welfare (defined most often as protection) was a fundamental responsibility of the Chilean state and one that justified the establishment of their authoritarian government. But the family was a double-edged sword for Pinochet. A range of social movements quickly began to attack Pinochet by turning his own familial claims against him. Thus beliefs about the responsibility or duty of the state to families, as well as how family welfare is interpreted, can serve as an important resource for all political actors engaged in struggles over the legitimacy of a government. The ideals of the Familial State provide one conceptual framework through which people make sense of and judge the adequacy of their political leaders and governments.

The underlying claims of the Familial State are related to, and often strengthened by, the second category, the Familial Nation. This category examines the use of the family as a metaphor for the nation by both state and societal actors. Feminist scholars have persuasively argued that idealized understandings of family and familial relations are central to how the "imagined community" of nations is created.[25] Chilean political rhetoric from the time of independence until today is replete with invocations of the nation as a family, which has strengthened the belief in the familial responsibilities of the Chilean state found in the previous category. Beliefs about the importance of Chilean families as the basic unit of society, and the base on which the Chilean nation-state is built, strengthen the political tendency to conflate actual Chilean families and the metaphoric Chilean national family.

Political actors use the beliefs of the Familial Nation in struggles over where to draw national boundaries and to justify who is deserving of state protection. For example, Pinochet claimed that many of his political opponents were not "true" Chileans, and he argued that their views endangered the Chilean national family. Thus he used the family to help justify his treatment of political opponents. In the later transition to democracy, the idea of a national family was used by the groups that made up the opposition's political coalition, the Concertación,[26] to recreate a sense of national unity and to redraw

25. The classic treatment of gendered nationalism is Yuval-Davis, *Gender and Nation*. See also McClintock, *Imperial Leather*; Verdery, "From Parent-State"; and Kaplan, Alarcón, and Moallem, *Between Woman and Nation*.

26. The Concertación is the name of the center-left coalition that united to defeat Pinochet in the 1988 plebiscite and has served as Chile's elected government since 1990. I discuss the Concertación in more detail in chapter 7.

the boundaries of the Chilean nation to once again include those individuals vilified by the military government.

Patriarchal Leaders and Militant Families

The particular political uses described in Familial State and Familial Nation are based in the continuing importance of the family in defining and explaining the ultimate ends of the state, the duties and responsibilities of the state vis-à-vis its citizens, and the relationships that bind citizens to one another as part of imagined communities. Both political leaders and citizens incorporate these beliefs into their public political speech and use them as symbolic resources in their attempts to pursue their political goals. The remaining two categories capture how familial understandings of the nation-state promote particular types of claims by either political leaders or citizens. The category of Patriarchal Leader describes how beliefs about who political leaders are and what they should do are understood through familial relationships, particularly with positions occupied by men. The final category, Militant Families, captures how beliefs about the importance of family and familial roles define the duties of citizens and help to justify political action by citizens, including action against political leaders and governments.[27]

Patriarchal Leader describes the use of parental symbols, especially paternal ones, to illustrate a political leader's character and ability to govern. Many male political leaders in particular argued that being seen as a good father indicated a good leader. During the period analyzed, men dominated politics and so the familial ideal espoused in Chilean politics remained rooted in patriarchal understandings of the family. This category therefore represents the ways that familial beliefs helped define the expectations of male political leaders. My analysis examines how male political leaders, especially Allende and Pinochet, drew heavily on these beliefs to present themselves as the valiant protectors, stern patriarchs, and benevolent fathers of the Chilean national family.

Thus the Patriarchal Leader represents a popular use of the family in politics. When particular leaders invoke the familial beliefs found in the Patriarchal

---

27. In 2005, the sociologist Julia Adams published a fascinating book, titled *The Familial State*, on the importance of patrimonial political structures and cultural beliefs in understanding the rise and fall of the Dutch Republic in the seventeenth century. While I developed the name of this category without knowledge of her work, I find it interesting that we both noted the importance of family in defining ideas about the ultimate goals of the state in radically different contexts.

Leader category, it strengthens the tendency of Chileans to expect their leaders to act as "good fathers" and to hold those leaders accountable when they fail to meet these expectations. As with the Familial State, it is not without risks for political leaders to present themselves as the metaphorical fathers of their countries. They can be judged by how well or how poorly they are fulfilling the duties believed to be the basic responsibilities of a political father. Groups within Chile that were working in opposition to both Allende and Pinochet criticized both men for having failed to be "good fathers" and used this failure to justify calls for their removal from political power.

Militant Families analyzes how political actors use familial identities to explain their political involvement and what galvanizes them into political action. Chilean citizens routinely invoke the need to protect familial welfare, or claim to be acting in the interests of the family to justify engaging in political action. If political leaders are tasked with upholding the state's responsibilities to Chilean families, then Chilean citizens can turn to their own familial responsibilities as grounds to pressure those leaders. Chileans called on their familial identities as mothers, fathers, wives, husbands, sisters, brothers, children, and grandparents to mobilize. As a mother, father, sister, or son, one might feel required to speak out and act. By taking public action, a person is also faced with the question of how to best present oneself publicly: as an angry citizen, a worker, a peasant, or a business owner? Along with these identities that represent recognized political interests, individuals frequently proclaim their status as family members and argue that these identities give them a right to speak and be heard in public.

This category helps explain the widespread invocation of motherhood as a political identity for women in Latin America.[28] In the period covered in this book, an amazing variety of women mobilized in pursuit of political projects.[29] Chilean women invoked their roles and responsibilities as mothers to explain what propelled them into public attacks against the legitimacy of both Allende and Pinochet. In the early 1970s, many women embraced the arguments of El Poder Femenino—a conservative and right-wing women's organization—and

28. Alvarez argues that in Brazil, motherhood was the "principal mobilizational referent for women's participation in urban social movements" and in what Alvarez termed "militant motherhood." See Alvarez, *Engendering Democracy*, 50. Alvarez's work on Brazil fits within a broad range of studies of the second wave women's movements in Latin America, many of which have noted the prevalence of women's familial identities and roles in providing the impetus for both individual political action and movement strategy.

29. For Argentina, see Taylor, "Making a Spectacle"; for Nicaragua, see Bayard de Volo, *Mothers of Heroes and Martyrs*; for El Salvador and Guatemala, see Schirmer, "Seeking of Truth."

took to the streets as mothers to protect their families from the political policies of Allende. Against Pinochet, women once again protested as mothers,
joining human rights groups, popular movements, and feminist groups.[30] As
mothers, they presented themselves as the voice of the Chilean family, thus
claiming both the right to speak and the space from which to speak. As the
accepted representatives of the family, women can claim that their demands
on those who have pledged to protect and promote familial interests are justified. While motherhood certainly represents a deeply felt and important personal identity for individuals, it is also true that mobilizing around familial
identities in general, and motherhood in particular, also served the larger political goals of many groups. Explicitly promoting groups as representing apolitical family concerns often represents a political strategy in itself.[31]

Militant Families provides a way to analyze not only women's frequent use
of motherhood to claim political representation, but also how men employed
their family identities as a way to create a space from which to speak, a topic
virtually ignored in current scholarship.[32] For example, the duty of men as
fathers to provide economically for the family has played a role in both the
labor and agricultural reform movements.[33] The importance of the citizenship
claims of Militant Families might also be greater when governments attempt
to minimize the ability of citizens to take political action, such as during the
Pinochet dictatorship. Pinochet repressed and attacked traditional public identities—such as activist, politician, and worker—as part of the military's project
of depoliticizing Chilean society. In response, both men and women often
turned to their familial roles and identities, forcing Pinochet to justify the repression of Chileans who claimed to be acting on behalf of families. Pinochet's

30. Popular movements designate a range of political activism that originated with Santiago's
lower-working-class urban dwellers, including communal kitchens, land occupations (*tomas*), and
housing protests. These political activities were based around organizing in order to meet people's
basic needs (housing and sustenance). While I base the claims for Militant Families in my own
empirical research, the widespread use of maternal identities in Chile has also been documented
by a number of other scholars. For women on the left, see Chuchryk, "Feminist Anti-authoritarian
Politics"; Agosín, *Tapestries of Hope*; and Valenzuela, *La mujer en el Chile militar*. For women on the
right, see Power, *Right-Wing Women*. For a comparison of women on both the left and the right,
see Baldez, *Why Women Protest*.

31. Baldez explores women's use of the politics of antipolitics in "Nonpartisanship as a Political
Strategy."

32. This aspect of motherhood as a political tool has been most thoroughly explored in the case
of the Madres de Plaza de Mayo. See, for example, Taylor, "Making a Spectacle"; and Fabj, "Motherhood as Political Voice."

33. For a discussion of the importance of men's identities in both campesino organizing and
governmental reform projects, see Tinsman, *Partners in Conflict*. See also Klubock, *Contested Communities*, for a discussion of gender identities in Chile's mining communities.

actions complicated his own use of familial welfare as a way to justify military rule. Thus the Chilean case—in which motherhood, fatherhood, and other types of familial identities were used in similar ways—underscores the need to analyze how familial beliefs are used to mobilize political action. Organizing around familial identities to protect familial welfare provides both men and women with tangible political advantages, especially when ideals of the family are used to help define and legitimate the state itself.

Rethinking Politics by Studying the Familial: Chile and Beyond

By shifting our attention to the familial, we gain a deeper understanding of how cultural beliefs shape the processes of political conflict and state development. The following analysis using this familial framework reveals three critical and interrelated aspects of Chile's contentious political struggles over questions of political legitimacy. First, familial beliefs were central to how Chileans understood and participated in the country's political struggles. Second, familial beliefs help to uncover how gender ideology is fundamental to the ways societies define political power, authority, and legitimacy, and therefore how they struggle over these issues.[34] Finally, the importance of familial beliefs to the political events in Chile examined here highlights the limited treatment of family more broadly within the discipline of political science.

As my opening vignette illustrates, often even a brief look at the speeches and rhetoric of people engaged in political action demonstrates that familial beliefs represent a major resource of language, symbols, metaphors, images, and arguments that become part of how people participate in and understand politics. Chilean political language certainly supports the claims of the cognitive linguist George Lakoff that family experiences and beliefs provide one of the basic metaphors through which we structure our understanding of both political and social ties.[35] More and more, I began to wonder about the uniqueness

---

34. I more fully develop the argument around the connections between familial authority and political authority and legitimacy in "The Ties That Bind." In that work, I argue that political legitimacy is an ongoing contested process that is shaped by the underlying values and claims about political authority in any given political community. I have also found Beetham, *Legitimation of Power*, helpful in thinking about political legitimacy in ways that do not treat it as a static concept.

35. According to Lakoff in *Moral Politics*, Republicans generally embrace a traditional, patriarchal, disciplinarian model of the family and politics, while Democrats follow a nurturant model

of Chile and its political culture. Chile is often considered to have a very traditional and conservative culture, heavily influenced by the Catholic Church.[36]
It was, after all, the last country in Latin America to permit divorce, which
only became legal in 2004. Was the widespread use of family as a resource in
Chilean political conflicts perhaps distinctive to its culture and history?

Once I began looking for family in politics, however, I found a wealth
of examples from other countries. Lakoff's work, for example, is based on his
analysis of current political divisions in the United States, a country much
more dominated than Chile is by liberal political theory and its formal separation of the political from the familial. To provide a few of these examples:
In the United States, invoking the need to protect "family values" and the "traditional family" has been a key political strategy of the Republican Party in
mobilizing political support at least since the early 1990s.[37] The development
of American public policies, including taxes, immigration, and agriculture,
cannot be explained without an analysis of the multiple functions that families serve in politics.[38] The political scientist Michael Schatzberg's recent work
on Africa has analyzed the continuing importance of familial metaphors in
shaping citizens' perceptions of political legitimacy. He argues that in much
of middle Africa, "political legitimacy rests on the tacit normative idea that the
government stands in the same relationship to its citizens that a father does
to his children."[39] The anthropologist Katherine Verdery, working in Eastern
Europe, has examined how idealized understandings of family shaped both
the state-building processes of communist governments and the more recent
shift to liberal states, which are transferring social welfare provisions back
onto individualized families.[40] Far from being limited to Chile, familial beliefs
seem to represent a widely used political resource in different countries and
across the ideological spectrum.

Within political science, it has been feminist political theorists who have

---

based in the equality of men and women within the family and a greater emphasis on caring for
the members of the family.

36. For a discussion of the importance of conservative values and the Catholic Church, particularly as they pertain to issues of gender equality, see Htun, *Sex and the State*; Blofield, *Politics of
Moral Sin*; and Blofield and Haas, "Defining a Democracy."

37. Patricia Hill Collins traces the term "family values" and its connection to the Republican
Party to a speech by Vice President Dan Quayle in 1992. See Hill Collins, "It's All in the Family," 62.

38. Strach, *All in the Family*.

39. Schatzberg, *Political Legitimacy*, 1. Here I am focusing on empirical work written by political scientists, though of course historians and sociologists have also done much work on this topic.

40. Verdery, "From Parent-State."

paid the most sustained attention to the importance of family in politics. For example, following the initial insights of Carole Pateman, numerous scholars have argued that our current definition of what counts as political and who is considered a citizen is rooted in a liberal political theory that justified the public, political rights of men through the private control of men over women, children, and other dependents within the family.[41] Feminist theorists have documented that this separation of the public and political from the familial and private, together with women's association with the familial and private, has justified women's continuing exclusion from full citizenship. The focus of much of this work, however, is to free women from the confines of the family by redefining what is "personal" and what is "political." Examining how the "political" is also "familial" at both the theoretical and empirical levels—as I do here—represents an alternative, and little explored, research agenda.

These insights from feminist theory and other disciplines have yet to be fully incorporated into political science. Even given the protests of feminist theorists and gender scholars, there currently exists a general lack of attention to even the obviously political aspects of the family. As the political scientist Patricia Strach found, since 1907, the top 28 political science journals have published a "paltry 72 articles" with the word "family" in the title, as compared to 2,734 articles in 29 sociology journals, and 702 articles in 44 history journals.[42] As she notes, "Political science is generally silent on the many ways that the family is used by political actors to achieve political goals."[43] This lack of attention is problematic as it has stunted the development of theories and empirical research into the relationships between the political and the familial.[44]

Because of the limited research on the intersection of the familial and the political, we do not know the extent of new insights that might be generated around many of the fundamental concerns of political science. The lack of

<hr />

41. Pateman, *Sexual Contract*. See also Shanley, "Marriage Contract"; Pateman and Grosz, *Feminist Challenges*; and Brown, "Finding the Man in the State."

42. Strach, *All in the Family*, 10.

43. Ibid., 6.

44. Important exceptions are the recent works by Schatzberg on middle Africa and Strach on the United States. An older literature explored the effects of early political socialization in families on individuals' political behavior (e.g., the level of involvement and the commitment to particular political parties) as adults. This research, however, continues to treat the family as a private institution that shapes individuals who then might have an effect on public politics, rather than how familial beliefs are an integral part of political processes and structures. See Schatzberg, *Political Legitimacy*; Strach, *All in the Family*; Clarke, "Family Structure"; Glaser, "The Family and Voting Turnout"; Connell, "Political Socialization"; and Beck and Jennings, "Family Traditions." I thank Patricia Strach for this point.

attention paid to these questions about the specifically political uses of family has weakened broader understandings of the political processes involved in the transitions between different forms of political rule, the legitimation of political authority, and the relationship between states and citizens. The analytic framework that emerged from my analysis of the specific uses of familial beliefs in Chile provides a foundation for future comparative work into the intersection of family and politics.

Asking and Answering Questions About the Familial: Definitions, Methods, and Sources

Fundamentally, I am interested in understanding how beliefs about family shape politics, political struggles, and political life. The central question I ask is: How do normative ideals about the relationship between the familial and the political shape the strategies of individuals and groups engaged in political struggle? More specifically, within the context of the rise and fall of two very different leaders and their respective governments, I ask: How were familial beliefs used in the struggles over the legitimacy of Allende and his elected socialist government? How were familial beliefs used in the struggles over the legitimacy of Pinochet and his military dictatorship? And finally, how were family beliefs used as Chile began its transition back to democracy? Because I was interested in tracing how beliefs about the family were employed in public political struggles and to influence political outcomes, I focused my research on sources that were produced for public consumption. I examined a range of media sources for each time period. Primary sources included newspapers, congressional debates, magazines, press releases, presidential speeches, and televised political ads. I gathered this material during sixteen months of field research between 1999 and 2001, and short research trips in 2005, 2006, and 2009. For all periods, I included sources identified as generated by and relating to either the ruling government or opposition groups.

The family is at the center of this study. In the following analysis, I define the family in terms of how it was understood and portrayed in Chilean politics. As discussed above, the family most often invoked by individuals and groups as they pursued their political goals was an idealized form of the nuclear family. Less frequently, it was an extended family, including a greater kinship circle of grandparents, aunts, uncles, and cousins. Often, the mother-child dyad was used to represent the family, though occasionally the father-child dyad was used. I also examined portrayals that invoked the roles and relationships within a family. For example, an ad that featured a small child and asked readers to imagine themselves as the parent of that child was relevant because the use of the child was designed to invoke a familial relationship (parent-child) with the reader. I also paid attention to the invocation of social expectations for different family members. In particular, political rhetoric and images that portrayed the inability of men to provide for their families or of women to adequately mother their children were analyzed.

Portrayals of men, women, and children that did not evoke family or familial relationships were not included. For example, while I included political propaganda that referenced job loss in terms of how unemployment interfered with men's ability to provide for their families, I excluded instances where men's identities as workers and the importance of having a job focused on masculine identity in general, even if such references indirectly hinted at men's roles as fathers and husbands. Although this conservative criterion risks excluding some familial references, it maintains a narrow focus on explicit invocations of family and familial beliefs that have a particularly political use rather than the much broader and more diffuse familial references that are part of larger Chilean society. While important connections between political uses and the broader cultural references can be found in ordinary speech, tracing the complex interrelationships between these areas is beyond the scope of this project.

Given the potentially immense amount of information that could be analyzed, I began by surveying the secondary literature in order to identify the key events and issues that generated significant public political debate and conflict for each period. As Anselm Strauss and Juliet Corbin note, it is important for the inductive researcher to "come to the research situation with some background in the technical literature and it is important to acknowledge and use that."[45] Major sources for the different governments and opposition movements vary somewhat given both changing political climates and new media technology. Each time period experienced unique political conflicts, and the examination of these different struggles necessitated careful selection of archival sources of political discourse.

To examine the rise and fall of Allende, I analyzed political speech produced around events where Allende and his opponents directly confronted each other. These public struggles were directed at persuading Chileans about the relative merits of the different groups and thus drew on symbols, rhetoric, and

---

45. Strauss and Corbin, *Basics of Qualitative Research*, 50.

images that depended on broader areas of cultural consensus. In particular, I analyzed the public rhetoric and propaganda produced during the 1970 presidential contest and the 1973 congressional elections. To analyze these invocations of family, I conducted an initial content analysis on the political ads found in the two most important newspapers of the time from different ideological standpoints, *El Mercurio* (which represented the center-right) and *El Clarín* (populist and left). In this analysis, I coded which candidates or political parties produced the ads, the types of persuasive strategies being used in the ads, and the use of family, either textually or visually, in the ad. This initial content analysis helped to confirm my suspicions about the widespread use of the family in political conflict. The control and censorship of the media during the military government, coupled with my inability to access much of the increasingly televised political propaganda, limited the usefulness of content analysis after the military took control. To trace the growth of civil society resistance and social movements, I also examined the public discourse associated with the anti-Allende popular mobilization in media outlets such as newspapers, magazines, and advertisements.

In order to understand how Pinochet and the military employed familial beliefs in their ongoing attempts to legitimize military rule, I examined a range of documents produced over the seventeen-year period that were disseminated purposefully to present the military government's arguments about why it had assumed power and what justified its continued control of the state. Given the importance of the familial framing promoted by the anti-Allende women's movement, I also paid particular attention to Pinochet's attempts to maintain women's support. I examined the magazines, documents, and activities of the Mothers' Centers and the National Secretariat of Women to trace these attempts. I also examined the government's public campaigns around housing and malnutrition, two areas that received a lot of attention from both Pinochet and his opposition. More generally, I was able to examine "Somos Millones," a general public propaganda television campaign produced in 1987, which was designed to increase public support for Pinochet before the 1988 plebiscite (in that referendum, Chileans were asked to vote for either a continuation of Pinochet's military government or a transition back to democratic governance).

I trace the rise of Pinochet's opposition by examining public political discourse produced both by and about the women's, human rights, and *poblador* social movements. Under Pinochet, political censorship and repression limited where examples of dissent could be published. I had to rely particularly on the archives of the Vicaría de la Solidaridad, which is part of the archbish-opric of Santiago. The protection of the Catholic Church permitted the Vicaría to exist as a space of dissent during the military government. Since the return to democracy, it has maintained extensive archives of the few opposition mag-azines that managed to be published under Pinochet. It also stores a great num-ber of primary documents, including press statements, conference proceedings, and seminar papers produced by the groups and individuals associated with the different social movements.

Finally, I analyzed the political uses of family in the 1988 plebiscite on Pino-chet's rule and the 1989 elections that finally returned Chile to democracy. During this time, television ads became particularly important. The televised electoral advertisements (or *franja*, as the collection of ads are called in Chile) became the venue for a direct confrontation between Pinochet's military gov-ernment and the opposition. Each night, both sides tried to persuade Chileans of their position. I supplemented my analysis of the televised campaign with newspaper and magazine sources. The discourses associated with both the plebiscite and the subsequent presidential election provided a unique oppor-tunity to examine how familial beliefs were mobilized during the transition to democracy.

Given that I focus on the language and images prevalent during political conflict, this study draws on the importance of discourse and its analysis. Dis-course analysis seeks to understand the constructed nature of social reality.[46] At its core, discourse analysis depends on the belief that human society is cre-ated by human interactions that are bound in webs of cultural significance.[47] As researchers, discourse analysis draws our attention to how ideas about pol-itics and power are embedded in the language, metaphors, symbols, identities, and public actions of individuals and groups. As a method for studying poli-tics, Neta Crawford argues, discourse analysis "can help us decipher the under-lying meaning, deep assumptions, and relations of power that are supported by and constructed through a discourse."[48] Thus discourse analysis directed my attention toward the uses of familial beliefs to construct, maintain, and criti-cize particular meanings of citizenship, political power, and legitimacy. The political invocation of familial beliefs analyzed in the following chapters was

46. Hardy, Harley, and Phillips, "Discourse Analysis and Content Analysis," 19.
47. For a discussion of how discourse analysis is understood in the social sciences, as well as a good discussion of how to use discourse analysis, see Gill, "Discourse Analysis."
48. Crawford, "Understanding Discourse," 23.

used by both state elites and everyday citizens to understand, organize, and participate in the political struggles of Chile.

I also found discourse analysis a useful approach because it incorporates both linguistic and visual text into a single analytical framework. Mark Laffey and Jutta Weldes argue that discourse analysis is the study not merely of language, but also of the "structures and practices" through which people make sense of and create the social world in which they live. How familial beliefs were used and what they meant often depended on the interaction between images and texts. The ideas depicted in drawings, pictures, and images, and the ways political actors physically and symbolically represented themselves, were as important as the words used, the arguments invoked, and the metaphors employed. Indeed, "discourses manifest themselves in both linguistic and non-linguistic practices . . . [and] cannot be limited to the study of texts or language narrowly defined."[49] The usefulness of incorporating both images and language can be seen particularly in my analysis of television propaganda. In Pinochet's "Somos Millones" campaign, for instance, the language of the advertisement referred to the general progress of Chile, but the visual story illustrated the improvement in the life of a particular Chilean family. A good example is a spot in which the language focuses on statistics about the expansion of TV ownership in Chilean society. The accompanying visual narrative tells the story of how the acquisition of a television improved the life of one family by allowing a father and son to bond over watching soccer matches.

Once I had decided to focus specifically on how familial beliefs were mobilized around conflicts over political legitimacy, I began by categorizing the familial uses of political actors. These categories eventually became the analytical framework developed above, which explains the dominant uses of familial beliefs and what these uses reveal about Chile's political struggles. My analysis, based in a process of analyzing and reanalyzing material, fits the model of developing a "grounded theory."[50] For this analysis, Chile does not represent a simple single case study. Instead, its unique political history allowed me to deploy my four categories across a series of related, paired cases (elected left democratic government and its right-wing opposition, a conservative military dictatorship and its democratic opposition). My work thus supports broader claims about the importance of the family in shaping how we understand

49. Laffey and Weldes, "Methodological Reflections," 28.
50. See Strauss and Corbin, *Basics of Qualitative Research*, for a discussion of the importance of "grounded theory."

political authority, political legitimacy, and the relationship between states and their citizens.

Overview of the Book

The subsequent chapters develop my analysis of the roles played by familial language, symbols, and images in Chile's political conflicts. Chapter 2 traces Chile's historical development through the lens of familial beliefs and provides the political context for subsequent chapters. I examine Chile's historical development in terms of how familial beliefs were mobilized in the development of different forms of states, each with their related political projects, types of political leaders, and understandings of citizens. The chapter ends by discussing how Chile's three major political traditions—the right, center, and left—viewed the relationship between the family and the state at the beginning of the 1970s.

The following five chapters analyze the struggles over the political legitimacy of both Allende and Pinochet and their respective governments through the familial framework developed in this introductory chapter. Chapters 3 and 4 examine the rise and fall of Salvador Allende's Popular Unity government. Chapter 3 includes an examination of the uses of family in the presidential election of 1970 and explores how political candidates and their parties invoked familial beliefs in their efforts to assume power. The uses of Familial State and Patriarchal Leader emerge most clearly in the political propaganda of the three presidential candidates: Jorge Alessandri on the right, Radomiro Tomic in the center, and Salvador Allende on the left.

The political struggles that led to the fall of Salvador Allende are the subject of chapter 4. I examine how the belief that the state is responsible for familial welfare (Familial State) was transformed into a biting critique against Allende by analyzing the political discourse surrounding both the March of the Empty Pots and Pans and the creation of an anti-Allende women's movement. The march also provides the first look at the uses of the family by ordinary citizens as part of Militant Families. The importance of familial discourse in the ongoing struggle over the political legitimacy of Allende's government was clearly evident in the 1973 congressional elections and in ongoing debates that immediately preceded the 11 September coup d'état that overthrew Allende and set the stage for military dictatorship.

Chapter 5 analyzes how Augusto Pinochet drew on familial beliefs to justify both the military's usurpation of political power and his continued control of that power. Invoking the ideals of Patriarchal Leader, he became the traditional father of the Chilean national family, protecting it from the threats of communism, societal violence, and challenges to "traditional values." Drawing on the beliefs of the Familial State, Pinochet further argued that his government was legitimate because it was fulfilling its basic responsibilities to Chileans and their families. The uses of familial beliefs by Pinochet's opposition are the focus of chapter 6. Focusing on three of the most vibrant parts of the opposition—the human rights movement, the housing movement, and the women's movement—I analyze how these groups contested Pinochet's portrayal of himself as a Patriarchal Leader and his government as upholding the Familial State. These groups portrayed Pinochet and his government as politically illegitimate by judging him against the criterion of family welfare. I also explore the importance of Militant Families in how these movements sought to mobilize and justify their political actions.

Chapter 7 explores the ongoing struggles between Pinochet and his opposition, now led by the Concertación, within the context of the 1988 plebiscite. I examine how the ideals of the Familial State and Patriarchal Leader provided the context for the debate over the political legitimacy of Pinochet and his government. The chapter concludes with an analysis of the Concertación's skillful uses of the beliefs of the Familial Nation both to recreate a Chilean political society open to political diversity and dissent and to reestablish the societal commitment to democracy.

In the conclusion, I explore the factors that either enable or constrain the use of familial beliefs as a political resource, and I show how my analytical categories provide a conceptual framework that could travel outside Chile. I also turn to the election in 2006 of Chile's first female president, Michelle Bachelet, examining how her election has challenged the particularly paternal understandings of political leadership. But I also argue that her presidency has also relied on, and possibly strengthened, the beliefs of Familial State. President Bachelet cast herself as a maternal protector of Chilean families, particularly during the economic crisis of 2008, when she greatly expanded state programs to protect Chileans from the ravages of rising unemployment. In the end, to understand politics, we need to pay attention to how politics shapes and is shaped by beliefs about the family and its relationship to political authority and the state.

★ TWO ★

THE HIDDEN STORY
Familial Beliefs and Political Conflict

The State recognizes the family as the basic and fundamental cell of the society, primary formative agent in the personality of men and the organic unity charged with transmission of experiences and values; [the State] recognizes that the family contributes to the formation and education of children and performs ethical, disciplinary, protection, guardianship and material assistantship functions, and [the State] also recognizes that its [the family's] stability is indispensable for the good equilibrium of the society and the Nation.

—SECTION 2, FROM THE PROPOSED LAW TO CREATE A MINISTRY OF THE FAMILY,
CHILEAN SENATE, 1971

On 2 March 1971, President Allende urged the Chilean Congress to create a Ministry of the Family as a new cabinet-level department. Allende claimed that the proposed ministry fulfilled the "constitutional mandate of the State" under which the Chilean government "is responsible to provide protection and defense to the family." Additionally, it was a concrete example of the Popular Unity's "political promise contracted with the people, expressed in the Program of the Popular Unity," to improve the welfare of the working class. For evidence of the current pressing need for the new department, Allende argued that the Chilean family was in crisis and that current challenges confronting Chilean families demanded governmental action. As the newly elected president, Allende was also following a long-standing Chilean political tradition of justifying the expansion of state power by invoking the state's responsibility for familial welfare.

The epigraph is drawn from Senado de Chile, *Diario de sesiones del Senado*, 37a, Anexo de Documentos, 1971, 1855. Unless otherwise noted, I have provided my own English translations of the Spanish primary sources.

Unlike many of the other items on Allende's political agenda that were greeted with stiff opposition, strongly shared political consensus around the importance of family and its present difficulties meant that this proposal received widespread support. Indeed, as the proposed Ministry of the Family progressed through the multiple levels of the Chamber of Deputies and the Senate—the two houses of the Chilean Congress—the speeches, debates, and statements made by deputies and senators revealed just how prevalent the agreement around key familial beliefs actually was in Chilean politics at the beginning of the 1970s. At the heart of the proposal was an image of the traditional family that could have easily been written by Chilean parties on the center or the right, instead of Allende's leftist Popular Unity coalition government. This political agreement also consisted of shared understandings of what constituted the ideal family, the importance of the family as the basic institution of Chilean society, the appropriateness of state action to promote familial welfare, and the intimate connections between familial welfare and the stability and progress of the nation-state. The language of the proposed Ministry of the Family also recognized the familial roles and identities of Chilean citizens as an important area of state interest. By drawing on widely shared beliefs about the centrality of the family to society and the state's familial responsibilities, Allende sought to expand the power of the state through creating a new ministry with the expansive mission of protecting and promoting familial welfare.

But how had these particular beliefs about the family and the state come to dominate Chilean political culture in the early 1970s? How were current understandings of the rights of citizens and the legitimate political power of the state influenced by past beliefs about the proper relationship between family and state? How had the political development of the Chilean state both shaped and been shaped by familial beliefs? To understand how Chileans used the familial ideals that ground my conceptual framework of Familial State, Patriarchal Leader, Militant Families, and Familial Nation, a broader knowledge of the historical relationship between family and state is needed. This chapter traces Chile's political development through the lens of familial beliefs by showing how and in what ways familial beliefs have been an integral part of the processes that produce different types of state structures (e.g., Spanish colonial rule, independent republics, welfare states) and their accompanying forms of rulers, subjects, and citizens (e.g., monarchs, founding fathers, citizen-patriarchs, patriotic mothers). At the end of the chapter, I return to the debate over the Ministry of the Family in order to explore both the areas of consensus that existed between Chile's political parties at the beginning of the 1970s and how that consensus could turn to conflict. Thus this chapter explains the development of the particular relationships between the political and the familial that informed the political struggles of the 1970s and 1980s examined in the following chapters.

Colonial Rule in Latin America: Kings and Patriarchs

A clear demarcation between the public and the private has not always dominated our understanding of what is meant by the political or the familial. Before the rise of liberalism in Europe and its colonies in the eighteenth and nineteenth centuries, political thought had been defined by the family analogy. As the political theorist Jean Bethke Elshtain notes, the "theoretical argument based upon the presumption that familial and political authority, governance, and order were analogous one to another, dominated political discourse for centuries."[1] Explicit connections between the familial and the political provided for the defense of monarchies found in the political ideology of patriarchalism. The historian Gordon Schochet argues that patriarchalism can be reduced to the following axioms: "(1) Familial authority is natural, divinely sanctioned, and . . . absolute and unlimited. (2) Political power is identical to the power of fathers. Therefore, political power is natural, divinely sanctioned, and—because it still enjoys the ancient and original rights of fatherhood—absolute and unlimited."[2] In other words, the political authority of monarchies was grounded in their presumed connection to the "natural" organization of patriarchal families. Patriarchalism, as a formal justification for political power, depended on the more generalized beliefs and support for the patriarchal principles found in the social, religious, and legal institutions of the time. These patriarchal principles included a belief in the natural superiority of men—a superiority that justifies men's control over the reproductive and productive labor of women within family networks—and placed a special emphasis on the authority of fathers within the family.[3] Until the nineteenth

---

1. Elshtain, "Preface: Political Theory," 4.
2. Schochet, *Authoritarian Family*, 269.
3. This definition is taken from Stern's discussion of patriarchy in colonial Mexico in *Secret History*, 21–22, and Schochet's examination of seventeenth-century England in *Authoritarian Family*, 64–72. The explicit connections between patriarchy and patriarchalism made the defense of female monarchs difficult within this perspective. Ruling queens were often faced with challenges to their authority that were based on the contradictions between their lack of power within gender ideology

century, patriarchalism provided the ideological foundation for political communities and legitimate authority in Europe.

Patriarchalism was the dominant theory of political power in Spanish political thought and practice during colonial times.[4] State structures throughout the Spanish colonies were built around a "hierarchical system of government at whose apex the king sat in all his majesty." Below were arrayed the Spanish elites that served as viceroys, governors, and members of the governor's council, the *corregidores* (heads of local districts), and members of the *cabildos* (municipal councils).[5] For most of the colonial period, the cabildos were the only level open to creoles—local-born elites of Spanish descent—while the higher levels were mostly held by *peninsulares*—Spaniards born in Spain.[6] Promoted by both the Catholic Church and the Crown, patriarchalism as an explicit theory of political power and legitimate authority provided the ideological justification for the colonial system throughout Spanish America.

Patriarchalism is sometimes presented in historical scholarship as a relatively simple form of political control and an ideological tool used to justify the brutal rule of elite power. Recent work, however, has recognized the complexity and robustness of this system in influencing the relationship between politics and culture that developed in the colonies. As the historian Steve Stern painstakingly documents, in colonial Mexico the use of familial authority as an analogy for political authority provided both elites and popular classes with a model for the relationships between the different members of the political community. Arguments over the appropriate limits of political power and the duties and responsibilities that bound both elites and their subjects were often fought through appeals to different aspects of the idealized family. Both political elites and popular classes understood their relationships to one another through familial analogies. Male political elites, including the colonial representatives of the distant Spanish monarch, deployed familial beliefs as a tool to argue for their right both to rule and to expect obedience from their political "children" (nonelite men, women, indigenous peoples, and slaves). On the other side of the equation, members of the popular classes often deployed familial discourses to remind colonial rulers of their obligations to these political "children" and the need to temper authority with care.[7]

---

and the political power granted by their title. For a discussion of this tension, see Schochet, *Authoritarian Family*, 43–47.

4. Stern, *Secret History*, 11–20; Morse, "Toward a Theory of Spanish Government."

5. Collier and Sater, *History of Chile*, 22–23. See also Loveman, *Chile*, 55–56.

6. Collier and Sater, *History of Chile*, 23–24.

7. See Stern, *Secret History*, especially 70–111 and 189–216.

At the level of the family, the connection between familial authority and political authority was also part of the "contested patriarchal pacts"[8] that governed the relationships between men and women. Men often understood their gender privileges as absolute, while women often based their resistance to patriarchal authority on more contingent understandings of the relationship between rights and responsibilities. For example, whereas men might argue that their control over the reproductive and productive labor of their wives and children was an absolute right conferred by the natural inferiority of women and superiority of men, women might feel that their obligations to men were contingent on how well men lived up to their own gendered responsibilities of providing for and caring for dependent members.[9] In these struggles, women also turned to their rights under Spanish colonial law, which included guaranteed inheritance rights to their parents' wealth and land. Adult, nonmarried women also "could sign contracts, ratify official documents, make wills, and appear in court."[10] Elite colonial women drew on their class, race, and familial privileges to act within society, even though colonial law denied all women the legal power to govern others, including their own children.[11]

In the political and social context of colonial Mexico, neither patriarchy nor patriarchalism was seen as a simple justification for dominance. Instead, these interconnected forms of power gained cultural and political robustness from their ability to provide for forms of dissent and struggle that stayed within the boundaries set by the broader ideology. Stern's work shows how patriarchalism provided conceptual frameworks for defining and limiting the scope of different forms of power that governed the relationships between the king and his subjects, colonial elites and popular classes, men and women, and fathers and their children. Within colonial political thought, male political elites turned to patriarchalism to justify their political power. As political fathers, popular classes judged colonial elites by how well they fulfilled their duties.

8. Stern uses this phrase to describe the patterns of struggle and reconciliation in colonial Mexico, both between men and women and between political elites and subaltern classes. For the initial description, see ibid., 97.

9. In addition to Stern's exceptional work, see also Dore, "One Step Forward." For another discussion of patriarchalism in a different context, see Nicholson, *Gender and History*.

10. Dore, "One Step Forward," 12.

11. Chambers and Norling provocatively argue that one possible reason behind the support of loyalist women for maintaining colonial rule was their rejection of the republican separation of private and public and the growing emphasis on women's domesticity. Using the case of María Antonia Bolívar, the sister of revolutionary leader Simón Bolívar, they suggest that elite loyalist women saw themselves as important actors within larger family and kinship networks. See Chambers and Norling, "Choosing to Be a Subject."

These subaltern men and women exploited familial understandings of political authority and power to contest what they perceived as unfair demands on the part of the political elite.[12]

While a historical analysis of these complex cultural contestations during colonial times has not yet been written for Chile, given its colonial order and the strength of patriarchal norms in colonial Chilean society, similar patterns probably existed. Throughout its colonial period and well into the twentieth century, Chilean society was dominated by a small group of elite families whose power bases were the landed estates of the central valley, but who through marriage and kinship patterns also had ties to mining, trade, and the military.[13] As the historians Simon Collier and William Sater discuss, the colonial "formation of great estates ruled by a land-owning elite and worked by a semi-servile rural population" was "one of the fundamental processes of Chilean history."[14] Certainly, the ideal of the powerful patriarch who rules his family and his landed estate with a mixture of benevolence and discipline has dominated both historical and cultural depictions of Chilean society from colonial times to the present.[15] Many of the later political uses of familial beliefs, particularly the Patriarchal Leader and aspects of the Familial State, can be found in the ideological foundations of patriarchalism outlined above. In colonial times, familial beliefs provided the language and concepts for understanding, contesting, and mediating power, whether that power was the political power of male elites or the personal power of men as family patriarchs.

From Despotic Kings to Republican Patriarchs: Familial Beliefs in the Transition to Liberal Republics

Throughout the eighteenth and nineteenth centuries, the historical development and diffusion of liberal political thought challenged patriarchalism as the reigning ideology in Europe and its increasingly rebellious colonies in North and South America. The explicit connections between the familial and the political at the ideological level were severed to make way for a new understanding of political authority based on ideals of consent, contract, and individual

---

12. Stern, *Secret History*.
13. Collier and Sater, *History of Chile*, 18–22.
14. Ibid., 7. See also Loveman, *Chile*, 38–39.
15. The classic work in contemporary Chilean literature is Isabel Allende's *House of the Spirits*. For scholarly discussions, see Collier and Sater, *History of Chile*, and Loveman, *Chile*.

liberty. By drawing a distinction between public, political authority and private, patriarchal authority, Locke attacked the explicit relationship between patriarchal familial beliefs and the power and authority of the monarchy as a system of government. As documented by feminist political theorists, Locke hoped that by severing the analogy between men's familial authority and the king's political authority to question the assumed naturalness on which patriarchalism depended.[16]

A foundational premise of liberal political thought is that public, political authority is fundamentally different from the private authority of family and household. Men's control over women, children, and other dependents could be seen as just and natural, while a monarch's similar control over adult, propertied men became a violation of those men's rights to equality and liberty. Increasingly, legitimate political rule and authority were understood not as natural or divine, but as a type of conventional power created through agreements between men. This distinction allowed liberal thinkers to create a new understanding of political power (based in consent) while leaving intact the broader cultural patterns of patriarchy that helped justify elite men's continued dominance of society. Early liberal theorists, however, partly based men's new political equality on their private standing as heads of households. As feminist critics have pointed out, this means that in liberal theory the political equality of (some) men was created on the basis of the private inequality of women.[17] Elite men's private control of women and of other men became the base of early liberalism's fraternal social order. This can be seen not only in the political writings of early liberal theorists, but also in the varied requirements of male suffrage at the inception of liberal republics, which often included marital status, age, race, and property.

The tenets of liberal theory became the foundational political principles of a wave of revolutions, including those in the United States and France, and throughout Latin America and the Caribbean. But patriarchal beliefs were not simply banished from politics to reside only in the private world of the family. A growing scholarship examining the gendered process of nation-state development during this period reveals the fundamental roles that familial beliefs

---

16. Locke, *Two Treatises*; Pateman, *Sexual Contract*.

17. Pateman's work, especially *The Disorder of Women* and *The Sexual Contract*, is fundamental to this critique. Feminist political theorists continue to explore how women's attempts to gain equal citizenship rights and political equality in liberal democracies continue to be stymied by their association with the family. For other work that examines how the split between private and public authority has limited women's political participation and rights, see Okin, *Justice, Gender, and the Family*; Lister, *Citizenship*; and Stevens, *Reproducing the State*.

played in shaping the politics and political beliefs of the revolutions and the emerging nation-states.[18] Throughout the Spanish colonies, both revolutionary political leaders and their supporters turned to familial imagery to both explain the reasons for their rebellion against the Spanish Crown and to create the symbols needed to found their new "imagined communities."[19] Depictions of revolutionary struggle as a family drama in which adult sons rebelled against the unfair and unwarranted treatment of a neglectful father, or—even worse—an unnatural stepmother, were common tropes during the revolutionary wars in the United States, France, and Latin America.[20]

Napoleon's invasion of Spain in 1807 and overthrow of Spain's royal family fanned the fire of the Latin American revolutions. Now supporters of independence could easily argue that the traditional forms of rule and the ties that had bound together the king and his subjects had broken down. Chile's creole elite quickly moved to set up a national junta that could govern Chile and protect the interests of the legitimate, but now deposed, Spanish monarch, King Ferdinand VII. This taste of independence was a heady experience, and while Spain attempted to reimpose colonial rule after Napoleon's defeat, many Chilean elites now were committed to the cause of Chilean independence.[21] Chilean revolutionaries were quick to argue that "misfortune has interrupted our relations with the sovereign and we should . . . consider ourselves in the primitive state," thereby necessitating a new form of political order. Tellingly, for Chileans this primitive state was not a Hobbesian vision of individual strife and conflict brought to an end by a strong leader; rather, "in this state, each head of the family is its natural governor; from every district or federation of families the magistrate . . . is elected."[22] According to the historian Mary Lowenthal Felstiner, political evolution in the new Chilean republic was pictured as a type of family rule that brought about a new social contract. In Chile, it was the "family as the stage before nation, family heads as natural governors, federations

---

18. For Latin America, see Earle, "Rape and the Anxious Republic"; Dore, "One Step Forward"; and Dore, "Property, Households, and Public Regulation of Domestic Life." For France, see Hunt, *Family Romance*, and Landes, *Women and the Public Sphere*. For the United States, see Fliegelman, *Prodigals and Pilgrims*, and Kann, *Gendering of American Politics*.

19. Here I refer to Benedict Anderson's famous definition of the nation found in *Imagined Communities*.

20. For Chile, see Felstiner, "Family Metaphors." See also Earle, "Rape and the Anxious Republic"; Hunt, *The Family Romance*; and Fliegelman, *Prodigals and Pilgrims*.

21. For a discussion of Chile's struggles for independence, see Loveman, *Chile*, 98–109. Collier provides a definitive account of both the politics and the ideology of Chilean independence in *Ideas and Politics*.

22. *Aurora de Chile*, 28 May 1812, 63, quoted in Felstiner, "Family Metaphors," 161.

of families as electors," that provided the foundation for the newly created political community.[23] Early Chilean revolutionaries like Camilo Henríquez imagined political authority as beginning in a golden age dominated by the rule of families, and that "with time a family becomes a nation."[24]

In Chile's struggle for independence, "images of the polity as a family or a federation of families pervaded revolutionary ideology," and political elites "called up the image of the family, which justified both rebellion and family interest in the state."[25] The family trope can be seen in the language of an early patriot who described the creation of the Chilean nation: "But now, freed from her oppressors, she calls on her sons publicly to name her as Mother. . . . Thus the despotic name of *King* will nevermore be revived in our territory, and the enchanting name of MOTHER COUNTRY alone will resound."[26] Chilean male revolutionaries shifted their allegiance from the paternal figure of the king to the newly founded Chilean nation. And while the mother country of Chile might depend on the love of her sons for her freedom, she did not possess the *patria potestad* necessary to command obedience from those sons.

While liberal political theorists talked about the political equality of individual men, Chilean political elites clearly understood that their new state comprised a federation of elite families represented by male heads of households. As José Miguel Infante, one of architects of the new state, said in the 13 July 1826 session of Congress, "In the states where democracy has been best perfected, a child is not permitted to act as legislator nor as elector, since he does not possess discernment."[27] Infante's political children included nonpropertied and illiterate men, often of mestizo or indigenous heritage. Women's exclusion was assumed. The political fathers were elite landowners, but that group could be expanded to "rich farmers, . . . industrious capitalists, . . . active bankers, . . . [and] clever manufacturers."[28]

The dominance of familial ideology in creating the imagery, ideals, and institutions of new states was perhaps especially strong in Chile because of this far-reaching power of actual elite families. In Chile, "the great creole families that came to dominate the revolutionary process directly or indirectly,

23. Felstiner, "Family Metaphors," 161.
24. *Aurora de Chile,* 17 February 1812, 9, quoted in ibid.
25. Felstiner, "Kinship Politics," 79–80.
26. "Manuscritos patrióticos que trabajó un amante de la libertad chilena el 26 de febrero de 1817, contra los egoistas y contra los godos," quoted in Collier, *Ideas and Politics,* 209.
27. Quoted in ibid., 148.
28. *Mercurio Chilena,* 1 September 1828, 284, quoted in ibid., 149.

were a relatively close-knit and homogeneous group."[29] While the Chilean creole elite embraced the idea of republican government, in practice it was a limited form. Throughout Latin America, the revolutionary leaders were more interested in establishing their political power within newly forming nation-states than in radically challenging the class, race, and gender hierarchies of their societies. Reinscribing familial beliefs into the political foundations of the new states allowed these elites to both limit the extent of social change and to justify their continued political dominance.[30]

After the revolution, Latin American political elites turned to their extended families and patriarchal beliefs as the actual and ideological bulwarks of the new states. These elites "advocated a political model wherein male elders represented both the family to the state and the state inside the family . . . [and] sought to enhance the powers of the family patriarch and to link their own claims to political authority with the traditional prerogatives of the family father."[31] The cultural and symbolic connections between the familial and the political in postrevolutionary politics were thus strengthened by the role of actual extended networks of elite families in creating political order out of the larger institutional chaos that beset many new nation-states. These early leaders found that the weakness of early state structures could be balanced by a strong system of family networks.[32]

While independence from Spain ended the particular family analogy of the king as father, the new ruling creole elites actually broadened the political uses of familial metaphors. They attempted to reconstruct their political communities and to justify new forms of political power by reforming rather than rejecting public patriarchy. Talking about the new nation-states as a family allowed male political leaders to present themselves in the role of the patriarch of the national family, thereby justifying their political authority by invoking a patriarch's authority over his family. In using paternal metaphors, they constructed fellow nonelite Chileans as children, who when obedient would be rewarded, but when disobedient would need to be disciplined.[33]

This ideological reinscription of elite men's dominance of political power did not go uncontested by excluded groups. But like the revolution itself, these

29. Collier, *Ideas and Politics*, 7.

30. For a thorough discussion of Chile's path to independence and the dominant role of elite families in that process, see ibid.

31. Dore, "One Step Forward," 15.

32. Kuznesof and Oppenheimer, "Family and Society"; Dore, "One Step Forward."

33. See, for example, Dore, "Holy Family," for a discussion of this particular use in the Nicaraguan case. Schatzberg presents a very similar argument regarding middle Africa in *Political Legitimacy*.

struggles often took place through contesting invocations of family. Nonelite men embraced an expanded discourse of patriarchal privilege to justify their positions within their families and local communities. The historians Florencia Mallon and Sarah Chambers have documented how in both Peru and Mexico, ideals of patriarchal privilege could be used to craft pacts between elite and popular men, and how these agreements afforded popular men more power within independent republics.[34] Elite women, taking advantage of the opportunity for questioning social hierarchies during moments of revolutionary change, argued for expanded social and political participation by crafting appeals to "republican motherhood" and demonstrating their loyalty to the new political order. Throughout the liberal republics, women and their male allies justified greater access to educational and economic opportunities by stressing the importance of women as the bearers of future citizens. But these new opportunities took place within more general trends of men's legal patriarchal control, particularly of wives, as a way to promote political stability. In fact, recent gender scholarship argues that the creation of liberal republics did not necessarily advance women's social, political, or economic interests, particularly during the nineteenth century.[35]

The political uses of family during the creation of new nation-states established important historical patterns that shaped not only how the Chilean nation was imagined but also how the duties, responsibilities, and privileges of the state, political leaders, and citizens were understood. Familial welfare, now linked to the survival of newly emerging nation-states, became a foundational part of what constituted the appropriate ends of political communities. Male political leaders continued to invoke the idealized understanding of fathers to justify their political power. For nonelite men, being a father and a patriarch also increasingly garnered political rights and privileges in the liberal

34. Chambers offers a detailed examination of how nonelite men presented themselves as "honorable" through their hard work and social behavior, and therefore deserving of the rights of citizens. But the expansion of men's rights often came at the cost of increased scrutiny of women's behavior and a strengthening of men's patriarchal power. See Chambers, *From Subjects to Citizens.* Mallon, in her analysis of the importance of popular understandings of liberal ideology in the transition of Peru and Mexico from colonies to independent republics, argues that plebian communities were bound together through reciprocal relationships between families and communities, where older men assumed positions of power and responsibility in both. Ideals of justice and fairness were discussed through a familial language, and community patriarchs could interfere with the privileges of individual patriarchs if their actions were seen as possibly endangering broader community relations. See Mallon, *Peasant and Nation,* especially chapter 3.

35. See Dore, "One Step Forward," 17–26; Dore, "Property, Households, and Public Regulation of Domestic Life"; and Guy, "Parents Before Tribunals."

republics, as legal systems strengthened the control of all fathers over their dependents (*patria potestad*) and citizenship was limited to heads of households (which continued to exclude all women and many men).[36] While personally and culturally significant, women's familial identities as wives and mothers did not yet grant them access to formal political power.

The importance of images of the founding fathers and political patriarchs of the revolution has created a lasting link between political and familial power. Paternal images and metaphors have continued to be readily used by both elected presidents and military dictators throughout the nineteenth and twentieth centuries across Latin America to describe political power and leadership (Patriarchal Leader). In addition, the family was enshrined as the basic unit of society, and the stability and prosperity of the state was seen as dependent on the stability and prosperity of the family (Familial State). For the political elite of the nineteenth-century liberal states, the stability and prosperity of society and family were best promoted by strengthening the political and social power of patriarchs.[37] While the theoretical foundations of liberalism are based on a distinction between political and familial authority, the historical development of Latin American states shows how familial beliefs continued to strengthen the political and cultural legitimacy of the early liberal republics.

Creating Responsible Families: The Development of the Welfare State

During the twentieth century, the rise of organized working classes, growing middle-class sectors, and the political left representing these groups created pressure for political, social, and economic change. The creation of welfare states both incorporated older beliefs and sought to create new ideas about the relationship between the familial and the political. The history of Chile from the early 1900s to the 1973 military coup is a narrative about the increasing

36. Dore, "Property, Households, and Public Regulation of Domestic Life"; Guy, "Parents Before Tribunals."

37. In terms of legal rights, women often lost rights in the transition between late colonial society and liberal republics. For example, under Spanish colonial law, women as wives were entitled to one-half of the estate upon the death of their husbands, and daughters were also guaranteed equal inheritance along with their brothers from the parents' estate. See Felstiner, "Family Metaphors," 170. In Argentina, Donna Guy has documented the unwillingness on the part of state courts and magistrates to interfere with men's patriarchal rights over wives and children, even in cases of violence and abuse that were recognized as being beyond acceptable norms. See "Parents Before Tribunals."

scope and power of a social welfare state coupled with the expansion of democratic practices and the widening of political power to marginalized groups.[38] The shift from the older, oligarchic liberal republics and the development of a modern welfare state was spurred by expanding the role of the state in promoting familial welfare. While the political elite of the eighteenth century strengthened the control of men over their wives and children as a way to ensure the political and social stability of a newly created state, promoting the economic and social welfare of nonelite families increasingly came to be seen as an appropriate area for state interest. Often, the expansion of both state power and citizens' participation was justified by the need to protect the welfare of Chilean families in order to promote the health and progress of the national community. The stability and progress of the state was increasingly seen as dependent on the welfare of all Chilean families, not just that of the elite families.

Both social reformers and liberal politicians invoked the need to promote the health and welfare of families to justify the expansion of state power into areas such as labor laws, public health programs, and educational reforms. For example, many of the first labor protection laws in Chile were built around beliefs about the importance of families and the state's responsibilities toward families. This consensus allowed legislators from the then-dominant political parties, the Conservatives and the Liberals,[39] to craft and pass the first social legislation protecting both new mothers who worked and, by extension, the health of Chilean families. Chile's political parties, however, remained deeply divided over whether to pass protective legislation for male workers.[40]

During the 1930s and 1940s, growing agreement among different sectors of the political center and left about the need to promote better wages for working-class men formed the basis of the coalition governments that created Chile's welfare state. Called the Popular Front, the center-left coalition of the Radical, Socialist, and Communist parties governed from 1938 to 1952. The

38. See, for example, Salazar and Pinto, *Historia contemporánea de Chile.*

39. The ideological differences between the Conservative and Liberal parties were related to the position of the Catholic Church in Chilean society. Conservatives tended to want to protect the traditional influence of the Catholic Church in terms of education, marriage, family life, and the state. Liberals were committed to a secular state and to expanding the power of that state by limiting the power of the Catholic Church. They promoted such policies as the creation of public schools, state control of birth and death registries, and the establishment of the legal control of family through civil law. Both Liberals and Conservatives generally embraced free-trade economic policies and saw a very limited role for the state in the economy. For an excellent discussion of the very beginning of labor laws and the welfare state in Chile, see Hutchison, *Labors Appropriate to Their Sex*, especially chapter 7.

40. Ibid., 199.

historian Karin Rosemblatt has documented how Popular Front leaders crafted the needed political compromises by invoking shared beliefs about the family. At their base, the welfare reform projects were directed toward "constituting male-headed nuclear families in which husbands acted as stable breadwinners and women as housewives and mothers."[41] The Popular Front governments embraced reforms aimed at improving the economic and social standing of "respectable male workers while limiting that of women and disreputable or unmanly men."[42] Indeed, "political leaders validated and promoted a masculine identity that defined men as workers and family heads, [and] they justified increased material benefits and political enfranchisement for men by insisting that men's productive labor and their contribution to their families fortified the nation."[43] Shared beliefs around family built coalitions between members of the different factions of the Popular Front, between representatives of the new state programs and the men and women positioned as their clientele, between the political parties of the left and the increasingly unionized male working class, and finally between the political parties on the left and those on the right.

The increasing emphasis on male-headed families and women's domesticity was also strengthened through Chile's ties to the outside world. The North American companies that ran Chile's copper mines turned increasingly to promoting this family ideal as a way to create a stable, productive, and less contentious workforce. And these organizations often worked closely with the Chilean state. According to the historian Thomas Klubock, processes of acceptance, compliance, and resistance to the attempts on the part of the state and the companies to promote this ideal fundamentally shaped the development of working-class identity and struggle. As "male workers and their wives . . . strove to fulfill the company's promise of social mobility and middle-class domesticity, they compared the material hardships of life and labor in the camp with the company's ideal of middle-class domesticity . . . [which] exacerbated their antagonism toward North American supervisors, and solidified their sense of class and community."[44]

The continued expansion of Chile's welfare state during the 1950s and 1960s solidified the patterns laid down in the first half of the century. State programs continued to promote the formation of male-headed families as the

41. Rosemblatt, *Gendered Compromises,* 45.
42. Ibid., 253.
43. Rosemblatt, "Domesticating Men," 263.
44. Klubock, *Contested Communities,* 287.

normative family ideal. State leaders presented themselves as concerned about and responsible for the welfare of Chilean families, and strong families were seen as the basis for the stability and development of Chilean society. The rich oral history of the historian Heidi Tinsman's work shows how both men and women embraced, contested, and incorporated the gendered ideals of reform projects into their ongoing struggles over rights and obligations within the family. For example, agricultural reform, a central project of the Christian Democratic president Eduardo Frei (1964–70), was built on "a version of patriarchal family [that] remained foundational to the way rural society was rebuilt." Agrarian reform was envisioned as "a process in which male citizen-producers would responsibly provide for domesticated, if better educated and more civic-minded, wives and children."[45] Further, while these programs often embraced the ideal of gender mutualism (mutual respect and support for the respective roles of husbands and wives), most often the people working at the multiple state organizations implementing the new programs did not promote such equality. Women were granted more respect and greater freedom within the family, but these changes were not seen as fundamentally challenging the belief in men's natural position as the head of the household. As with the earlier reform projects of the Popular Front, men as the idealized breadwinner and head of household were more often the direct beneficiaries of new state programs, while women's incorporation was mediated through their relationships with men.[46] Thus agrarian reform projects incorporated the same gendered familial ideals that had been a part of the earlier reforms directed toward the urban working class and unionizing mine workers.

Recent historical work illuminates how Chilean political elites, social reformers, and organized working classes all turned to shared beliefs about family welfare to craft political compromises and pursue political goals. These appeals shaped the foundation of the welfare state and Chilean politics in the twentieth century. Politicians sought to expand state control over society through promoting an ideology that saw family welfare as a priority for governmental policies, thereby cementing the ideals of the Familial State. Chilean social reformers and organized working classes turned to arguments based in familial welfare to justify access to more benefits. The ideological basis for the vision of citizenship found in Militant Families was indelibly shaped by these political struggles. While the liberal state had limited participation and citizenship

45. Tinsman, *Partners in Conflict*, 3.
46. Tinsman, in ibid., argues that this did not change under Allende's shorter-lived agrarian reform project.

rights for elite male heads of households, the welfare state sought to expand participation, first to men and then to women, by legitimating these changes in terms of family. Social programs sought to help men support and provide for their families, and then to take care of those women and children when this did not happen. Promoting men's positions as fathers, husbands, and heads of households—roles shared across class and racial divisions—formed a basis for the political justifications and compromises used for the creation and expansion of new state programs and greater access to citizenship.

Women's participation in the state and in state programs directed at women's welfare also greatly expanded throughout the twentieth century. The first wave of the women's movement in Chile utilized a language of familial welfare to argue for a whole range of changes needed to improve women's political, legal, and social position. Early women reformers and their allies argued that changes to women's legal and social status were justified because expanding women's rights and political participation would benefit Chilean families. Because of this, women's greater political and social participation would also benefit the health, stability, and progress of the state. The familial focus of state programs was carried through in the creation of state-sponsored Centros de Madres (Mothers' Centers, or CEMA). Directed toward poor and working-class women, these centers provided a space for women to learn about issues and problems specific to their status, and to receive training in gender-appropriate work and household management, and served as a form of collective representation for women. By the 1970s, CEMAs both distributed material benefits to Chilean women and were used by Chile's political parties to incorporate women into their projects.[47] Thus women's familial roles helped justify improvements in the political, economic, and social position of women.[48]

The struggles of everyday Chileans to expand their political participation recast ideas of citizenship for Chilean women and many Chilean men. Early feminists turned to maternalism to argue for such diverse goals as increasing women's access to education, improving the health of mothers and children, and reforming civil codes to give married women greater control over property and wages. Suffrage activists argued for women's citizenship by connecting civic duty to women's familial roles as wives and mothers.[49] Expanding citizenship to working-class and peasant men, however, was also deeply connected to beliefs

47. See Tinsman, *Partners in Conflict*, 146–56, and Power, *Right-Wing Women*, 107–18. I discuss the role of Mothers' Centers under Pinochet in chapter 5.
48. Lavrin, *Women, Feminism, and Social Change*.
49. For a discussion, see ibid.

about the importance of creating responsible heads of households. Nonelite men argued that as dedicated supporters of their families, they deserved the rights and responsibilities of full citizenship. Changes in both state structures and ideals of citizenship during the twentieth century reshaped how the familial was incorporated into the political, but they did not displace familial issues from political beliefs. Increasingly, familial identities became important political identities not only for elite men but also for working-class, peasant, and poor men and for all women. Again and again, politicians, social reformers, and everyday citizens drew on familial beliefs to help create and justify new state structures designed to promote social welfare and to expand citizenship rights to more groups.

Chile's Political Parties: Crafting Compromises Around Family

Chile's powerful political parties also shaped these processes. Unlike many other Latin American countries, where political parties remained weak and noninstitutionalized, a dominant feature of twentieth-century Chilean politics was the power and capacity of its political parties. Three main political tendencies have dominated Chile's political development: (1) a political left that generally embraces a vision of class struggle and argues for an expanded role of the state; (2) a political center that includes traditional liberal parties and those inspired by progressive Catholic social thought; and (3) a political right that combines conservative Catholic social traditions with a commitment to free-market economic policies.[50]

By the 1970s, the Chilean right was represented by the National Party (Partido Nacional, PN). Both Chilean men and women have embraced conservative beliefs about the family and politics. Some Chilean women have been fervent supporters of the right because of the importance it places on upholding traditional understandings of both the family and gender roles. Elite conservative women also have a long history of public involvement, beginning with extensive charity work. During the early twentieth century, conservative women

---

50. For a general discussion of the development of Chile's political parties, see Oppenheim, *Politics in Chile*; Collier and Sater, *History of Chile*; and Loveman, *Chile*. For a discussion of the development of political parties on the left, see Drake, *Socialism and Populism*. For the development of the Christian Democratic Party, see Smith, *The Church and Politics*. Valenzuela's *Breakdown of Democratic Regimes* provides an excellent account of how the internal dynamics and political goals of Chile's political parties helped bring about the intense political polarization preceding the military coup.

organized working-class women into Catholic unions that would "uphold and defend the interest of those women who worked for a living without attacking the principles of order and authority."[51] Women's connection to the Catholic Church led the Chilean right to become an early supporter of women's suffrage. In 1917 the Conservative Party[52] became the first party to formally propose a law for women's suffrage. In 1934, Chilean women won the right to vote in municipal elections, but it was not until 1949 that they were granted equal suffrage with men. Women first voted for president in the 1952 elections. The political right has consistently courted women voters, efforts that often yielded political dividends. As the historian Margaret Power notes, while women voted in smaller numbers than did men, "from the 1930s until the 1960s, the majority of voting women cast their ballots for conservative candidates."[53]

In the 1960s and 1970s, faced with intense political competition and determined efforts on the part of the center and the left to organize workers and peasants, the Chilean right increasingly saw women as an important base of support (especially those in the middle and upper classes). Women's incorporation into party politics, however, did not change the position of the Chilean right regarding the family; the National Party continued to promote the ideal of the traditional, patriarchal family arrangement. During this period, the National Party opposed proposals to legalize divorce and to eliminate the legal distinctions between legitimate and illegitimate children in inheritance laws. The PN also promoted programs that supported traditional values around the sanctity of marriage and the natural order of the family.

The Christian Democratic Party (Partido Demócrata Cristiano de Chile, PDC) dominated the political center in Chile in the 1960s and 1970s.[54] The

51. Ericka Kim Verba, "The Liga de Damas Chilenas: Angels of Peace and Harmony of the Social Question" (paper presented at the Latin American Studies Association meeting, Guadalajara, April 1997), quoted in Power, *Right-Wing Women*, 48.

52. While Chile's ideological spectrum has had a defined right, center, and left for the majority of the twentieth century, Chile's political parties have changed quite a bit. During the oligarchic republics of the nineteenth century, the Liberal Party represented liberal political tenets. But the growth of parties of the center and the left led to a decrease in support for the Liberal Party. In the 1960s, the remnants of the Liberal Party joined the Conservative Party to form the National Party. See Collier and Sater, *History of Chile*, for an extensive discussion of the development of Chile's political parties.

53. Power, *Right-Wing Women*, 69.

54. Before the ascendance of the PDC, the major centrist party was the Partido Radical (the Radical Party, or PR). The PR was founded in 1863 and known as an anticlerical, liberal party of the middle class. It emerged as a major political party in the 1920s and controlled the presidency in the 1940s as part of the Popular Front governments. Starting in the 1950s, the PR was increasingly in competition for the political center with the PDC. By the 1970s, the PR had splintered and its electoral influence was considerably weakened. See Oppenheim, *Politics in Chile*, 15–16.

original roots of the PDC were a group of youthful members of the Conservative Party in the 1930s who were interested in the "social question" (the problems of poverty and underdevelopment) and started to explore the progressive Catholic social thought promoted by theologians such as Jacques Maritain and Alberto Hurtado. In 1938, these young Conservative Party dissidents founded their own party, Falange Nacional. Renamed Partido Demócrata Cristiano de Chile in 1957, the PDC had by the 1960s replaced the secular PR as the dominant party of the center.[55] The Christian Democrats argued for the need to transcend both capitalism and socialism through a focus on "nonindividualist, community responses to social and economic problems" that would organically integrate the needs of different sectors of the community.[56] The PDC in the 1960s and 1970s combined a commitment to the need for moderate structural reforms to address the problems of poverty and underdevelopment with unfailing support for Chile's democratic process and institutions. This was captured in Eduardo Frei's 1964 presidential campaign slogan, "Revolution in Liberty."

The PDC was thus a complex mix of progressive ideals and conservative beliefs. Perhaps nothing captures this better than the party's views of the family. The PDC viewed the family as the fundamental social institution of Chilean society, and therefore as crucial to the success of its social reform projects. Embracing this ideal, its reform projects were directed at helping men to fulfill their responsibilities as the heads of households, while women were taught hygiene and household economics in order to fulfill their roles as mothers and housewives. As discussed above, President Frei's agrarian reform policies were also built around a vision of gender complementarity and mutualism. This approach to gender relations reflected broader changes in the position of the Catholic Church. As part of the progressive changes associated with the Second Vatican Council, the Catholic Church had altered its official position, from upholding men's authority over their wives and children, to a vision in which "the unity of marriage will radiate from the equal personal dignity of wife and husband, a dignity acknowledged by mutual and total love."[57] Increasingly, Catholic social thought argued that men should recognize the importance of women's contributions to the family and should refrain from violence against their wives. Further, this perspective held that women should expand their involvement into the public world, but with a continued commitment to the fundamental importance of their roles as wives and mothers.

55. Collier and Sater, *History of Chile*, 305–6.
56. Oppenheim, *Politics in Chile*, 25.
57. From *Gaudium et spes*, quoted in Htun, *Sex and the State*, 32.

At the root of the programs of the PDC was a firm belief in the traditional family and the mutually beneficial relationship between strong families and a strong state. During Frei's presidency, policies continued to treat women fundamentally as wives and mothers, and government programs were designed to help women to better perform these roles, thus strengthening the family. But the PDC also viewed men through the lens of the family. As husbands, men were supposed to support women's new opportunities for political and social participation, since the benefits of more educated and socially involved wives and mothers would accrue to the entire family. The PDC promoted reforms that would strengthen the family by providing both better material situations (through economic programs) and stronger emotional and spiritual connections (through greater mutual respect and understanding between men and women). Thus, while arguing for the "equal dignity" of men and women, the PDC remained committed to the image of the nuclear family built on the traditional roles of women and men.[58]

Chile's political left has been dominated by two parties, the Socialist Party (Partido Socialista de Chile, PS) and the Communist Party (Partido Comunista de Chile, PC). While there are important differences in the political development and ideological stances of the two parties, the left's general view of the family has been more or less consistent.[59] The left maintained that working women's welfare was best served by providing working-class men with sufficient wages and state programs that would allow them to support dependent wives and children. With Allende's election in 1970, a coalition between these two parties was the base for his Popular Unity (Unidad Popular, UP) government.[60]

58. In addition to Heidi Tinsman's work, the Chilean anthropologists Larissa Lomnitz and Ana Melnick in *Chile's Political Culture* document the importance of familial networks and Catholic social teachings in the political and ideological development of the PDC.

59. The Chilean Communist Party was founded in 1921 (although it had roots in the late 1880s) and the Socialist Party in 1933. One of the main divisions between the two parties was the membership of PC in the Third International. The PC has always been the smaller of the two parties, although sometimes the more politically moderate. In general, the PC did not advocate violent revolution, but argued instead for a broad alliance of all groups that supported social change and working through Chile's democratic institutions. The Chilean Socialist Party was always a nationalist party. It rejected allegiance to the Soviet Union, arguing that its policies and ideology should be based on an analysis of the culture and history of Chile and Latin America. The PS was generally committed to change through electoral means, though it always had a strong minority that argued for armed revolution. In general, the party was not very interested in establishing close ties with other progressive parties and groups, but all party leaders did not share this tendency (e.g., Salvador Allende was a strong supporter of coalition politics). For a discussion of the history of Chile's leftist parties, see Oppenheim, *Politics in Chile*, 18–20.

60. The left coalition, the Popular Unity (UP), that elected Allende also included two splinter groups from the Radical Party (the Democratic Radical Party [PDR] and the Left Radical Party

Like the center and the right, the Chilean left also supported an ideal family based on the man as breadwinner and head of household, while women were seen primarily as wives and mothers. As Allende was famously quoted as saying, "When I say 'woman' I always think of the woman-mother. . . . When I talk of the woman, I refer to her in her function in the nuclear family. . . . The child is the prolongation of the woman who in essence is born to be a mother."[61] Embracing an idealized vision of the nuclear family, leftist political parties argued for the need to increase the wages of working-class men and to expand the family allowances, most often paid to men, as a way to promote stronger families.

As compared to the right and the center, however, the left was more supportive of laws that would have helped equalize women's relative position within the family. Allende's government, for example, supported legislation that would have granted women "full civil capacity" and would have made community property the default marital property arrangement, rather than recognizing the husband as the "chief of the conjugal society" who "may freely administer his property and that of his wife."[62] Leftist parties were also more willing than others to acknowledge women's oppression within the family. Under Allende, the Popular Unity argued for creating state programs that would help women to manage conflicts between their roles as workers and as mothers. For example, Allende's government experimented with small programs such as communal food preparation and cooperative laundries, as well as the expansion of child-care facilities. These initiatives were aimed at decreasing the burden on working mothers, but they did not question the traditional gender norms that made women more responsible for children and the home than men.[63] In the final analysis, while the changes promoted by the UP produced significant material gains for working-class and poor women, Allende's programs posed virtually "no threat to the patriarchal structures at either the micro or macro levels . . . [and] Allende and the UP coalition felt no need to expand

---

[PIR]), two splinter groups from the Christian Democrats (Movement for United Popular Action [MAPU] and the Christian Left [IC], which represented the most left-leaning tendencies within the Christian Democrats), and three other very small parties (Popular Socialist Union Party [USOPO], the National Democratic Party [PADENA], and the Independent Popular Action [API]).

61. Quoted in Chaney, "Mobilization of Women," 269.

62. Article 134 of the Chilean Civil Code in effect in 1970s, quoted in Htun, *Sex and the State*, 73. These reforms were never passed, and even today the default marital property regime recognizes the husband as the overseer of the joint property of the marriage. Chilean couples have to specifically ask to be married under the common property regime, which recognizes the equality of both parties over marital property.

63. For a discussion of these programs, see Shayne, *Revolution Question*, especially 73–89.

their gendered programs beyond the nuclear family."[64] While many of Chile's feminist activists had strong ties to leftist political parties, they were not able to fundamentally challenge the patriarchal beliefs embedded in the programs and policies of the PS and the PC.

Thus Chile's political parties of the right, center, and left shared a strong commitment to an idealized vision of the traditional patriarchal family. This is not surprising, as the idealization of the traditional family was widely shared in Chilean society at the time. For example, in their 1968 analysis of the perception of women's and men's roles in Chile, the sociologists Armand and Michèle Mattelart argued that the dominant ideal for women in Chile was to be "a good mother and a good wife."[65] For most Chilean men and women, the dominant ideal of family life remained one where women passed "without any detours from the house of her father to the house of her husband, there to fulfill her destiny as the mother of children and the dutiful wife who carefully performs all her domestic tasks with a view toward her husband's comfort and convenience."[66] During the 1960s and 1970s, women's most important duties and responsibilities remained centered on motherhood, the family, and the home. Women's central roles and identities remained within the family, even with a growing acknowledgment of and support for women's participation outside the home. For men, their public identities as worker and citizen and their familial role as the father, breadwinner, and authority figure remained constant.

The Politics of the Ministry of the Family

When President Allende proposed a Ministry of the Family, he sought to continue Chile's political pattern of expanding state power through invoking shared beliefs about the family and the state. The debate around the Ministry of the Family provides a concrete demonstration of how consensus around familial beliefs shaped the interactions between Chile's political parties. Even at the beginning of the 1970s, a widespread consensus for a certain view of the "ideal"

64. Ibid., 88. The inability or unwillingness of the Chilean left to question traditional gender roles is part of a broader pattern of leftist politics in Latin America. This pattern led Maxine Molyneux to formulate her analysis of women's practical and strategic gender interests in her classic article "Mobilization Without Emancipation?," which sought to understand the successes and failures of the Sandinista government in Nicaragua to address women's inequality and oppression.

65. Mattelart and Mattelart, *La mujer chilena en una nueva sociedad*, 60.

66. Ibid., 35.

family, and men's and women's appropriate familial roles, was shared across the political spectrum. In addition, the proposal contained shared views about the relationships between state and family, including a belief that the family represented the basic nucleus of society and the foundation of the Chilean nation-state. Those proposing the ministry argued that this privileged position meant that the state had a duty to protect and promote familial interests. Finally, most political actors agreed that for a variety of reasons the family was threatened and in special need of aid from the state. A growing recognition that many Chilean families failed to achieve the idealized form was seen as a sign of a deepening societal crisis rather than an argument for a broader valorization of different types of families.

Presented to the Chilean Congress on 2 March 1971, the Ministry of the Family's explicit goal was to create a cabinet-level department that would coordinate the existing myriad of state programs directed at Chilean families. Additionally, the ministry was tasked with the creation and promulgation of national familial policies that would integrate the family more fully into state policies and provide solutions to the pressing problems facing the family. Allende framed his proposal in two ways: as a concrete example of his and his government's commitment to Chilean families, and as a necessary response to the current problems facing the family. Allende believed that "a great part of our people live in conditions that make a healthy and authentic family life practically impossible."[67]

As the legislation progressed it was clear that the veneration of the family and explicit connections between national interests and familial interests were not limited to the speeches of Allende and members of his government. Unlike many of Allende's other political projects, the creation of the ministry was initially praised and supported by all political parties.[68] Senator Valenzuela, a Christian Democrat, stated, "Today, the Christian Democrats, as with the rest of the parties of the opposition, approve the creation of the Ministry of the Family . . . because we are convinced that in this manner we are serving the permanent interests of Chile."[69] Deputy Monckeberg, an influential member

67. Cámara de Diputados, *Sesiones regulares y irregulares*, Sesión 22a, 3 March 1971, 1432 (hereafter cited as Cámara de Diputados).
68. See Cámara de Diputados, Sesión 36a, 11 May 1971, 2549–65. It is interesting to note that one other project that did not meet with fierce opposition was the nationalization of the Chilean copper mines. It also had widespread support and was seen as benefiting national interest. But that project was quickly passed, while the legislation for the Ministry of the Family was eventually politicized and languished without being passed into law.
69. Senado de Chile, *Diario de sesiones del Senado*, 74a, 7 September 1972, 4042.

of the conservative National Party, a medical doctor and fierce opponent of Allende, voiced his support of the ministry during the initial hearings in the Chamber of Deputies, stating, "This project of law [will] . . . give to the family the true transcendence it must have for the survival of our *patria*,[70] because it is precisely the base of the moral, spiritual, and economic formation of our society. It is there [in the family] where the future of our children is cast, and within the family . . . that all sectors receive the necessary support for the power to live with dignity and educate their children."[71] Clearly, Deputy Monckeberg could find common ground with Allende around shared beliefs in the family as the base of the current Chilean nation, its important role in shaping Chile's future through the education of children, and the state's obligation to the family based on the connection between familial flourishing and state survival. But as a member of the rightist National Party, he stressed the moral and spiritual aspects of family welfare. Thus political elites shared an understanding of the family as the basis of the nation, and familial welfare as crucial to national interests.

But what types of family are behind these invocations? Based on the transcripts recording the debates of both the Senate and the Chamber of Deputies, most politicians clearly understood family along the lines of the traditional arrangement of a husband, wife, and children. Allende, in his original message to the Chamber, stated that "behind the great structural reforms that we want to implement, there is a man, a woman, and a child who have been born to be happy."[72] In case of any doubt about the family outlined by President Allende, Deputy Allende of the Socialist Party noted the importance of the ministry in promoting the legal organization of the working-class family: "the husband, the wife, the child . . . the working family."[73] Deputy Allende affirmed that the parties of the Popular Unity were "conscious that what families worry about is that the head of the household has work . . . [and] that the housewife's work be valued and recognized as fundamental for the family."[74] The fact that the original proposal had not contained a definition of "family" perhaps points to the strength of the consensus around this normative conception of the family.

70. The term *la patria* in Spanish can be translated in a number of ways, including as "nation," "homeland," "fatherland," or "motherland." I have chosen to not translate this term in order to maintain the contextual nuance and shifting meaning.
71. Cámara de Diputados, Sesión 23a, 1 December 1971, 1772.
72. Cámara de Diputados, Sesión 22, 2 March 1971, 1433.
73. Cámara de Diputados, Sesión 36a, 11 May 1971, 2565.
74. Ibid., 2561.

While there existed a widespread consensus around the ideal family, Chilean lawmakers were certainly aware that many Chilean families did not conform to this vision. In trying to formally define the scope of the proposed ministry, Chilean lawmakers were loath to limit it to only nuclear families. Instead, the committee assembled by the Chamber of Deputies finally agreed on the following definition: "A group of persons united by the bond of matrimony, [the bond of] paternity, legitimate, illegitimate, or by adoption." Additionally, the family was defined as a "group of persons, [who] through a stable cohabitation are generally recognized as a family in their relations with the community." If an individual did not fit into the broad definition of the law, the proposal went on to say that all individuals were to be considered part of a family, because the ministry was aimed at "all members of the national community."[75] Thus, in trying to write a definition that pinpointed the family as the target of state policies, politicians ultimately ended up defining all Chileans as somehow part of a family. This broad definition reaffirmed the fundamental belief in the importance of the family as the base of society. The recognition of multiple experiences of family, however, did not demand that lawmakers fundamentally rethink their commitment to a specific familial form as the ideal. More often, the recognition of different family forms supported another area of consensus in the debate: the belief that the family was in crisis, and that there was a need for state actions to strengthen the traditional family.

President Allende, for example, justified the need for a Ministry of the Family through invoking current dangers to the family, arguing that the "social decomposition that characterizes the underdevelopment of our country has its most dramatic reflection in the familial environment[:] . . . high levels of illegitimacy, rupture of the familial bonds . . . low scholarly performance, mental deficiencies, juvenile and adult delinquency, alcoholism, drug consumption, [and] abortion practices."[76] Other problems that threatened the family included a lack of public housing, unemployment for men, and the lack of social and cultural opportunities for women.

These concerns reveal that political elites felt that the functioning and progress of Chilean society depended on the existence of healthy nuclear families. During the debate, an amazing variety of society's ills were discussed in terms of how they might affect the family's abilities to fulfill its duties. For example, Deputy Bulnes of the National Party noted that his party had been convinced

---

75. Cámara de Diputados, Sesión 23a, 1 December 1971, 1761.
76. Cámara de Diputados, Sesión 21, 30 November 1971, 1546.

of the need for the legislation because of problems such as unemployment, alcoholism, and malnutrition that affected a large number of Chilean families, "especially in the poorest sectors."[77] Indeed, many social problems were defined not as individual afflictions, but rather as family problems, impairing men's and women's abilities to fulfill their familial roles. The current plethora of familial problems endangered the production and socialization of future Chileans and the maintenance of the Chilean nation. Thus, as Deputy Saavedra noted, the law was a "justified response to the necessities of the Chilean family."[78]

Although most politicians agreed that the state had a duty to protect the family and that Chilean families were presently facing great risks, determining the causes of these threats, and which threats were most pressing, depended on the political ideology and policy goals of different parties. Each major party stressed different problems as the most critical and proposed distinct roles for the state in addressing these issues. In general, the parties of the Popular Unity government viewed threats to the family as rooted in the exploitation of workers in the capitalist system. Indeed, it was the "capitalist man" (a man formed within the capitalist system) who "destroys his family, who goes to the bar, who does not worry about the little ones . . . who gets drunk," so that when he comes home he will not have to hear about the problems with the "nutrition of the little ones . . . it is this man who abandons his children."[79] Thus working-class men were unable to fulfill their gendered familial responsibilities within a capitalist system.

Many UP deputies and senators also felt that capitalism threatened the family by exploiting women and not respecting their roles as wives and mothers. Because of men's insufficient wages, women were driven into the workforce, where they could be both exploited as workers and used as surplus labor to depress the wages paid to men. Capitalism's material exploitation also caused emotional problems in family life. Socialist Deputy Palestro argued that it was the fault of capitalism that "the family does not have any connection and permits the daughter to convert into a prostitute, that the son converts into a delinquent, that the father goes without work or that the mother does not have anything to put into the pot . . . [except] for a piece of bread."[80] From this perspective, the root cause of the multiple crises that affected the family was the current economic system. To protect working-class families from

77. Cámara de Diputados, Sesión 36a, 11 May 1971, 2557.
78. Cámara de Diputados, Sesión 21, 30 November 1971, 2558.
79. Cámara de Diputados, Sesión 23a, 1 December 1971, 1780–81.
80. Ibid., 1774.

these threats, special attention from the state was needed. The proposal for the Ministry of the Family included the left's vision of class and community uplift, which depended on men and women upholding ideals of male and female behavior that embraced hard work, rejection of vice, and mutual respect.[81] Once the revolution was implemented, the problems facing the family rooted in economic exploitation and the moral failings of capitalism would disappear. In the meantime, the family deserved the help and support of the Popular Unity government.

For Christian Democrats, the current and immediate threat to Chilean families was rooted in the radical processes of development that Chile was experiencing as it underwent modernization. Christian Democrats believed that a Ministry of the Family could "attend in more profundity to the problems related to the familial nucleus and its normalcy within a society in revolution."[82] Like the members of the UP, the Christian Democrats placed some of the blame for problems within families on Chile's unequal economic progress and continuing underdevelopment. Consistent with Catholic social teaching, they also promoted the idea that the family had to be the base of social and political changes, since only the family could teach the proper cultural and moral values that supported these changes. Within Christian Democratic thought, all members of the family had a special contribution to make in the success of the reforms and the creation of a more just society. In particular, cooperation between husbands and wives within the family unit would provide the glue to hold together both the family and Chilean society as they grappled with the changes brought on by modernization and development.

The National Party, on the other hand, stressed the importance of nonmaterial factors in the current crisis. Members constructed the threats to the family as arising not from the process of modernization or capitalist exploitation, but from challenges to the spiritual, moral, and religious values of Chilean society. Deputy Monckeberg, for example, criticized the Popular Unity's proposal for focusing too much on the material and not enough on the spiritual role of the family. The proposal needed to recognize that the "indisputable work of the family is the education and transmission of values to the children and the emotional development of persons."[83] Deputy Bulnes noted that the National Party believes that "it is necessary to . . . eliminate or diminish a series

81. Rosemblatt, "What We Can Reclaim."
82. Senado de Chile, *Diario de sesiones del Senado*, 74a, September 1972, 4039.
83. Cámara de Diputados, Sesión 36a, 11 May 1971, 2554–55.

of problems and conflicts that originated in an atmosphere of alcoholism, in unemployment, in malnutrition, problems that are of a social nature, economic nature, cultural nature, and inclusive of a conjugal nature."[84]

An examination of the entire debate surrounding the proposed Ministry of the Family reveals the centrality of family in Chilean politics and political culture. In the view of many Chileans in the late 1960s and 1970s, it was the family that held together Chilean society and that produced and socialized future generations. The family and familial interests were often used to symbolize the nation and national interests in the discourse of politicians at the time. Given the shared understanding about the importance of the family among the dominant political factions, it is not surprising that the health and well-being of Chilean families was framed as a central political concern. Political elites of all political persuasions strongly felt that the Chilean state had a responsibility to protect or promote familial welfare, even though they disagreed over exactly what this meant in practice. Thus the legislation proposing the Ministry of the Family provides a concrete example of how widely shared these familial beliefs were, how areas of agreement promoted state policies, and how even crucial disagreements between political parties contained areas of consensus.

Conclusion

The historical development of Chile, as well as other Latin American states, illustrates the complex connections between the familial and the political. Past uses of family and familial beliefs to create new political communities, justify different types of states, promote institutional development, and create specific types of citizens became embedded in cultural understandings about politics, political leaders, and citizens. These historical understandings inform the current symbolic repertoires of politics and the meanings that are mobilized in the ongoing pursuit of political goals. By tracing this historical development, we see how the foundations for the four categories of political uses of family were crafted through previous political projects. The basis of Patriarchal Leader was created during colonial rule, strengthened by the liberal republics, and extended during the twentieth-century welfare period. The understandings of Familial State were located more in the state-building projects of the early

---

84. Ibid., 2559.

independence period and were recast and strengthened as the state expanded its control and influence through social welfare policies. But the intertwining of political and familial forms of authority, rule, and power that sustained colonial political order should not be overlooked. Familial symbols and metaphors of the nation (Familial Nation) helped justify the creation of the Chilean state and have influenced national imaginings ever since. Familial understandings of citizenship (Militant Families) were shaped during both the establishment of Latin America's independent republics and the reform projects of the twentieth-century welfare state.

These understandings about the connections between familial and political authority are part of broader cultural beliefs about the roles, rights, and responsibilities of the state, political leaders, and ordinary citizens. Given this history, it is not surprising to find that familial beliefs played a prominent role in the political struggles of the 1970s and 1980s. These connections would assume even greater importance in the coming political struggles as both political elites and Chilean citizens sought to make sense of emerging political issues, justify their political positions and actions, and persuade others to join their struggle.

★ THREE ★

COMPETING FATHERS
The 1970 Presidential Election

In July and August 1970, Chilean political life was dominated by a fiercely contested presidential election between three strong candidates: Salvador Allende, Radomiro Tomic, and Jorge Alessandri. All three were well-known standard-bearers for Chile's dominant political tendencies. For the left, Salvador Allende ran as the candidate of the Popular Unity, a coalition comprising the Chilean Socialist Party, the Chilean Communist Party, and a number of smaller parties. The centrist Christian Democratic Party supported Radomiro Tomic as the successor to the current PDC president, the popular Eduardo Frei. The former conservative president Jorge Alessandri[1] ran as an independent candidate, but he was supported by the rightist National Party.[2] Two of the candidates, Alessandri and Allende, were seasoned presidential campaigners; in fact, they had competed against each other in the 1958 presidential election, which Alessandri won with a narrow plurality (31.6 percent), defeating Allende by only about thirty-three thousand votes.[3] Chile's vibrant multiparty system meant that Chilean presidents were often elected with less than 50 percent of the vote. In 1970, the three candidates represented well-known ideological differences among the parties about the role of the state in the economy, what reforms were needed, the pace of reform, and the relationship between citizens and the state.

In presenting their candidacy and political projects, all three candidates depended on specific familial understandings of the state, political leaders, and citizens. In this chapter, I examine how in campaign ads and political speeches

1. Under Chilean law, the current president was barred from seeking reelection for a consecutive term, though past presidents were allowed to run again after their break from office. Thus, while Frei could not present himself for reelection, Jorge Alessandri, having left office in 1964, was once again eligible to run.
2. In disarray after electoral defeats in the 1966 congressional elections, the Conservative Party and the Liberal Party had merged to create the National Party. For a discussion, see Collier and Sater, *History of Chile*, 305–29.
3. Loveman, *Chile*, 264.

each candidate drew on an ideal of the Patriarchal Leader. My analysis also reveals the centrality of questions of familial welfare in defining the roles and responsibilities of the state. In crafting their electoral strategies, the three candidates thus drew on and strengthened cultural beliefs of the Familial State, linking familial welfare to the general interests and well-being of the national community. In their campaigns, the three presidential candidates routinely framed issues such as employment, urbanization, lack of adequate housing, and high rates of inflation in terms of their impact on the abilities of Chilean families, rather than individuals, to prosper. Finally, during the campaign, candidates appealed to both men and women through their family roles, and it was through these family roles that citizens' demands were seen as legitimate.

Fathers and Families in the 1970 Presidential Campaign

The reform projects of President Eduardo Frei set the stage for the 1970 election. In 1964, fearing that Allende and the left would emerge victorious (and lacking its own strong candidate), the right threw its support behind Frei. After winning the election with a historically high majority of 56 percent, Frei pursued a policy of moderate structural reforms designed to modernize agriculture and incorporate the urban poor into state programs through an emphasis on housing and job training, and he sought to decrease the power of foreign monopolies (particularly in Chile's copper industry).[4] Frei firmly believed that problems of poverty, inequality, and social injustice could be addressed through "nonindividualist, community responses" based on progressive Catholic social teaching. Frei positioned the Christian Democrats and his "Revolution in Liberty" as a "third option to the unbridled capitalism on the Right, on the one hand, and the Marxism of the Left, on the other."[5] Frei was partially successful in all three areas, but as the political scientist Brian Loveman notes, "for every successful program there were more people left out than included. The backlog of need and poverty made even significant improvements . . . a political defeat."[6] Allende and the leftist parties hoped to capitalize on these unmet expectations by pledging to increase and deepen reform. Arguing that Frei's third way had not been able to meet the needs of the poor and working class, Allende promised to bring about socialist goals through

---

4. Oppenheim, *Politics in Chile*, 24–26; Loveman, *Chile*, 224–25.
5. Oppenheim, *Politics in Chile*, 25.
6. Loveman, *Chile*, 239.

democracy, proposing extensive structural reforms (e.g., more extensive land reforms, nationalization of industries, expansion of social welfare) to begin the shift away from a capitalist economy.[7]

The success of the PDC also generated growing opposition on the right. While Chilean conservatives had supported Frei in 1964 to prevent a victory by Allende, by 1970 they felt betrayed by Frei's policies and what they saw as the increasing radicalization of society. They particularly resented Frei's land reform projects, the increasing mobilization of rural labor, and their loss of political control of the countryside. These changes threatened not only elites' control of agricultural land but also their traditional base of political power.[8] The Chilean right rallied behind former president Jorge Alessandri, who was technically running as an independent and who promoted free-market economic policies and conservative social values and policies. Alessandri's emergence as a strong candidate demonstrated that those on the right had reorganized, and further that they were invested in the presidential campaign.[9] Caught between two strong candidates, the PDC candidate Tomic chose to run on the successes of Frei's programs, promising to deepen and extend Frei's social reforms. Hoping to consolidate his base and to attract middle-class progressives (who continued to worry that Allende was too radical), Tomic highlighted the importance of mediating socioeconomic inequality through modernization and the expansion of social welfare programs, rather than through an embrace of socialism.

The candidates in 1970 presented Chileans with a clear choice among competing visions of Chile's future. While politically distinct, all three campaigns incorporated specific familial beliefs to frame the candidates' political positions. In the two months leading up to the election of 4 September, 1,083 campaign ads appeared in the two largest newspapers of the time—*El Mercurio*, the standard-bearer of the center-right, and *El Clarín*, a popular leftist paper that boasted the widest readership in Chile.[10] Nine percent of the 689 ads in

7. For a discussion of the basic platforms of the three candidates, see Oppenheim, *Politics in Chile*, 35–42.

8. Brian Loveman, in *Struggle in the Countryside*, traces the history of rural labor conflict in Chile. He shows how control over land and rural politics was the base of national political power for Chile's traditional elite. He argues that for most of the twentieth century, the Chilean left sold out the interests of the *campesinos* in exchange for Conservative support for urban labor issues. Ultimately, he argues, it was the agrarian reforms of Frei and Allende that threatened the political power of the elite, and their reaction to this threat was a major cause of the breakdown of Chile's democracy.

9. See Power, *Right-Wing Women*, for a discussion of the evolution of the Chilean right during the 1960s.

10. I conducted the coding during my field research in Chile. I am confident in the overall analysis I present, but it is highly probable that I might have missed a few scattered ads (the holdings of the National Library were sometimes incomplete, occasionally missing a day or a few pages). But

El Mercurio and 21 percent of the 394 ads in *El Clarín* referenced family. Campaign ads that presented the candidates' policy positions or proposals, but without appealing to the family, made up 12 percent of the ads in *El Mercurio* and 7 percent in *El Clarín*. Overall, the most common type of ad was candidate endorsement, which included ads extolling the support of civil society groups (neighborhood councils, retired groups, professional associations) and individuals for one of the three candidates (22 percent in *El Mercurio* and 11 percent in *El Clarín*). Closely following were ads publicizing the campaign rallies of the three candidates (19 percent in *El Mercurio* and 12 percent in *El Clarín*). The majority of the remaining ads in both publications were designed simply to put the candidates' names in the paper, rather than to explain issues. These ads often listed only the candidate's name and his position on the electoral list (Tomic was 1, Alessandri was 2, and Allende was 3). Consequently, the ads with familial references are even more significant than their numbers suggest, given the level of detail needed to make a textual or visual familial claim.

The number of familial ads for each candidate reflected their electoral strategies and political ideologies. Of the ads in *El Mercurio*, 5 percent of Alessandri's ads referenced the family, with Tomic at 13 percent and Allende at 20 percent. In addition, of the ads that attacked communism and Allende but were published by groups other than his opponents' official campaigns, 17 percent referenced the family. Acción Mujeres de Chile (Women's Action of Chile) and Chile Joven (Young Chile) produced the majority of these anticommunism ads. In *El Clarín*, 63 percent of Allende's, 21 percent of Tomic's, and 4 percent of anti-Alessandri ads featured the family (Alessandri's campaign did not place ads in *El Clarín*). Anti-Alessandri ads were designed to combat the anticommunist ads and were produced by groups such as the Comite de Fumigación Nacional (Committee for National Fumigation) and the Campaña de Información Pública y Orientación Popular (Public Information and Popular Orientation Campaign). In all the campaign ads, familial images were used in three main ways: (1) to portray the candidate's political leadership and personal characteristics; (2) to appeal to voters through their familial roles; and (3) to present the family as the ultimate beneficiary of the candidate's proposals. In the anti-Allende and anti-Alessandri ads, the family was presented as the social entity most threatened by the candidate in question.

A content analysis of the campaign propaganda reveals the prevalence of

---

as with most political campaigns, newspaper ads were often repeated, and it is unlikely that I missed the larger ads that featured more complex arguments.

familial references across the political spectrum. The comparative importance of these references, however, also sheds light on broader campaign strategies of the three presidential candidates. The strength of familial references in Allende's campaign, for example, reflected a concerted effort on the part of the Chilean left to strengthen its appeal to women voters. Since winning suffrage in 1949, women had voted in smaller numbers for the parties of the Popular Unity than had men. In 1958, for example, when Allende had previously lost to Alessandri, he received only 22 percent of women's votes in comparison to 32 percent of men's. And it was this gender gap that helped Alessandri win his slim victory. In 1964, against Eduardo Frei, Allende had received 32 percent of women's votes compared to 45 percent of men's.[11] In the last two months before the 1970 election, Allende's campaign published detailed, half-page newspaper ads two to three days a week in *El Clarín*, aimed specifically at women as wives and mothers. These ads—addressed in bold type to the "Chilean woman"—invariably constructed women through their families, even if at times women were also addressed as workers or citizens. Allende also positioned himself as the defender of poor and working-class women and their children, and the left's campaign sought to appeal specifically to women by explaining how the Popular Unity would protect their families. Given the amount of campaign propaganda and the complexity of the ads directed at women, the Chilean left saw increasing women's support as a necessary element of victory. While some of the ads with familial content also addressed men, Allende's electoral ads primarily targeted these sought-after women voters.

The relatively smaller number of ads featuring familial discourse in Alessandri's campaign also reflected specific campaign strategies. While supported by the conservative PN, Alessandri had decided to run as an independent and therefore focused his campaign on his personal character, leadership, and political experience as a past president. Alessandri's ads frequently trumpeted his personal qualifications rather than discussing policy proposals. But his status as a bachelor limited the use of the familial references in these claims, whereas both Allende's and Tomic's campaigns featured ads with images of their families in order to present them as family men. The relatively smaller number of ads with familial content in Alessandri's campaign might have also reflected the right's confidence in the strength of its female support, as well its use of alternative ways of appealing specifically to women. Alessandri's supporters organized an extensive radio campaign directed at women and employed other

11. Power, *Right-Wing Women*, 73, 95.

strategies, such as "meetings and teas organized by and for women."[12] Finally, Alessandri might have counted on the extensive anticommunist campaign conducted by groups not officially connected to his campaign to maintain women's distrust of Allende and the political parties on the left. As Margaret Power has argued, "The official Alessandri campaign focused on projecting a positive image of the candidate, while those from Acción Mujeres de Chile and Chile Joven portrayed the horrors that a UP victory would, they claimed, inevitably entail."[13] According to these groups, a victory by the left would mean the destruction of the three pillars of Chilean society: families, traditional Christian values, and democracy.

The family's centrality in both the Christian Democratic Party's official ideology and cultural identity was certainly reflected in Tomic's campaign.[14] Many of Tomic's ads explicitly presented his proposed policies as helping all family members—men, women, and youth—to fulfill their respective duties to the family. As with Allende, women were addressed predominantly as wives and mothers. Tomic's victory also depended on women, who were emerging as a crucial constituency for the Christian Democrats. In 1964, women had driven Frei's resounding victory, as he received 60 percent of the female vote. As president, he had implemented and expanded government-funded programs, such as the Mothers' Centers, to incorporate women into the party's base.[15] Tomic's campaign, much more than the campaigns of his opponents, also appealed to men through their familial roles as husbands and fathers.

The three campaigns thus turned to familial images and beliefs to pursue specific instrumental purposes of appealing to voters, presenting the candidates' leadership abilities, and explaining policy priorities. But to understand these uses, the analysis must move beyond a simple content analysis of the ads. The following discourse analysis reveals how the persuasive appeal of these instrumental uses depended on and drew meaning from the role of familial beliefs in constituting a broader understanding of the duties of political leaders, the role of the state, and the identities of citizens. This analysis shows the larger

12. Ibid., 127.
13. Ibid., 128.
14. In *Chile's Political Culture*, Lomnitz and Melnick argue that the family is both a central concept and a focal institution in Chile's Christian Democratic Party. PDC activism is closely related to experiences of family political participation, particularly having a mother committed to more progressive social Catholicism. The family is also the focal point of social networks and lifestyles. Christian Democrats think about their political identities in terms of being "a good father, good mother, one who struggles for social justice" (146).
15. See Power, *Right-Wing Women*, 99–125.

historical patterns, complex nuances, and idealized understandings of leaders, citizens, and the state embedded within the campaign propaganda's texts and images.

Three Competing Versions of the Patriarchal Leader and the Familial State

ALESSANDRI AS THE STRONG PROTECTOR

Alessandri, the oldest of the three candidates and a former president, focused on the importance of protecting Chilean families in his uses of Patriarchal Leader and Familial State. His campaign portrayed him as an independent leader who could safeguard peace and security for Chilean families without being beholden to special interests or submerged in petty political squabbles.[16] Alessandri's campaign cultivated his image as a strong protector by visually surrounding him with people who needed care and protection. Many of his ads featured large photos of a baby or a child. These were the "innocents," the ones who needed to be protected by the actions of a strong leader. For example, one ad featured the picture of a young girl looking up into the camera, accompanied by the following text: "These eyes look at the world without understanding the conflicts that convulse it. She is unaware of the violence and hate that are so close. She doesn't know how fragile freedom is, how little it takes to lose it. She doesn't know the meaning of a life without dignity and justice. Her mother is aware of the current dangers and wants to eradicate them forever. She knows that the future of her children will be decided today."[17] The language of the ad contrasts the innocence, youth, and purity of the child with the violence and danger that only Alessandri's victory can keep at bay. It calls on women as mothers to act to protect both the future of their children as well as the "fragile" values of freedom, dignity, and justice.

As this example suggests, Alessandri's campaign positioned him as protecting women's ability to be good mothers. It was hoped that women would recognize that only an Alessandri victory could guarantee their families' welfare. This appeal to women based on beliefs about the duties of mothers was repeated again and again in Alessandri's advertising. For example, underneath a

16. For another gendered analysis of Alessandri, and especially how his campaign was part of the "Campaign of Terror" waged by the right against the left in the 1964 and 1970 presidential campaigns, see ibid., 126–37.
17. *La Tercera de Hora*, 11 July 1970, quoted in Power, *Right-Wing Women*, 128. The ad also appeared in *El Mercurio*, 10 July 1970, 29.

picture of a young woman staring somberly at the camera, the text reads, "My children will start school very soon. I do not want them growing up in the middle of violence and chaos. Chile should continue to be a democracy in which trust and stability rule. When dealing with the world in which my children will live, I do not accept threats . . . nor chaos. I want to live and progress in order and peace. For these reasons I need the government of a just and strong citizen."[18] Here, readers are asked to either identify with the young woman (perhaps as mothers themselves) or sympathize with her desire to protect her children's futures. The text argues that if Alessandri loses, Chile's democracy, order, and peace are in danger from other politicians who do not have Alessandri's experience or strength of character. The young mother sees Alessandri as protecting her family and the country from these threats. Another ad (fig. 3.1) featured a close-up of the face of a baby being held in his mother's hands. The accompanying text states, "In eighteen years he will be a man who can decide his destiny and that of his patria in the voting box. Now his destiny is in the hands of his mother. His future depends on her; whether he will develop in a world of order or chaos, of violence or serenity . . . of progress or stagnation, depends on the decision that she is making now. And this woman knows that her son's future will be decided today."[19] This ad depicts the future of Chilean children as dependent on the decisions of their mothers. Women as mothers possess the special ability to recognize the current dangers threatening their families. It was hoped that motherly intuition and a mother's commitment to her children's welfare would assure an electoral victory for Alessandri.

Rather than pledging to support specific programs, such as better jobs or housing, Alessandri promised to protect the family by providing a safe and secure environment in which parents could raise their children. He was the resolute defender of Chilean families and of the Chilean democratic traditions that allowed families to flourish. Other ads featured children of various ages, often calling on their parents to protect their future by voting for Alessandri. In a similar way, a young boy says to the reader, "My mother . . . urges me to study and to work so that I will be useful to my country when I am older. She does not want to expose me to a life of sacrifices and frustrations because the government made a mistake."[20] According to Alessandri, a government run by either of his opponents would mean a life of "sacrifices and frustrations" for Chilean children.

18. *El Mercurio*, 21 July 1970, 23.
19. *El Mercurio*, 3 July 1970, 31; and 31 July 1970, 30.
20. *El Mercurio*, 17 July 1970, 30; 17 August 1970, 33; and 18 August 1970, 29.

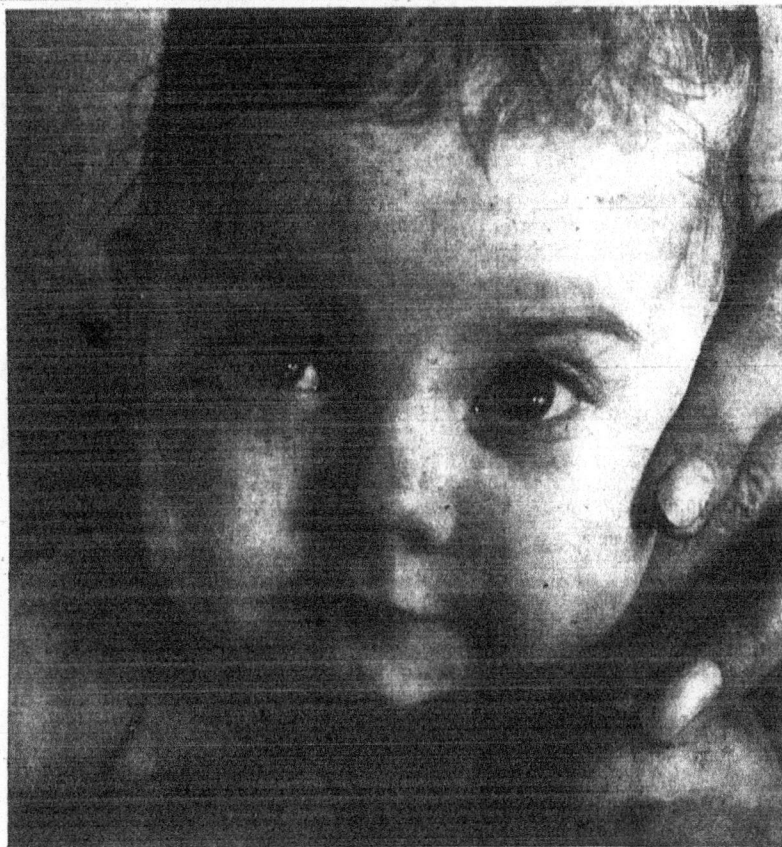

Dentro de 18 años, este será un hombre
que podrá decidir en las urnas su destino y el de su patria.
Ahora está en manos de su madre.
Su porvenir depende de ella;
si su vida se desenvolverá en
un mundo de orden o caos, de violencia o serenidad,
de cohesión o libertad, de progreso o estancamiento,
depende de la decisión que ella tome ahora.
Y esa mujer sabe que el mañana de su hijo se decide hoy.

Es por eso que está con Don Jorge Alessandri

Fig. 3.1 "That is why she is with Don Jorge Alessandri." (*El Mercurio*, 3 July 1970.)

Alessandri's version of the Patriarchal Leader was based on his ability to protect rather than to provide materially for Chilean families. His ads focused on his individual abilities to guarantee safety and security for women and their children. Alessandri's campaign did not focus on the promise of better material conditions, but rather on the importance of a secure and ordered environment that would allow families to flourish. In his ads, Alessandri was always addressed with the honorific "Don," which in Chilean society is often associated with the upper class and the traditional landed elite. The image of Alessandri as a stern but fair patriarch emanated from his campaign. Additionally, the representation of Alessandri as a past president and the son of a past president invoked nostalgia for the past, when leaders were supposedly "above politics." Alessandri could be counted on to govern independently and to restore social order.[21]

Alessandri's campaign neatly dovetailed with the ongoing anticommunist campaign being run by Acción Mujeres de Chile, Chile Joven, and other groups.[22] Often referred to as "scare campaigns," ads produced by these groups claimed that an Allende victory, and more generally the defeat of the right, meant Chile's descent into authoritarianism, violence, and chaos. These ads presented voters with concrete examples of the dangers threatening the family to which Alessandri's campaign alluded. For example, an ad published by Acción Mujeres de Chile featured an anxious-looking mother consoling her son (fig. 3.2). The text asks, "Where is the father?" The ad answers, "In many communist countries, this question will not have an answer. Hundreds of men have been snatched from their homes and are found in jails, concentration camps, or have disappeared, for having spoke out or written against the government."[23] This critique has no subtleties: if communism (Allende) wins, then Chilean families will be destroyed, in this case by the imprisonment or death of fathers. The ad speaks to both men and women. It asks women to imagine their families without their husbands, while it asks men to imagine being jailed and thus unable to fulfill their familial duties to protect and provide for their wives and children.

Communism could also threaten the family by destroying the traditional relationships between parents and children. In an ad from Chile Joven, two pictures, side by side, feature the same nicely dressed woman (black dress, pearl

---

21. Collier and Sater, *History of Chile*, 258.

22. For a more detailed treatment of the actions of these two groups in the larger anticommunist drive of the Chilean right, see Power, *Right-Wing Women*, 128–37.

23. *El Mercurio*, 1 August 1970, 33. Knowing the history of disappearances committed by Pinochet, in hindsight this ad appears extremely ironic.

¿DONDE ESTA EL PAPA...?

En muchos países comunistas, esta pregunta no tendrá respuesta. Cientos de hombres han sido arrancados de sus hogares, y se encuentran en cárceles, campos de concentración o desaparecidos, por haber opinado o escrito en contra del gobierno.

LUCHEMOS PARA QUE CHILE SIGA SIENDO LIBRE

CHILE
acción mujeres de Chile

Fig. 3.2   "Where is the father?" (*El Mercurio*, 1 August 1970.)

earrings) holding a framed picture of her young son, who appears to be about ten years old (fig. 3.3). On the left, the son is dressed in a neat school uniform, carrying his satchel. On the right, he is wearing a military uniform and beret, pointing a machine gun toward the reader. Through his outfit and disposition, this young revolutionary mimics one of the leaders of the Cuban Revolution, Ernesto "Che" Guevara. In bold text, the caption reads, "Your son . . . or your enemy?" Below, the text claims that in communist countries children were

Su hijo...¿o su enemigo?

En los países dominados por el comunismo, los hijos son
lanzados contra sus padres para aplastar cualquier intento
de liberación de quienes han sido sometidos por el terror.
No permitamos que esto ocurra en Chile.

¡RECHACEMOS A LOS QUE PROPAGAN
LA VIOLENCIA Y A LOS
INCAPACES DE EVITARLA!

Fig. 3.3   "Your son . . . or your enemy?" (*El Mercurio*,
3 July 1970.)

used against their parents to crush any attempt to return to freedom. The ad
ends with the following: "We reject those who incite violence and those incapable of preventing it."[24] This text is meant to imply that Allende and the parties of the UP "incite violence," while Tomic and the Christian Democrats are
"incapable" of confronting the threats of communism. The class markers in

24. *El Mercurio*, 3 July 1970, 27. See also *La Tercera de Hora*, 1 July 1970.

the ad (the dress of the woman, the school uniform) indicate that the endangered family belongs to either the middle or upper class. Chile's upper classes were the most fearful of a possible Allende victory and therefore strongly supported Alessandri. This ad also plays on growing fears of a generational conflict in which children rebelled and parents lost their control and influence in the family. The 1960s, in Chile as in other countries, were a time of cultural ferment and the questioning of traditional values, a challenge associated with the left. Many Chileans, especially conservatives, worried that the growth of youth activism in universities and in social justice causes signaled a breakdown of the traditional patriarchal authority of the father and a challenge to women's prerogatives as mothers.[25]

An Acción Mujeres de Chile ad presented a slightly different understanding of the dangers posed to the family by communism. It asks the reader, "Your child . . . or a number?" and claims that communist states endanger the family by removing children from the loving care of their mothers and placing them in state-run facilities. By this action, communism denies the individual, human worth of children. The text of the ad goes on to claim that it is the "loving care and education" mothers lavish on their children that produce "men free and dignified." Under communism, however, children are reduced to numbers in a system and stripped of their subjectivity.[26] By removing children from a mother's care, communism endangers not only actual families but the metaphoric national family as well.

In many anticommunist ads, the destruction of the Chilean family and the destruction of Chilean democracy and social values are inextricably linked. Conversely, protecting Chilean families also protects the Chilean nation, national values, and democratic governance. The rhetoric of these campaigns was familiar to Chilean voters due to the massive scare campaigns previously launched against Allende in the 1964 election. In her analysis of these campaigns, Power found that men were addressed as "husbands and fathers . . . responsible for ensuring the survival and sustenance of their wives and children," while women were presented as mothers. Those 1964 ads similarly warned "that an Allende victory would mean the loss of their children, the

---

25. For a discussion of the challenges to traditional authority in the Chilean countryside, see Tinsman, *Partners in Conflict.* Isabel Allende's *House of the Spirits* provides a literary exploration of the ways in which young adults in the 1960s and 1970s were challenging their parents' social and political values. In "*Barbudos,* Warriors, and *Rotos,*" Florencia Mallon explores the constructions of a radical leftist masculinity and its connection to generational conflict.

26. *La Tercera de Hora,* 29 July 1970, 30.

destruction of their homes, and the end of motherhood."[27] Acción Mujeres de Chile, a right-wing women's group founded in 1963, was active in both campaigns, and it is possible that the group received covert funding from the CIA in both 1964 and 1970.[28] The anticommunist ads in both 1964 and 1970 made it brutally clear that the possible victory of Allende would endanger the family, particularly the traditional patriarchal family.[29]

This strategy of using threats to the family as a way to criticize opponents was not exclusive to the political right. While Power's excellent analysis of the 1964 and 1970 scare campaigns reveals the importance of familial beliefs in shaping the right's appeal to men and women, her exclusive focus on that side of the political spectrum misses how the left turned to its own familial understandings of citizens' identity and the state's responsibilities. During the campaign, independent leftist groups attempted to counter the anticommunist campaign by arguing that Alessandri represented the true threat to Chilean families. Calling themselves the "antifascists," these groups explicitly challenged Alessandri's candidacy by doubting his ability to "father" Chilean children. Against his self-representations as a patriarch able to defend Chilean families, the antifascists portrayed Alessandri as a failing old bachelor who was not strong enough to assume the presidency. In response to the ads that called on parents to vote for Alessandri in order to protect the "fragile freedom" of their

27. Power, *Right-Wing Women*, 80–81.

28. Margaret Power makes a convincing argument that this group was probably the "right-wing women's group" referred to in the investigations by the U.S. Congress into CIA actions against Allende. At this time, U.S. foreign policy in Latin America was driven by a desire to contain the spread of communism and communist-leaning groups. Allende, and more broadly the PS and PC, were the targets of U.S. interventions designed to undercut their support in Chile and to help their opposition. The U.S. Senate report *Covert Action* estimates that the CIA funneled between three and four million dollars into anti-Allende activities, including this scare campaign (*Right-Wing Women*, 90–93). In 1964, the PDC and Frei were the beneficiaries of this political activity. In the 1970 election, the extent of the scare campaign was limited by organized attempts by the left, including a break-in at the offices of the public relations firm in charge of the campaign, Agencia Andalién, to expose the complicity of both the Chilean right and the United States (ibid., 130–33). In addition, while Allende was the main target in 1964, the reformist Tomic was also targeted in 1970, uniting the PDC and the parties of the left in outrage over the campaign. As I discuss in the next section, the left also organized its own scare campaign, which often used a similar familial discourse to present the right as the real threat and the actions of the Chilean elite as complicit with foreign powers.

29. Who exactly composed these groups and where they received their funding has generated considerable interest and debate. The Chilean Congress in a later investigation determined that ads and radio broadcasts with very similar content were reproduced in twenty-two newspapers and on forty-five radio stations during May, June, and July of 1970. The investigators estimated that the total number of radio spots added up to eighteen hours a day for three months, and that the total cost of this publicity campaign was around 16.3 million Chilean escudos. Investigations by both the Chilean Congress and the U.S. Congress support claims that the CIA provided at least part of the financing for this campaign. Power, *Right-Wing Women*, 132.

children, groups associated with the left ran an ad featuring a small boy intently concentrating on his homework. The caption reads as follows:

> He is starting the long road of learning. His knowledge will make him a free man and the master of his own life. In order to fully carry out this destiny, respect for his rights will be needed, [namely, the rights of] equality of opportunities and liberty of expression. However, a cruel, heartless, and egotistical leader who never was a father, eliminated, ten years ago, breakfast and other small benefits in the school's budget. For this reason, the children of yesterday, who are the same as the children of today, . . . look at him with disdain and fight against his unprecedented pretensions to return a government that will once again mistreat the youth. For this reason, [they] are against Alessangre.[30]

"Alessangre" combines "Alessandri" with "sangre," which means blood in Spanish. Alessandri's victory would mean violence and bloodshed. Using the same familial logic as the opposing side, this ad argues that it was really Alessandri who represented the true danger to Chilean children. According to the ad, Alessandri lacks a basic qualification for the presidency: the ability to "father" children. Further, instead of providing for today's children, his government will strip them of their rights and destiny. The ad calls on Chileans to resist Alessandri for the sake of today's children.

This same critique was central to another ad, this one addressed to the "Chilean woman," which argues that as president Alessandri did not protect Chilean families. Completely abdicating his duties as a Patriarchal Leader, Alessandri ordered a massacre of poor workers and, adding insult to injury, failed to provide materially for the widows and orphans left behind.[31] In this context, insinuations that the never-married Alessandri was gay—an extremely damaging attack given the social mores of Chile in 1970—were also part of the attacks against his leadership abilities and personal characteristics.[32]

Tomic's Version: The President as the Good Provider

If Alessandri's version of the Patriarchal Leader was as the stalwart protector, Tomic cast himself as the good provider and focused on his ability to guarantee

30. *El Clarín*, 23 July 1970, 3; and 25 July 1970, 3.
31. *El Clarín*, 1 September 1970, 18.
32. For a discussion of the use of the charge of homosexuality against Alessandri, see Sigmund, *Overthrow of Allende*, 102–4.

material benefits for Chilean families. In his campaign, Alessandri embodied the Chilean right's greater concern with issues of order and stability. The responsibility of both the president and his government was to protect families so that, in turn, families would be able to reproduce the traditional values on which the country was built. From the perspective of both Alessandri and the generalized anticommunist campaign, Tomic's and Allende's respective reform proposals threatened social peace and stability by catering to social groups that had been previously marginalized, particularly workers, the urban poor, and peasants. It was these groups, as well as middle-class social reformers, that Tomic's campaign sought to persuade through his invocations of the ideals of Patriarchal Leader and Familial State. His version combined material and moral protection for the entire family.

In contrast to Alessandri, Tomic often turned to his own identity as a father to illustrate his qualification to be president. As one large ad—featuring a picture of Tomic, his wife, Olaya, and his nine children—argues, "This man taught his nine children to read. Help him educate all the children of Chile."[33] This portrayal of Tomic and his family draws on the connection between familial and political authority found in the Patriarchal Leader category. Tomic's familial position demonstrates his political abilities. Another ad with a similar argument shows a smiling mother holding her baby (fig. 3.4). She states, "I am not ungrateful . . . I will do my duty for Chile . . . I like Tomic because he is sincere. A man who has nine children knows what this means."[34] The text includes the woman's name and age (Elena Fuentes, twenty-five years old) to emphasize that she is a real person. These ads argue that Tomic's individual familial identity—as a good father in his private life—directly reflects on his ability to be a good president—to symbolically "father" the Chilean nation. In addition, the specific use of language and image in the second ad positions Elena Fuentes as a woman belonging to the lower class (*pobladoras*), a group that had strongly supported Frei and his policies. Frei's government had targeted these women for incorporation into the PDC through the creation of Mothers' Centers and other social policies. The ad reminds pobladoras of the benefits they have received and argues that not voting for him would be a sign of ingratitude and a lack of respect for Tomic, a man clearly deserving of their high regard.[35]

33. *El Clarín*, 3 September 1970, 9.

34. *El Mercurio*, 23 July 1970, 13.

35. I am indebted to Karin Rosemblatt for pointing out to me the classist subtext of this ad and how it reflected worries on the part of PDC leaders that they were losing support among lower-class Chileans.

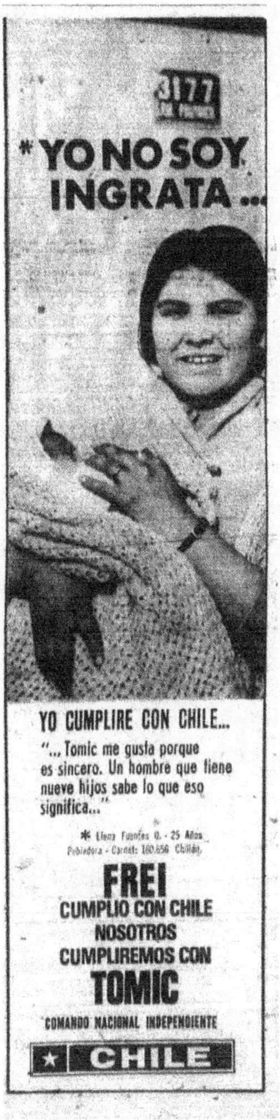

Fig. 3.4   "I am not ungrateful."
(*El Mercurio*, 23 July 1970.)

Another example of Tomic's appeal as a father was found in an ad addressed to the "Women of Chile," which contained a full page of names of women supporters. One of the five reasons listed for their support of Tomic was "because through his life and with his large family [he] has demonstrated that he has the moral and humane character . . . that the country . . . demands from its government."[36] The fact that Tomic was a good father and provider for his own family meant that he possessed the necessary qualifications to lead the country.

36. *El Mercurio*, 2 September 1970, 37.

Through his position as a father of nine children and his commitment to his duties as the head of the family, Tomic represented the ideal candidate of the Catholic Christian Democratic Party and the symbol of its commitment to promoting Chilean families.

Throughout his electoral campaign, Tomic was presented as the successor to President Frei. Tomic's campaign created an overall picture of Tomic and the Christian Democrats as committed to directing the resources of the state to guarantee not individual prosperity but rather the welfare of Chilean families. A vision of the state as fundamentally responsible for familial welfare lay at the heart of Tomic's campaign. A full-page spread in *El Clarín* on 2 September 1970 exemplifies this view of the relationship among the state, family, and citizens: "Chilean woman! Tomic guarantees for you, for your children, and for your husband: Work, Housing, Education, Health. . . . Tomic has said: 'The family is the foundation of society; therefore, it is the responsibility of the state to provide all the necessary means for its free and harmonious development. . . . A Vote for Tomic Is a Vote for Chile.'"[37] In the text, Tomic pledged to fulfill the "responsibility of the state" to provide for Chilean families, because doing so also supported the foundation of Chilean society. According to this view, the future of Chile depends on the healthy development of families, which can only be promoted by policies that guarantee work, housing, education, and health. Harmony is achieved by helping all members of the family according to their specifically gendered roles and responsibilities. Men are guaranteed work, children education, and women benefit through these provisions, as well as through the state's help in taking care of all members of the family by providing health and housing. The ad also promises that by helping all family members, including children, to fulfill their respective roles, Tomic's government would guarantee social harmony, progress, and democracy. The accompanying photo strengthened the construction of Tomic as a paternal president dedicated to providing for Chilean women and their families, featuring him surrounded by happy women, including his own wife, and children.

Tomic's connection to Frei also figured heavily in these ads. A standard story line in the campaign presented President Frei's social policies as having already improved the lives of many Chilean families; it argued that the six years of Frei's mandate was too short a time frame to implement all the necessary reforms. Tomic vowed to continue and extend the benefits of Frei's programs to

37. *El Clarín*, 2 September 1970, 10; and 3 September 1970, 10.

many more Chilean families. Material improvements were concretely shown in the ads by presenting a "before" picture, depicting how families lived before Frei's policies, and an "after" picture, showing the benefits. For example, in an ad about urban poverty, under the caption "Those who lived like this before . . ." is a picture of a man, dressed in old clothes, holding a wheelbarrow and standing in front of his wife and three small children (fig. 3.5).[38] The ad clearly depicts a family living in one of the shantytowns that "represented the grimmest underside of Chilean life" in 1970.[39] Brian Loveman estimates that between 20 and 25 percent of Santiago's population (up to a half million people) were living in the capital's shantytowns.[40] The rising rate of rural-to-urban migration had swelled the number of urban poor. Unable to find good jobs and affordable housing, many Chilean families, like the family pictured in the ad, were living in shacks in neighborhoods that lacked electricity, running water, and other services.[41]

The picture of the impoverished family was easily recognizable as symbolizing one of the most pressing problems of Chilean society, urban poverty. Under Frei, the PDC had made a conscious effort to address the physical needs of these sectors through a variety of programs, including Operación Sitio (a self-help housing program where the government provided land on which poor families could build), Mothers' Centers, and neighborhood councils and youth clubs, which were used to funnel resources to poor families and to increase political participation.[42] In the "after" picture, under the heading "and improved their situation," the family members are presented as beneficiaries of these programs. They are dressed in clean, neat clothes. The father and mother hold their young, smiling children while standing proudly in front of a solidly constructed wooden building. The success of the Christian Democrats' program in bringing families out of poverty is the ad's easily understood visual narrative.

In the ad, Tomic took up the mantle of Frei's past successes and pledged to continue programs designed to promote the welfare of Chile's less fortunate families. The text under the two contrasting pictures emphasizes this message. The ad claims that Frei's reforms had benefited "hundreds of thousands of Chileans," but "six years is very little time" to address the problems of the

38. *El Mercurio*, 29 July 1970, 15.
39. Collier and Sater, *History of Chile*, 294.
40. Loveman, *Chile*, 239.
41. Collier and Sater, *History of Chile*, 291–94.
42. Schneider, *Shantytown Protest*, 50–51.

Fig. 3.5 "Those who lived like this before." (*El Mercurio*, 29 July 1970.)

entire country. A Tomic government would continue the programs, without which "the country will never advance, nor have social peace ... [because] without justice for all there is security for none."[43] In addition, promoting the familial welfare of Chile's poor and working classes protected the general interests of social peace and Chile's much-vaunted democracy.

43. *El Mercurio*, 29 July 1970, 15; 3 August 1970, 41; and 31 July 1970, 43.

Tomic's campaign again and again turned to familial imagery to promote its vision of the role and responsibility of the president, as well as that of the Chilean state more generally. In another ad, the "before" picture depicts a lower-working-class laborer in a run-down outdoor shop. The "after" picture features a man dressed in a suit and tie. The two pictures represent the transformation of the man from a day laborer into an office worker, or from poverty to middle class. But the ad's visual narrative makes it clear that the benefits accrue not only to the man as an individual but also to his family. In the "after" picture, he holds the hands of two girls, clearly his daughters, who are both wearing school uniforms. He has obviously just picked them up from the clean, well-managed school in the background.[44] The overall message was Tomic's promise to dedicate the resources of the state to helping men be good fathers. Symbolically, by showing him with children only in the "after" photo, the man is transformed into a father through the success of the state's programs. Tomic's programs create good family men who are both financially viable and dedicated to their children (e.g., picking up the daughters from school). The story presents economic progress as familial progress: when a man is provided with a good job, his children are able to attend good schools and take advantage of better opportunities.

The pledge of a better life for all Chilean families was also used to appeal specifically to women as wives and mothers. Featuring an image of a woman bent over a wooden tub, washing dirty clothes by hand, the caption of one ad states, " . . . BEFORE 1964, thousands of Chilean women lived like this. Thanks to the changes realized by President Frei, the majority of them have achieved human dignity. . . . But six years is very little time. It is necessary to continue and accelerate the changes until there is no woman who feels that to have a child is a misfortune. Only by terminating poverty can social peace be achieved."[45] On one level, the ad argues that Tomic, like Frei, was dedicated to improving the lives of individual women. Progress is defined as moving women away from the picture of unremitting toil and poverty presented in the image. But ultimately women's progress did not lie in individual gains or freedoms, but in the benefits that accrued to Chilean families.

This is the case even in the ad's implicit reference to birth control and abortion ("to have a child is a misfortune"). Although all nontherapeutic abortions were illegal at this time, it was estimated that at least one in four pregnancies

---

44. *El Mercurio*, 26 July 1970, 48; and 3 August 1970, 41.
45. *El Mercurio*, 5 August 1970, 35; and 20 July 1970, 44.

in Chile ended in an abortion.[46] Botched and nonsterile abortions posed a serious health threat for many Chilean women. Deaths from clandestine abortions were a significant cause of Chile's extremely high rate of maternal deaths (28.3 deaths per 1,000 fertile women in 1965).[47] Responding to long-standing concerns over Chile's high rates of maternal and infant deaths, as well as pressure from both national and international groups, President Frei had sponsored Chile's first nationwide birth control programs.[48] These initiatives presented access to birth control and family planning as one crucial aspect of the overall welfare and health of families, in line with the Christian Democrats' broader goals of development, modernization, and poverty reduction.[49] The ad featuring the woman washing clothes subtly implied that women might be forced to contemplate abortion because of their economic situation. At the very least, women were not able to celebrate their pregnancies and did not always welcome more children. Therefore, by improving women's economic ability to care for their children through state programs, Tomic would be protecting Chile's future children. The ad was in line with the family-planning campaigns of the Christian Democrats that emphasized the health of families rather than women's control over their sexuality. This strategy deftly supported the PDC's reproductive health policies while not directly confronting the abortion issue (possibly to avoid confrontation with the Catholic Church). In his promise to provide women with the necessary resources to have and raise children, Tomic and his policies symbolically fulfilled the husband/father/provider role of Chilean presidents.

Tomic's ads also frequently featured children and positioned the readers as either mothers or fathers. One ad in *El Mercurio* pictured three poorly dressed boys sitting in the dirt outside a rough shack. The caption in bold letters read, "If Your Children Lived Like This!" and continued addressing both men and women directly as parents: "You would demand more justice, faster changes, more compassion from fellow citizens who live better." The ad used emotional ties between parents and children to appeal to those Chileans not currently living in poverty to recognize the common ties between all Chileans as mothers

46. Given the illegality of abortion and the taboo nature of the subject, statistics vary. Collier and Sater report the rate of one in four (*History of Chile*, 295). Tinsman cites statistics from the Association for Family Promotion (Asociación Chilena de Protección de la Familia, APROFA), a private affiliate of the International Planned Parenthood Federation, that place the rate as high as one abortion for every two live births (*Partners in Conflict*, 157).

47. *Boletín APROFA*, July 1965, quoted in Tinsman, *Partners in Conflict*, 157.

48. Tinsman, *Partners in Conflict*, 156.

49. Ibid., 156–70.

and fathers. The ad then proceeded to argue for the need to elect Tomic in order to continue the work begun by Frei: "Thanks to the substantial social changes of the government of President Frei, the great majority [of people] have improved their situation, until they have achieved human dignity. . . . But six years is very little time. It is necessary to continue to accelerate the changes until no Chilean has to live like this."[50] Tomic's campaign thus asked men and women, as parents, for their support because of Tomic's commitment to familial welfare.

In a similar vein, Tomic and the Christian Democrats also touted the benefits that had accrued to the family due to the party's housing policies. One of Tomic's most discussed campaign promises was to provide an individual house "for every Chilean family." The housing ads featured a series of five pictures that followed different families in search of a house and enjoying the benefits that a house gave each family. In these ads, having a house signified myriad benefits for the Chilean family, including progress, modernization, and familial harmony. A typical example follows a man from his work, where he was talking to a coworker about how to obtain a house, to the last frame, where he is at his own house, trimming a tree in his front yard and surrounded by his family. The caption reads, "What happiness . . . ! If one could say my 'own house' it would be much greater. In the last six years—under the government of President Frei—close to two million people began to say 'my own house.' . . . In the plans of Tomic there is a house for every Chilean family. There will not be a family without a house."[51] Again, it is the family that benefited from past policies and that would continue to benefit under a Tomic government. Tomic, like a good husband and father, would provide all Chilean families with their own houses.

Tomic's promise to provide houses not only fulfilled his party's commitment to the material welfare of Chilean families but also promoted an ideal of family happiness, harmony, and security. The multiple ways in which Tomic's campaign promoted this ideal can be seen in an ad featuring two young girls (fig. 3.6). In the narrative, the two girls compare how their families live. The first girl's family has recently acquired their own house, while the second girl's family continues to rent. The first girl remarks to her friend, "How nice it would be if you all also had your own house." The story ends with the second girl sitting down with her mother, sister, and father, now in their own home. The father

50. *El Mercurio*, 2 August 1970, 65.
51. *El Mercurio*, 9 August 1970, 56.

asks the mother, "Did you notice how early the girls return home now . . . ?" Underneath the last picture, the caption reads:

> The mother and siblings are at home . . . It is "their" house. Lately, Papa has been saying, "Now we have our own house," and it seems that this is very important. But then she realizes that other little girls do not have a house and they would also like to feel her same happiness . . . and security. And it is because the home is the principal refuge of the human being . . . and for that reason it is a sacred right. Tomic's plans include a house for every Chilean family. There will not be a family without a house.[52]

Having a house symbolized class mobility, because it meant the husband/father was earning enough to provide his wife with her own space to oversee the raising of their children. This ad was designed to appeal particularly to those families suffering from the deficit of adequate housing in Santiago. Many young couples, especially from the lower class, often lived in overcrowded conditions, with other family members or as boarders. The promise of their own house symbolized having the space for a married couple to raise their children. The ad presents a picture of family togetherness that would appeal to many parents. In addition, having a house reinforced the ability of parents to watch over their children. The images of girls safely in the home rather than out in the street was probably especially appealing to parents worried about the growing freedom of young women.

The ads featuring housing illustrate how Tomic's slogan of "Work, Housing, Education, Health" epitomized the centrality of families, rather than individuals, in his campaign. It was the family that was the ultimate target and beneficiary of Tomic's policies. Stronger and happier families, the base of Chilean society, were the ultimate goal of programs that provided men with good jobs, children with good schools, and women with better lives. In the campaign, housing policies not only provided dwellings but also helped Chilean families escape the problems of poverty and material insecurity and strengthened family unity and harmony. For Tomic, housing was a governmental priority because it strengthened families. The visual and rhetorical power of the ads depended on these broader beliefs about the importance of family welfare and the responsibility of the government.

52. *El Mercurio*, 11 August 1970, 14.

Fig. 3.6 "There will not be a family without a house." (*El Mercurio*, 11 August 1970.)

Allende's Version: The Working-Class Father in Charge of the State

For many Chileans, the iconic figure of the left was the valiant miner who fought against the twin evils of capitalism and imperialism. In Allende's 1970 presidential campaign, however, the central protagonist was the working-class family. Allende's campaign ads trumpeted the Popular Unity coalition's commitment to the needs of working-class families, often symbolized by mothers and children. Like Tomic, Allende embraced arguments about the responsibility of the state to Chilean families and presented himself as the candidate best positioned to realize this vision. Allende's campaign argued that both the conservative candidate Alessandri and the centrist reformer Tomic were fundamentally unable to fulfill the responsibilities of president because of their support for the capitalist system. As one ad claimed, "The strong and united family is the only guarantee of a strong and united country. The United Left of Chile wants to make the patria a sovereign nation, free and dignified, . . . whose roots are in the family."[53] By framing Allende as the working-class family's stalwart defender, the campaign fused a general commitment to the welfare of the working class with a concrete response to anticommunist scare campaigns, which presented the left as antifamily.

Allende's version of Patriarchal Leader presented him as defending the working-class family, particularly mothers and children, by providing extensive state social benefits and programs. In campaign propaganda, women and children were often depicted as victims, and Allende—and by extension the organized left—was presented as saving them from the excesses of the Chilean capitalist system. For example, one ad that ran in *El Clarín* featured a picture of a mother holding a small child on her lap (fig. 3.7). With their pleading eyes turned toward the camera, they demand the concern of the reader. The ad's text provides a lengthy indictment of capitalism as a system that forces children to work to help support their impoverished families. By making children work, the ad argues, the capitalist system ultimately hindered the viability of progress for the entire working class by denying children necessary schooling. The ad stresses how Allende personally witnessed the effects of this type of abuse of innocent children during his visits to factories, and "that only the United Left can rescue women and children from hunger and misery."

While the text of the ad appeals to both men and women to protect children, the visual depiction of the mother and child positions women and their

53. *El Clarín*, 23 July 1970, 6.

Fig. 3.7 "*Chilena*, for you and for your children." (*El Clarín*, 15 August 1970.)

children as victims who need the protection of a strong (male) defender. Allende, referred to by name in the text and as "three" (his position in the electoral list on the ballot) in the tagline, becomes the symbolic father and husband to the pictured woman and child, completing the picture of a traditional nuclear family. The ad implies that his government will assume the duties and responsibilities of a good family patriarch, promising the "Chilean woman" that "for you and for your children, we will overcome with the three [Allende], the only one of the three [candidates] that is worthy."[54] Allende stands ready to defend Chilean women and children.

Allende's 1970 campaign was clearly focused on wooing women voters. The campaign produced detailed ads that appeared in *El Clarín* almost every Tuesday, Thursday, and Saturday for the two months before the election. In these ads, Allende explicitly discussed the exploitation of women under capitalism, the burden that the double day placed on working mothers, and the economic precariousness of housewives. The text in one ad, for example, reads, "When a woman works, not only does she need to complete her duty at work, but also she needs to return to the house to worry about the children, the husband, and the home. When she is only a housewife she must watch the children, cook, clean, and iron. She does not have a retirement or a hope of rest. . . . All

54. *El Clarín*, 15 August 1970, 6; see also 20 August 1970, 6, for use of the same image but with different text.

of the doors close for poor women."[55] The ad presented a bleak picture for
Chilean women caught in the double bind of the capitalist system. Either as
workers or housewives, women suffered from capitalism.

How did the left plan to address these problems? Exhorting women to "rise
up . . . for the patria, your home, and your family," the left promised that under
Allende women would have "a comfortable and dignified house . . . abundant
milk and food for their children . . . a pregnancy watched over by doctors . . .
and hospitals, medicine, and protection." This would all add up to "Security,
Happiness, Order, Life."[56] The ad claims, "We want [to take] the following
actions, to give a good salary, homes, and health care. That is to say, the left
wants to finance the family." The left vowed to make women's lives better by
providing a better life for their family through more material resources. In a
similar ad, women are urged again to rise up "for la patria, your home, and
your family" (fig. 3.8). It argues that Allende will respect the work women do
at home, in contrast to the regime of the "momios" (Chilean slang for members of the conservative upper class), under which women's intensive household labor of "washing clothes, cooking, cleaning the house, shopping,
administrating family finances, ironing, taking the children to school" was neither recognized nor paid. In his government, Allende would create a Ministry
of the Family and provide child-care centers, cooperative laundries and kitchens.[57] By making these claims, Allende confronted the antifamily accusations
leveled against him, framing the real terror facing Chilean families as six more
years of a government not committed to the needs of working-class families.[58]

Drawing on long-standing tenets of socialist and communist political ideology, Allende's campaign attempted to recognize women's roles and identities as workers and mothers who needed state support to help balance work
and family obligations. Allende also wanted to provide women with extra protection, given their greater vulnerability within the capitalist system. But the
positive presentation of women as both workers and wives/mothers always
existed in an uneasy tension with the left's commitment to more traditional
understandings of the family and gender roles. In government policies and
programs, such as the family assignments that paid extra money to legally
married male workers to support their families, the left had enthusiastically

55. *El Clarín*, 23 July 1970, 6.
56. *El Clarín*, 18 July 1970, 6.
57. *El Clarín*, 4 July 1970, 6.
58. See, for example, *El Clarín*, 30 July 1970, 6; and 11 August 1970, 6.

La mujer en el régimen de los monies y el
capital extranjero realiza un intenso trabajo que
no es reconocido ni pagado por nadie:

—Lavado de ropa.
—Cocinar.
—Limpiar la casa.
—Hacer las compras.
—Cuidar los niños.
—Administrar la plata para la casa.
—Planchado.
—Mandar los niños a la escuela.
—Servir la comida a la familia.
—Hacer que la casa esté bonita.
—Atender a los familiares del marido.

−ALLENDE, LIDER
DE LA IZQUIERDA

Dignificará el trabajo del hogar e incorporará a la
mujer chilena a la vida moderna y sus como-
didades.

El Gobierno de la Izquierda crea el MINISTERIO
DE PROTECCION DE LA FAMILIA, que pone en
marcha:

—Lavanderías populares mecanizadas.
—Comedores populares: Buena alimentación.
—Jardines infantiles.
—Guarderías infantiles.
—Diferentes escuelas para la capacitación
profesional de la mujer.
—Trabajo y jubilación a través de la creación
de cooperativas en los centros de madres.
—Entretenimientos: bailes, teatro, canciones.

SEGURIDAD
ORDEN
ALEGRIA
NUEVA VIDA

ALZATE CHILENA: Por la patria, tu hogar y tu familia

CLARIN — Página 6   Sábado 4 de Julio de 19

Fig. 3.8 "Rise up, *Chilena*: For *la patria*, your home, and your family." (*El Clarín*, 4 July 1970.)

embraced the familial ideal of a male breadwinner and a female housewife.[59] In the many ads, questions about who would receive the benefits and in what ways were answered with statements similar to the following: "With a just salary, decent housing, and the possibility of health for all, it will be more easy to marry and the single mothers will gradually disappear."[60] In other words, the best way to protect mothers and their children was to guarantee good jobs to working-class men. With good jobs, men would marry and be able to support families. Women would not have to do paid work, thus saving them from exploitation within the capitalist system.

Condemning Chile's capitalist system because of the threat it posed to children was also a recurrent theme of the campaign. In another ad, a photo of a small child lying in a hospital bed, looking up at the camera, is paired with the following text: "This is the sad destiny of the children of the people [del pueblo] under the capitalist regime. Changes in this situation depend on you, *Chilena* [Chilean woman]." It continued, "*Chilena*: Only the Popular Government will guarantee to your children a half liter of milk a day. Only Dr. Allende

59. Rosemblatt in *Gendered Compromises* discusses this tension during the Popular Front governments of the 1930s and 1940s. Writing in 1978, the Chilean sociologist Luis Felipe Lira credited Chile's high rates of legal marriages and low rates of cohabitation and illegitimacy (as compared to other countries in Latin America) to government policies that rewarded marriage ("Aspectos sociológicos").

60. *El Clarín*, 23 July 1970, 6.

CHILENA:

SOLO el gobierno popular garantizará a tus hijos medio litro de leche al día.

SOLO el doctor Allende se ha comprometido a entregar libros gratis a los escolares.

SOLO la Izquierda Unida está interesada en que los niños sean los únicos privilegiados de Chile.

SOLO tú puedes lograr que esto sea realidad, uniéndote a las mujeres de la Unidad Popular.

ESTE ES EL triste destino de los hijos del pueblo bajo el régimen capitalista. De ti depende, chilena, que esta situación cambie.

MUJER: *por ti y para tus hijos,* **VENCEREMOS** *con el "tres", el único capaz de los tres*

CLARIN — Página 4   Lunes 17 de Agosto de 1970

Fig. 3.9   "Woman, for you and for your children, we will overcome." (*El Clarín*, 17 August 1970.)

has promised to provide books free to the schools. Only the United Left cares about making children the only privileged in Chile" (fig. 3.9).[61]

Again, the ad constructed the poverty and misery of Chile's women and their children as stemming from the failure of previous governments to protect Chilean families from the capitalist system. In the prior ad, women and children were forced to work. In this second ad, children are sick. As a medical doctor, Allende was presented as both knowledgeable and concerned about the health and well-being of Chile's children. In the campaign, Allende and his supporters often accused their opponents of ignoring the welfare of Chile's families in order to protect the interests of the rich, particularly imperialist foreign interests. They claimed that their opponents' promises to support Chilean families were really lies meant to obscure the failures of the previous governments. As another ad argues, the elite represented by the right promoted "higher prices" in order to gain "higher earnings" for their companies. The text went on to claim that "these rises produce hunger and misery that translate into high levels of infant mortality. Further, they maintain an unjust system, because when [the capitalists] are not interested in the children they die of malnutrition."[62] At the bluntest level, this critique accuses Alessandri and

61. *El Clarín*, 17 August 1970, 6.
62. *El Clarín*, 18 July 1970, 6.

his partisans of supporting policies that guaranteed more profits for the rich while killing the children of Chile's working classes. Allende and the Popular Unity, however, would defend mothers and their children by protecting them from the foreign businesses and monopolies. These groups pursued profits at the expense of the health, welfare, and even the survival of Chilean families. Thus the left framed previous governments and the other two candidates as unjustly favoring unworthy social groups (e.g., rich capitalists). Under Allende, children would be the focus of state protection (the "only privileged") and state policies would promote familial welfare.

Allende and the Popular Unity vowed to protect the family through marshaling state programs in its defense. The UP framed its political goals as dedicated to ending privileges for the rich in order to prioritize the most vulnerable members of Chilean society—mothers and their children. Additionally, the UP claimed to be the only party that really represented women's true interests because of its willingness to make Chilean children the "only privileged" in Allende's future government. Connecting the Chilean nation and the Chilean family, many ads argued that only Allende could protect them from capitalist foreign interests that did not care about the welfare of Chile's children or its future as a nation.

In his campaign, Allende hoped to appeal to working-class men and women through their familial roles and responsibilities. He recognized the specific problems faced by working-class mothers (single motherhood, the double day, child labor) and promised a solution: providing better jobs for working-class men and more state programs that helped working-class women fulfill their responsibilities as mothers. He approached women through their roles as workers and mothers, but he placed more emphasis on their identities as mothers and presented himself as willing and able to use the state to protect and defend them and their children. In the ads directed at Chilean women, such as in figure 3.6, Allende was often positioned as a symbolic father/husband completing a picture of the idealized nuclear family. While men were not as often directly addressed in their familial identities, they often represented a secondary audience, as Allende's solutions could appeal to men through the promises of state support for the family, including better jobs and pay. Like Tomic's and Alessandri's, Allende's campaign incorporated familial images and identities in pursuit of specific strategic goals. Allende's ads argued that he was the better choice because of the failure of previous governments to act responsibly toward Chilean families. His campaign presented him as the best Patriarchal Leader for the Familial State because he and his future government would be able to protect Chilean families, particularly mothers and children, from capitalist exploitation.

Conclusion

In the fiercely fought campaign, the candidates turned to multiple and varied invocations of the family and its connection to the political. The discourse of the three campaigns drew on and strengthened the general societal tendency to turn to familial beliefs to understand both the duties and responsibilities of Chilean presidents and the state they governed. All three candidates presented themselves as a version of the Patriarchal Leader who would protect and provide for Chilean families and recognized familial welfare as a fundamental responsibility of the state (Familial State). Chilean citizens, particularly women, were addressed through their familial roles, and their political interests were often defined through claims about familial welfare. Taken together, the uses of the family in the 1970 election show how relationships among the state, political leaders, and citizens are defined partly through familial beliefs. While at times the three political candidates interpreted this relationship very differently, all agreed that the government owed specific duties to Chilean families and promised to uphold these duties as president. In the end, in a historic vote on 4 September 1970, Allende won the election and became the first democratically elected socialist president. He won with 36.2 percent of the vote, while Alessandri received 34.9 percent, only thirty thousand votes short. Allende's victory, however, did not mean the end of political debate over his ability to rule. And as we will see in the next chapter, political conflict continued on familial terrain.

★ FOUR ★

A FEUDING FAMILY
Mobilizing For and Against Allende

Winning the election was only the first of the political struggles faced by Salvador Allende. Many members of the Chilean political right first refused to accept his election and then actively resisted the attempts of the Popular Unity to implement its program of social and economic reforms. Over the course of his tragically short presidency, Allende faced both growing political polarization and a deepening economic crisis, caused in part by determined efforts on the part of the Chilean business elite and the U.S. government. Scholars have extensively studied the importance of class conflict, extreme politicization, and the fateful mistakes of political leaders in helping to bring about the eventual military overthrow of Chile's democracy.[1] But how were these conflicts understood? What was the actual language of these conflicts at the time? How were political and economic problems framed and interpreted by Chilean political leaders and mobilized citizens? In public debate, who was responsible for the political and economic situation? Allende and his government? The Chilean upper class? Foreign imperial powers? These struggles over the interpretation and meaning of the political and economic crisis indelibly shaped Allende's presidency and helped pave the way for the military coup.

Chilean political leaders and everyday citizens turned to familial beliefs about the responsibilities of the state (Familial State), the role of political leaders (Patriarchal Leader), and citizens' rights and identities (Militant Families) as they struggled over how to understand and react to the economic and political challenges besetting the country. Starting with the March of the Empty Pots and Pans in December 1971, societal groups and political elites turned to these familial understandings to either question or uphold the political legitimacy of Allende and his Popular Unity government. Intertwining the ideological claims of the Familial State and the Patriarchal Leader, Allende's opponents

---

1. I discuss this literature in detail in chapter 1.

questioned his capabilities as president and the legitimacy of his government by arguing that neither he nor his government was fulfilling his responsibilities toward Chilean families. Referencing rising levels of violence and political polarization, Allende's opponents portrayed the security of Chilean families, and by extension the nation, as endangered by the current government. Increasingly, Chilean citizens, particularly women, mobilized through a discourse of familial identities, invoking ideals of Militant Families to criticize the current Popular Unity government. Allende and his supporters actively contested these claims by extolling their commitment to Chilean families. In this chapter I show the centrality of the familial framework in these struggles between Allende and his opponents by analyzing three major political events: the March of the Empty Pots and Pans and the subsequent mobilization of anti-Allende women, the 1973 congressional elections, and the debate over Allende's educational reform during the months before his overthrow on 11 September 1973. Throughout Allende's presidency, political struggles were fought on the discursive terrain over which political party, individual, or group better protected the family and promoted familial welfare.

The March of the Empty Pots and Pans

On 1 December 1971, Chilean women took to the streets in the "first mass mobilization against the Allende government."[2] Before the March of the Empty Pots and Pans, as it came to be known, the political opposition to President Allende had been disheartened by the failure of various attempts to prevent him from taking office. While Allende had won the election, Chilean law held that if the top candidate did not win an absolute majority of the vote, then the Chilean Congress could choose between the top two vote getters.[3] While the Congress traditionally upheld the will of the voters and appointed the winner of the popular vote, in this case the Chilean right attempted to subvert the process. They tried to convince the Christian Democrats to vote with the National Party for Alessandri, who had pledged to immediately resign to allow for new elections.[4]

Far-right military officials and civilians took a more extreme path in their opposition. They attempted to kidnap the chief of the armed forces, General René Schneider, who had staunchly refused to involve the military in politics.

---

2. Oppenheim, *Politics in Chile*, 64.
3. Ibid., 38.
4. See Collier and Sater, *History of Chile*, 328–29, and Oppenheim, *Politics in Chile*, 38–39.

The plan was to frame the extreme left for the kidnapping, thus provoking military intervention to prevent Allende from assuming the presidency. In a tragic turn of events, General Schneider was killed in the attempt. The investigation into his death quickly revealed the identities of the conspirators, the plot, and some contact between the participants and the CIA.[5] Ironically, given the hopes of the right-wing conspirators, the immediate result of the kidnapping was to assure that the Chilean Congress would follow tradition and confirm Allende's victory.

The Schneider assassination and the confirmation of Allende as president left the right demobilized and without a clear path to oppose the new Popular Unity government. The Christian Democratic Party, divided between moderate and liberal factions, also did not have a unified approach to the new Allende government.[6] Taking advantage of this disorganization and division, Allende launched a series of radical reforms designed to socialize the economy and to redistribute wealth. Initially, Allende advanced reforms begun by President Frei, and he counted on political support from the more liberal members of the Christian Democrats. Allende seized the banner of Chilean patriotism by pushing ahead with a plan to fully nationalize the copper mining industry, a measure that enjoyed widespread popular and political support. The bill passed in the Chilean Congress unanimously. In the first year, the Popular Unity also expanded the agrarian reform program of Frei, speeding up the pace of land appropriations and creating state-owned cooperative farms.[7]

The government also aggressively pursued the nationalization of Chile's industrial sectors while increasing the salaries of the Chilean working class and fixing prices on basic consumer goods. The net effect of the government's programs was a decrease in unemployment in Santiago—Chile's manufacturing center—from 8.3 percent to 3.5 percent. At the same time, real wages increased and the "share of national income going to labor increased from 55.0 percent in 1970 to 65.7 percent in 1971."[8] Further, the gross national product "soared by 8.3 percent."[9] The initial success of Allende's economic reforms,

5. Baldez, *Why Women Protest*, 62–63; Collier and Sater, *History of Chile*, 329; Oppenheim, *Politics in Chile*, 61–62.
6. For a good discussion of the internal dynamics of the right and the Christian Democrats during this time, see Oppenheim, *Politics in Chile*, 38–40, 53–54.
7. The rise and fall of Allende and the UP government has generated an extensive scholarship. In this discussion, I am relying mostly on Oppenheim, *Politics in Chile*; Collier and Sater, *History of Chile*; and Brian Loveman, *Chile*.
8. Stallings and Zimbalist, "Political Economy," 72.
9. Collier and Sater, *History of Chile*, 343.

coupled with the enthusiasm of his supporters and the disunity of the opposition, helped the Popular Unity win roughly 50 percent of the vote in the municipal elections in April 1971, a considerable gain from the 36 percent Allende received in the 1970 presidential election.[10]

By the end of 1971, however, the political honeymoon was over and Allende's policies began to generate stronger opposition. While the nationalization of the mostly foreign-owned copper industry had enjoyed widespread support, the expropriation of Chilean-owned businesses and large agricultural estates put Allende and his government in direct confrontation with the Chilean upper class. Additionally, the Christian Democrats were increasingly unwilling to compromise with Allende, as a more conservative faction, under the leadership of former president Eduardo Frei, regained control of the party.[11] Unable to get the needed support in Congress to pursue his agenda, Allende increasingly bypassed the legislature and made changes by executive order. The UP government, through creative legal interpretations, began using existing laws that allowed state control of any industry "deemed 'essential' to the economy" if it broke the law or failed "to operate efficiently," criteria that allowed the government substantial leeway in interpretation.[12] While furthering the Popular Unity's overall goals, this strategy also promoted common ground between the Christian Democrats and the National Party. This political opposition was mirrored by a growth in societal opposition, in particular on the far right by groups such as Fatherland and Liberty, and Solidarity, Order, and Liberty.[13]

In December 1971, women took to the streets, banging pots and pans to protest the visit of Fidel Castro and to express their disapproval of Allende's government. The March of the Empty Pots and Pans reshaped the Chilean political landscape.[14] The historian Margaret Power argues that the march fueled the organization of conservative women and contributed to the growth of the opposition to Allende. It switched the strategy on the part of the right to "street

10. Oppenheim, *Politics of Chile*, 54.
11. Ibid., 64.
12. Collier and Sater, *History of Chile*, 342.
13. Baldez, *Why Women Protest*, 69.
14. In current scholarship, Power offers the most thorough discussion of the debates surrounding who organized and participated in the march. See *Right-Wing Women*, especially 144–47. See also Baldez's discussion in *Why Women Protest*, 77–80. An older generation of scholarship is also important, although the debate over the class characteristics of the women marchers sometimes overshadows other important issues. See Chaney, "Mobilization of Women"; Crummett, "El Poder Femenino"; and Mattelart, "Chile." Bunster's examination in "Watch Out for the Little Nazi Man" raises important issues about the persuasiveness of traditional understandings of politics and gender for fueling political violence.

demonstrations and direct actions," an approach that was "more confrontational, more challenging, . . . and more likely to build a movement."[15] Political scientist Lisa Baldez agrees with Power's assessment about the importance of the march, arguing that it "catapult[ed] men to action," ending the political lethargy of the opposition and unifying the political opposition to the Popular Unity government.[16] The march marked the beginning of the use of mass street demonstrations, which would dominate Chilean political life until the 11 September 1973 coup d'état. According to Baldez, the march "set off a series of events that changed the fate of both the opposition and the government in significant ways."[17]

While scholars agree on its overall political importance, what remains open to debate are the questions of who organized the march, who participated in it, and what their political goals were. For the purposes of this study, getting to the truth of these questions is less important than understanding how these questions were framed, portrayed, and debated within the public discourse of the time.[18] The march not only brought conservative women onto the streets but also provided powerful discursive strategies for framing and justifying attacks against Allende and the political legitimacy of his government. The march provided an initial framework for attacking Allende that helped set a pattern for the next two years. The arguments promoted by the march provided an enduring general framework for attacking Allende. The critical advertisements for the march accused Allende and his government of threatening the survival of Chilean families. The ads also positioned women as guardians of the family and claimed that they had been driven to protest because of threats to familial welfare. The newspaper advertisements, for example, claimed, "We also say to the President of the Republic that the scarcity of food and the rising expense of the basic supplies, when they can be found, is an attempt against the life of our families. You need to walk the markets, the department stores, and grocery stores so that you personally comprehend that the [press] releases of your ministers and technicians do not have anything to do with the realities that the Chilean woman suffers."[19] An article in *La Tribuna* called on women to "bring empty pots and pans with them in order to highlight the

15. Power, *Right-Wing Women*, 167.
16. Baldez, *Why Women Protest*, 76.
17. Ibid.
18. Those interested in exploring these issues further should consult the scholarship discussed above in relation to the debate over women's participation in the march.
19. Ad inserted into Cámara de Diputados, Sesión 24a, 3 December 1971.

lack of food."[20] Another ad claimed that women daily saw that "there is no meat, chicken, milk, noodles, and other essential food, and when we do find these products we have to pay prices that are beyond our resources."[21] In the press conference held by the organizers two days before the march, on 29 November, Nina Donoso claimed that "politics will not be key"; rather, the demonstration was called for because "we [women] have no formula to feed our babies and they get sick with diarrhea. . . . Our husbands are forced to attend political meetings in order to keep their jobs."[22] Chilean women were urged to take to the streets to protect their families, which meant upholding both women's traditional role as caretaker of the family and men's position as breadwinner. Government policies were presented as threatening familial welfare by interfering with the ability of women to fulfill their basic duties as wives and mothers to feed their families.

Such framing allowed organizers to present the march as stemming from the central roles and identities of Chilean women, which cut across class, ethnic, regional, and political lines. Often, as in an opinion piece in *El Mercurio* published on the morning of the march, the women were lauded as Chilean mothers for "courage and valor" in providing for the daily sustenance of their families.[23] Poor mothers were singled out for praise for the sacrifices they endured in order to help their children and husbands. The piece lauded the valiant mothers who were being forced to protest by banging on empty pots and pans because the government had failed in its promise to improve their families' lives. According to an editorial in *La Tercera* by María Oyarzún, poor Chilean mothers were protesting in order to protect their families. In concrete terms, mothers would take to the streets because they "don't have pasta to make soup for the babies and [the babies] are sick with diarrhea."[24] Framing the march along the lines of women protesting a lack of basic consumer goods might have worked to obscure the class interests of many of the women organizing the march who, as members of the upper class, certainly did not lack access to food. Other reasons given for the march included the increasing politicization of daily life, which, according to the ads, meant that men were forced to attend political meetings to keep their jobs, and parents could not educate their children in liberty and democracy because of changes in school curricula.

20. Power, *Right-Wing Women*, 150.
21. *La Tribuna*, 29 November 1971.
22. *El Mercurio*, 29 November 1971, quoted in Power, *Right-Wing Women*, 151.
23. *El Mercurio*, 1 December 1971.
24. *La Tercera*, 1 December 1971.

The actions of the women marchers were also presented as driven by apolitical and selfless worry over their families. The organizers invoked women's familial identities as mothers to present themselves and the other participants as outside traditional politics.[25] Drawing on gendered understandings of women as selfless and uninterested in politics, the rhetoric surrounding the march claimed that women had been spurred to act as mothers to protect the general interests of their families and the nation.[26] Unlike male politicians, who were motivated by their own particular interests—and therefore could be blind to the dangers posed to the nation by the current government—women were presented as clear-sighted critics. For example, in the call to the march printed on the front page of *La Tribuna* on 29 November, the rhetoric makes a distinction between the sectarianism of political society versus the general concern of women as mothers: "The sectarianism, the arrogance of the government officials, has filled us with worry about the future of our patria and the destiny of our children."[27] In addition to the material welfare of the family, the ads positioned women as defenders of the Chilean nation. The ads called on women to demonstrate because "the facts, at first isolated, later more frequent and today constant, have demonstrated that the government, the parties that form its political base, are making an attempt against the life of the nation, oblige us to break our silence and publicly demonstrate our rejection."[28] Thus, the legitimacy of the women's familial and national concerns was contrasted with the illegitimate political goals of the government.

How was the case made that the government threatened the life of the nation? The answer can be found in an ad for the march in *La Tribuna* on 1 December 1971, which criticized Allende and his government for dividing Chilean families and so too the Chilean nation: "Our nationality is in crisis, and national solidarity . . . is being destroyed by the criminal divisions between the class[es] . . . fabricated by communism to destroy the Chilean family. Chilean women . . . cannot remain impassive before the anguished moment that Chile is facing. Conscious of our responsibility to the nation and our children we will lend our unconditional support to the march."[29] The ad draws an explicit link between the responsibility of mothers for the survival of both their own families and the Chilean national family. The rhetoric leaves no room for ambiguity:

25. Power, *Right-Wing Women*, 148.
26. Ibid., 151–52.
27. *La Tribuna*, 29 November 1971, 1.
28. Ad inserted into Cámara de Diputados, Sesión 24a, 3 December 1971.
29. Quoted in Baldez, *Why Women Protest*, 92.

the destruction of Chilean families, and by extension the nation, was the ultimate aim of the Chilean left. This language invoked the massive anticommunist "scare campaign" of the 1964 and 1970 presidential elections.[30] According
to the ad, Allende and his government "fabricated" political conflict and division in order to destroy Chilean families.

Allende's presidency placed the family in physical and spiritual danger because "hate has been sown, [along with] the lack of respect for authority and
those values that for us are fundamental."[31] According to the march organizers,
these values included Chile's revered democratic traditions, including freedom of speech, thought, and religion. These values were endangered by the
UP's attempts to politicize societal institutions, such as attempts by leftist students to oust the conservative rector of the University of Chile. The ads con-
strue this action as an attempt on the part of the left to insert political ideology
into the educational system at all levels and to remove parental control.[32] Therefore, the loss of Chile's democratic traditions and values was not simply a
political matter; family and nation were threatened by attempts to erode the
values and morals that supported the traditional authority of parents over
their children.

In the march's publicity, therefore, organizers drew heavily on the complex
interconnection of beliefs that bound the family and the nation-state. Running throughout the public discourse surrounding the march was a consensus
that the state and political leaders had a fundamental duty to protect the family. The public statements and advertisements surrounding the march presented the current problems facing Chile as threatening the family, and it laid
the blame at the feet of Allende. Problems such as the scarcity of consumer
goods, struggles over education reform, and the politicization of employment
were framed as endangering familial welfare and presented as evidence of
Allende's failure to fulfill his responsibilities toward Chilean families. In addition, the conflation of family and nation in the language surrounding the march
meant that by destroying the family, the nation was threatened, and that by
destroying the nation, Chilean families were endangered. Their harsh attacks
against Allende were justified through the general understanding that the state
is to protect the family, and by extension the nation.

30. For an excellent discussion of the history and effects of the scare campaign in Chile, especially as it pertains to the uses of gender in the campaigns, see Power, *Right-Wing Women*. See also
chapter 3 of this volume.

31. *La Tribuna*, 29 November 1971.

32. See the ad inserted into the Cámara de Diputados, Sesión 24a, 3 December 1971, and Power,
Right-Wing Women, 150.

The centrality of the family in the discourse over political legitimacy also helps explain the repeated invocation of women's familial roles. March organizers turned to societal beliefs about the centrality of women's familial identities as mothers and wives to appeal to women and to construct their actions as a defense of the family and the nation. Women were presented as the true "voice of the people" because they were acting out of apolitical motivations as mothers. They were spurred into political action out of their selfless concern for the future of their children, their families, and their nation. The power of women's familial identities as wives and mothers rested not only in cultural beliefs about appropriate gender roles but also in the specific political claims that these identities invoked. If a fundamental duty of the state is to protect families, then given women's responsibilities for the family, women have a reciprocal duty as citizens to criticize the state. Thus familial identities serve to justify political claims and to legitimate public action.

The March and Its Meanings

As Power persuasively documents, women were the public leaders of the march, even if they were supported by specific men and male-dominated political organizations. The march permit, granted on 26 November, was given to Silvia Alessandri, a National Party deputy, and the principal organizers were all middle- or upper-class Chilean women.[33] The explicit framing of the march as organized by women and for women to express their concerns as mothers and housewives was at the time unique and made the march even more newsworthy. Appealing to women through their familial roles proved to be an effective strategy in generating support. The *New York Times* reported that five thousand women had participated, while the opposition press claimed higher attendance, including the probably inflated figure of one hundred thousand reported by *El Mercurio*.[34]

The march began around 6:30 P.M. when "thousands of women converged at the Plaza Italia and began to march" toward the central avenue and the Moneda, the Chilean presidential palace, banging on empty pots and pans.[35] While the majority of marchers were women, men from the youth groups of

---

33. Power, *Right-Wing Women*, 146–47, 151; *El Mercurio*, 30 November 1971.
34. Baldez discusses the differing reports of the size of the march in *Why Women Protest*, 78.
35. Baldez, *Why Women Protest*, 78.

various opposition parties, as well as the far-right group Fatherland and Liberty, accompanied the marchers in order "to provide security for the women."[36] Shortly into the march, violence broke out. Skirmishes between opposing youth groups, supporters of the UP throwing objects at the marchers, and construction workers throwing bricks were all reported. Fights between groups associated on one side with the National and Christian Democratic parties and the right-wing Fatherland and Liberty, and on the other side with the youth groups that supported Allende, such as the communist Ramona Parra Brigade, the socialist Elmo Catalán Brigade, and the Movement of the Revolutionary Left, fueled the violence.[37] At the Cerro Santa Lucía, a wooded park in the center of Santiago, police barricades had been erected and officers were given orders to stop the marchers and not let them proceed closer to the Congress and the Moneda. When the marchers attempted to bypass the blockade, the police sprayed them with tear gas, and new confrontations between the marchers, the police, and supporters of the UP broke out. During the march, ninety-nine people were reported injured—sixty men and thirty-nine women. Skirmishes continued well into the night, and the government declared Santiago an emergency zone on 2 December.[38]

The march immediately became the focus of an intense interpretive struggle between supporters of Allende and his opposition. In constructing the political meaning of the march, the opposition pursued a number of strategic moves. First, it focused on a specific version of the violent incidents associated with the march. The newspaper reports in the opposition press ignored the role of fierce interactions between the mostly male youth groups. Instead of ongoing altercations between different politicized groups of mostly young men, the opposition claimed that the government had actually supported the violence against the marchers, who were invariably represented as Chilean mothers. The opposition press repeatedly asserted that Allende had ordered the police to not interfere with the actions of the pro-Allende groups and to use tear gas and water on the women. For example, under the headline "Violent Incidents," *La Tercera* featured dramatic pictures of injured women marchers. One picture featured two women crying with one clutching her baby, while the text detailed how young women, carrying their children in their arms, were confused and scared during the tear gas attacks. The article explicitly blamed the

---

36. Power, *Right-Wing Women*, 153.

37. See Baldez, *Why Women Protest*, 79–80, for a discussion of the participation of these different groups.

38. Ibid., 155.

government for the violence, claiming that the government's support of radical leftist groups had tied the hands of the police in protecting the women and their children. In this account, the police were forced to abandon their duty to protect women and were ordered to condone the violence and unlawful actions of the government supporters. In the opposition press, the women marchers became the innocent victims of a government that had abandoned its duty to protect Chilean mothers and their children, even ordering the police to spray the women with water and tear gas, all due to the politics of a radical minority.[39]

The narrative of mothers forced to protest in the street in order to save their family and their nation, only to then be subjected to government-sponsored violence, was repeated in an ad taken out on 5 December in *El Mercurio* by the National Feminine Unity, a women's group that had helped organize the march. The ad justified the demonstration by calling on the tradition of the past "mothers" of the Chilean nation, and it portrayed the marchers as current mothers who acted out of their dedication to the welfare of their families and their nation:

> Our participants carried the national flag, the symbol of our respect for the Patria, and the white flag, emblem, in all the countries of the parliamentary world, of peace and not violence. We carried also our pots and baskets that expressed . . . the problem that today afflicts all housewives from Arica to Magallanes.
>
> We united as women and as mothers, without political or social distinctions: girls, young women, and old women.
>
> We are the voice of the people [*pueblo*], the feminine *pueblo* of the Patria . . .
>
> It was a journey never seen in the history of Chile.
>
> The spirit of the mothers of the Patria guided us, propelled us . . .
>
> *What would we have to fear if we marched through the streets of the Patria carrying our flag and singing our song?*
>
> We were wrong. . . . The seeds of fear and of violence, the bastard appetites of power . . . have sunk very deep into minority sectors of our country. . . . It is a stain that with difficulty we will forget and a regrettable balance of victims, violence, pain, and shame in all the homes of the Patria.[40]

39. "No nos aterrorizan," *La Tribuna*, 3 December 1971, 9.

40. "Violentos incidentes," *La Tercera*, 2 December 1971, 1; *El Mercurio*, 5 December 1971, 41. See also the ad, on p. 36, from the National Party that under the headline "Homage to the Chilean Woman" repeated the central claims of the National Feminine Unity.

This ad presents what was to become the dominant framing of the march within opposition discourse. The marchers are not just women, but mothers, both real and metaphoric. Further, they are the direct successors of the founding mothers who had helped create the Chilean nation. The women claim that their actions are justified because of their position as mothers of both the family and the nation. Further, their actions are legitimate because of Allende's failure to fulfill his duties toward family welfare, as shown by the current political and economic problems. The rhetoric of the ad claims that Allende and his government also failed to respect and protect these women. The government's actions are portrayed as stemming "from the bastard appetites" promoted by the political ideology of the left. This viewpoint promotes the rejection of the duty to protect women and children and leads men to violently attack women and children in the pursuit of political power and personal interests. The ad contrasts the legitimate and justified actions of the women with the venal and illegitimate actions of the government.

The march reshaped the discourse of the opposition parties, as both the PDC and the PN increasingly incorporated these family-based critiques in their attacks against Allende. Immediately following the march, the two parties launched a congressional investigation into the actions of the government around the March of the Empty Pots and Pans. Deputies Saavedra (PDC), Retamal (PDC), and Alessandri (PN), all women and march participants, became the spokespeople for the march within Congress. In their presentations, the three deputies stressed that Chilean women had been forced into action because of the seriousness of the everyday worries they were facing. In the words of PDC deputy Retamal, the marchers were not against change or Salvador Allende, but rather they "wanted to defend . . . the principles [of]: democracy for all, liberty for all, tranquility for our children, fiscal security of our men, for our husbands."[41] PDC deputy Saavedra pointed out the hypocrisy of the government in pushing for a Ministry of the Family while subjecting Chilean mothers to violence. She argued that "the family, especially the mother of the family, the head of the house," was not receiving the help from the government that the family deserved. The marcher was a "woman who is preoccupied by the educational content being given to her children . . . who has a husband in Public Administration that is feeling pressure, because [he] doesn't think the same as the government," and that this "is the insecurity" the march signified. Saavedra contrasted the march with the pending legislation to create

41. Cámara de Diputados, Sesión 24a, 3 December 1971, 1819.

the Ministry of the Family, asking fellow deputies why they were "creating an organization that we say will focus on the Chilean family, if they [the mothers and housewives] do not have, in practice, the protection or the attention that they deserve in this moment from the government?"[42] For all three deputies, women were the accepted and recognized representatives of the family. The deputies' speeches established a clear contrast between the legitimate action of the women marchers, who were acting to protect their families, and the illegitimate action (or inaction) of the government, which had failed to uphold its responsibilities to Chilean families.

In the congressional debates, members of the opposition repeated the charges that the government had condoned the violence. Deputy Arnello (PN) singled out for condemnation the actions of the police. He asserted that the "actions of Marxist brigades were favored by the unspeakable conduct, ordered by the police forces [and] . . . by the government and the minister of the interior. This conduct was extremely passive because of the relationship with the assaulting groups. . . . None of the assaults were repelled by the police." According to him, the failure of the police to protect the women represented a complete dereliction of duty by the government. This action showed that the communist ideology of the government "morally castrates" people and leaves them concerned only with political power and hatred for those who do not share their political beliefs. Arnello argued that hatred, rooted in the government's political ideology, was behind the cowardly and unchivalrous attacks on the women. The government's actions had justified the women's denial of "their support to the Marxist parties," an action based on their "feminine intuition." According to Arnello, "Chilean women, with their intuition, demonstrated, one and a thousand times, that they clearly comprehended that [one] cannot tolerate a doctrine, an ideology, that contradicts the essence of the great patria that they serve and the little patria, their homes and their families."[43] For Arnello, the march was a valiant attempt by women to protect both the national family and their own family from the threats posed by the present government and its ideologies. Family and nation are merged in this critique: women, because of their overwhelming concern for others, were better able to understand and resist the dangers posed by communism.

The argument and the tone of the congressional exchange were disseminated to the wider public by the publication of the entire debate in newspapers

42. Ibid., 1813.
43. Ibid., 1814.

and by a number of ads taken out by opposition parties and groups over the next month.[44] These ads continued to contrast the courage and self-sacrifice of Chilean mothers with the cowardliness and sectarianism of the Allende government. For example, the National Party in an ad in *El Mercurio* lauded women who demonstrated "the serenity and courage that is the pride of a consciousness of duty completed day after day, to sustain their homes and to form the present and future children of the patria." The PN contrasted the courage of the women with a government that had been "passive before the attacks on the women." Instead of protecting Chilean mothers from violence, the PN claimed that the government was actually reprimanding the women who marched, thereby adding insult to injury.[45] The March of the Empty Pots and Pans provided the opposition with a powerful critique that framed the government as a threat to Chilean families. Further, the experiences of participants in the march were used by the opposition as dramatic, concrete examples of the threat posed by Allende and Chile's left.

Capitalizing on the success of the march, many of the women who had participated decided to organize a group that could coordinate and plan future protests. The anti-Allende women's group El Poder Femenino (Feminine Power, EPF) was organized in early 1972 and presented itself as an organization of wives and mothers.[46] Mobilizing based on women's familial identities (Militant Families), the EPF created a movement of women dedicated to criticizing Allende and the Popular Unity government. From the beginning of 1972 to the coup of 1973, the EPF interjected a familial critique of Allende's political legitimacy into the ongoing struggle. The EPF promoted an understanding of the economic crisis in terms of its effects on women's abilities to fulfill their roles as wives and mothers. The group attacked the Juntas de Abastecimiento y Precio (JAPs), neighborhood groups organized by the UP government in an attempt to ensure the equitable distribution of food. The JAPs were supposed to ensure that Chilean households could purchase a "basket of basic goods—rice, cooking oil, sugar, and so forth" at the official prices.[47] The opposition charged that the JAPs "served only those who supported the UP government,"[48]

---

44. The congressional record was usually published in *El Mercurio*. What makes this slightly different is that the deputies present at the debate on 3 December approved a special request to have that session printed immediately not only in *El Mercurio* but also in the other major newspapers of Santiago as well as an important regional paper. See Sesión 24a, 3 December 1971, 1829–30.

45. Ad inserted into Cámara de Diputados, Sesión 24a, 3 December 1971.

46. Power, *Right-Wing Women*, 168.

47. Oppenheim, *Politics in Chile*, 75–76.

48. Power, *Right-Wing Women*, 188.

and the JAPs became a symbol for how the UP was willing to inject politics even into programs meant to provide basic sustenance to Chilean families. Thus it was Allende and the UP that were denying Chileans access to vital consumer goods because of political calculations. The actions of the EPF helped transform the growing lack of such goods into a biting critique of the legitimacy of Allende's government.

The lack of basic goods and the hardship endured by many women as they attempted to feed their families became a rallying cry for women who opposed Allende. To keep the importance of the march and its critiques visible, the EPF organized a nightly banging of empty pots and pans in neighborhoods across Santiago to dramatize the failure of the government to provide enough food to fill the family pot. In order to strengthen its ability to speak for all Chilean women, the EPF attempted to broaden the class basis of the movement. To do so, it appealed to women through their familial roles as wives and mothers. As Power argues, "The factor that most effectively helped anti-Allende women broaden their movement to include poor and working-class women was the economic crisis that beset Chile from late 1971 onward."[49] As an EPF ad stated, "We are the ones who must endure the *colas* [lines for goods]; we are the ones who struggle to feed and dress our children; we are the ones who suffer from a lack of foodstuffs; we are the ones who suffer from seeing the hate that divides us."[50] These everyday signs of the economic crisis especially affected women because of the division of gender roles in Chile. Women of the working and middle classes suffered because they did not have the money to spend on the black market, and they did not employ household help and thus they were the ones waiting in the lines.[51] Many women's lives began to revolve around waiting in these long lines, sometimes through the night, in order to procure basic necessities. In the public pronouncements and actions of the EPF, the economic crisis was not an abstract concept; rather, it was understood through the concrete dangers posed to Chilean families. The group's arguments against Allende were organized around the central claim that the current government was failing in its familial duties.

Beliefs about the responsibilities owed to families by the state provided a flexible framework for interpreting the threats posed by the economic crisis. For many Chileans, the economic crisis was experienced as long lines to purchase

49. Ibid., 186.
50. Quoted in Crummett, "El Poder Femenino," 111.
51. For discussions of the economic crisis and its effects on women, see Power, *Right-Wing Women*; Baldez, *Why Women Protest*; and Mattelart, "Chile."

goods, a booming black market, an increasing scarcity of goods, and a general uneasiness about the economic situation.[52] While there was no doubt that starting in 1972 Chile's economic situation deteriorated, at the time there was considerable political struggle over how the crisis should be understood. Was it the fault of Allende? Or was it the fault of the Chilean business elite and the actions of the United States? Ironically, while Allende's policies promoted income redistribution and higher wages, the goods that the lower classes could now afford were no longer easily available. Even women who supported the UP and Allende viewed the lines as interfering with their ability to provide for their families.[53] For many Chileans, the *colas* came to symbolize the failure of Allende and the UP. The political legitimacy of Allende and his government was debated through interpretive struggles over the state of familial welfare and the state's responsibility for Chilean families.[54]

THE GOVERNMENT AND ITS SUPPORTERS RESPOND

Allende and his supporters recognized the political threat posed by these developments. They quickly attacked the opponents' core familial claims. One key strategy of the government's response was to deny that the marchers were "authentic" Chilean mothers. Instead of the marcher as the self-sacrificing Chilean mother portrayed by the opposition, Allende and his supporters framed them as either dupes of the rich or members of political groups already hostile to the government. In an address to the crowd that had gathered in the National Stadium on 4 December to bid good-bye to Fidel Castro, Allende went on the offensive. To question the women's ability to speak for all Chilean families, he pointed out that the marchers "came from the high-class suburb to downtown Santiago," and that they "came and left in powerful cars." While the marchers banged on empty pots, Allende argued that in fact these women had "never known the lack of basic foods."[55] By highlighting the class position of the women, Allende questioned both the veracity of their material claims and the marchers' ability to symbolically represent Chilean families. Instead of apolitical mothers interested only in the welfare of children and the nation, the marchers were portrayed as upper-class women who were upset because

52. For a discussion of the overall economic situation of Chile during the time of the UP, see Oppenheim, *Politics in Chile*, part 2.
53. Power, *Right-Wing Women*, 196.
54. Ibid., chapter 6.
55. Cockcroft, *Salvador Allende Reader*, 139–40.

of threats to their class position. As exploiters of Chilean working-class families, the upper-class marchers could not claim to be self-sacrificing mothers. Thus the women could not legitimately speak for either the Chilean family or the Chilean nation.

This portrayal of the marchers was also promoted in the coverage of the march in the leftist press. For example, *El Siglo* claimed that the women who participated were from Las Condes, an upper-class neighborhood of Santiago, wore the latest fashions, and beat on pots and pans that they were holding for the first time (since they had maids to cook for their families).[56] This critique was encapsulated in a cartoon (fig. 4.1) published in *El Siglo* on 5 December, which featured five overweight, upper-class women with exaggerated features, bedecked in jewelry and holding pots and pans. This image accompanied a caption that read "empty pots and hollow heads."[57] Rather than the image of the valiant mother protecting her child, the left portrayed the marchers as rich, fat, stupid, unattractive, and overindulged. These women are clearly not motivated by concern about the welfare of others.

Casting aspersions on the intelligence of the marchers furthered the UP's claim that the women were actually being manipulated by political groups opposed to Allende. Senator Teitelboim of the Communist Party referenced this argument in his defense of the government on the floor of the Chilean Senate. He bluntly stated that the march was the result of agitation by members of the Chilean right as well as the U.S. government. According to the senator, the march should not be seen as resulting from a concern over the welfare of Chileans, but rather as an extension of the ongoing campaign to oust President Allende. He further argued that those on the Chilean right would do anything, including endangering women and children, in their attempts to discredit Allende and save their class privileges. He called the march a farce because people that had "full stomachs for centuries" used the sound of empty pots and pans to critique the government. The march showed the depravity of those on the right because they claimed that Allende threatened the family, when in reality it was these same groups—the real organizers of the march—that had perpetuated hunger and the "highest infant mortality rate in the world."[58]

For the government and its supporters, "true" Chilean mothers understood

---

56. See the coverage and editorials of the march in the 2–5 December editions of *El Siglo*.

57. *El Siglo*, 5 December 1971, 2. The Spanish reads, "'Ollas vacías' y cabezas huecas . . . "

58. Senado de Chile, *Diario de sesiones del Senado*, Sesión 36a, 7 December 1971, 1719–20. Margaret Power notes that while it is clear the CIA was covertly funding many right-wing groups, there is no clear evidence that the agency had a hand in planning the march. See *Right-Wing Women*, 162–63.

Fig. 4.1   "Empty pots and hollow heads." (*El Siglo*, 5 December 1971.)

that the "real" danger to Chilean families was posed by the forces that opposed the political changes promoted by Allende. For example, PC deputy Mireya Baltra called on women to recognize that "fascism wants to destroy our homes" and Chile's democratic traditions by attacking the legitimately elected government of Allende. According to her, it was the opposition that wanted to "divide the people and the families" and "that generates fanaticism through crime, assaults, and lies; [that] corrodes with hatred all that it touches."[59] The left's supporters argued that true Chilean women would never sell out their families to the foreign interests of the United States by protesting against the elected government of Salvador Allende. Instead, they would work with the government in its attempts to solve the problems of scarcity caused by illegal speculation.[60] As *El Siglo* put it, the true face of the Chilean woman was seen in those who fought and sacrificed for the "dignity of her patria and her family" by supporting the current government.[61]

59. *El Siglo*, 12 December 1971, 12. Following the march, between 5 December and 21 December, no fewer than eighteen articles in *El Siglo* were printed defending the government and promoting a "counter-march" to be held on 20 December.
60. *El Siglo*, 12 December 1971, 12.
61. *El Siglo*, 8 December 1971, 5.

Allende and his supporters also attempted to counter the politically dangerous claim that the government had not protected innocent women and children, arguing that members of far-right groups had purposely provoked the altercations at the march. The left pointed to the various groups of men accompanying the women marchers as evidence of the violent intentions of the opposition. In a speech on 4 December, Allende called attention to their presence: "The people should know that that large demonstration was not a women's demonstration. It was preceded by groups of 70 or 80 boys with helmets and masks. They carried clubs with metallic projections, and they were probably armed. The women were flanked by organized groups of men who were similarly attired."[62] Thus it was the male march participants who had come prepared for violence. The women's presence was simply a screen that the opposition was using for its attacks on the government. Allende and his supporters attempted to portray the opposition as endangering women and children. It was the opposition that had sponsored a women's march in order to create a violent clash with the police that could be used to further the right's portrayal of Allende and his government as violent and illegitimate.

Finally, the UP sought to contest the symbolic power of the march by quickly planning a counter-march on 20 December. The government claimed that these women counter-marchers "were going out to defend their nation and their family against the violence of fascism" and represented the "true conscience of the Chilean woman."[63] To generate support for the march, *El Siglo* conducted on-street interviews with ordinary Chilean women voicing support for Allende. One such woman was Orfelina Hernandez, who claimed that the number of women who "support the government are a thousand times more that those that want to disparage it."[64] Maria de la Cruz Gonzalez, who claimed that she had always been apolitical, stated that she would be joining the march because of the material improvements she had experienced under Allende, including the fact that "the prices of the primary needs articles are less than in previous years. It's the truth that now one can buy much more."[65] The UP thus utilized the testimonials of "authentic" Chilean mothers to contest the assertion that Allende was not taking care of the material needs of families.[66]

62. Cockcroft, *Salvador Allende Reader*, 139–40.
63. *El Siglo*, 16 December 1971, 3.
64. *El Siglo*, 17 December 1971, 17.
65. *El Siglo*, 18 December 1971, 18.
66. Shayne argues that Allende and other male UP elites were hesitant to promote the counter-mobilization of leftist women, and that they undercut the attempts on the part of UP women activists

The political impact of the March of the Empty Pots and Pans was felt throughout the remainder of Allende's government. The interpretive power of the opposition's invocation of the Familial State and Patriarchal Leader can be seen in how the worsening economic situation in Chile was increasingly understood as a failure on the part of Allende to provide for familial welfare. The dominance of these familial understandings of the responsibilities of governments and leaders in the attacks against Allende was visible on the first anniversary of the march. Politicians from the opposition used the event as an opportunity to rake Allende and his government over the coals as a build-up to the upcoming congressional elections. For example, PDC deputy Saavedra in an editorial in *La Tercera* reminded readers of the reasons for the original march and the attacks on the women marchers. She pointed out the hypocrisy of Allende and his government, whose rhetoric claimed to support women but whose deeds continued to make it difficult for women to fulfill their roles as wives and mothers. Indeed, she claimed that the actions of Allende and his government "cannot produce a result more dramatic, nor more grotesque, nor more anguished" than the newest institution of Chilean society, the *cola*. Saavedra argued that because of Allende and his policies, women daily confronted "the problems of maintaining their homes ... shuffling their time and money between an empty market or the black market."[67] Another editorial in *La Tercera* criticized the government for the attacks "against our families, against our women, mothers, wives, or daughters."[68] The ongoing banging of empty pots and pans in neighborhoods across Santiago also kept the women's discontent visible.

The actions of both sides demonstrate the power of existing societal consensus around key beliefs, including the duty of the state to protect families. This consensus meant that Allende and his supporters did not contest the general foundations of the opposition's critiques. They conceded that his government had a responsibility to families, that familial welfare was intimately connected to the flourishing of the Chilean nation, that concerns about familial welfare represented a legitimate reason to mobilize, and that women as mothers had a special right to speak on behalf of families. Instead, Allende sought to discredit his opponents by presenting the myriad ways his government did

---

to mobilize a pro-Allende women's movement. This lack of support for a specifically women's response (as compared to a general response) was based on the strength of traditional gender understandings of both women and the family within the Chilean left. See *Revolution Question*, 87–88.

67. *La Tercera de la Hora*, 1 December 1972, 4.

68. *La Tercera de la Hora*, 4 December 1972, 3.

in fact support true Chilean families. In other words, both sides agreed on the use of familial welfare as a legitimate criterion for judging the success of the government (Familial State) and the president (Patriarchal Leader). What they fundamentally disagreed about was whether Allende and his government were fulfilling their duties to Chilean families. The discourses prompted by the march provided a conceptual framework through which Chileans could easily understand the growing economic and political crises.

Who's the Better Father for the Familial State? The 1973 Congressional Elections

The familial framing of the current political debates was incorporated into the rhetoric and images in the 1973 congressional campaigns of candidates from all political parties. By the time of the elections in March 1973, Chile was facing serious economic and political crises. The growing economic instability stemmed from a combination of problems in the UP's management of the economy, active resistance by the Chilean elite to economic measures taken by the government, and an "invisible U.S. blockade." In keeping with the anticommunist policies of the Nixon administration, the United States pressured international lending agencies to limit funds to Chile and tried to cut off exports to Chile of critical goods and services produced by American suppliers. Overall, Chile's foreign aid from the United States decreased from $260 million (1967) to $3.8 million (1973).[69] Taken together, these factors created a vicious circle. The increase in wages pushed by the UP meant that there were more people able to purchase goods. But Chilean industries often could not produce the goods to cover the rising demand due to a variety of causes, including deliberate sabotage by owners and inefficient takeovers by both the government and workers. The UP had to turn to importing food to meet basic needs, further depleting its monetary reserves. The government also had to deal with growing inflation, declining industrial production, and pressure from its own coalition to speed up and extend the nationalization of industries. By 1973, the UP was strapped for resources and facing both an intransigent national opposition and a hostile United States.

For both sides, the congressional elections represented a high-stakes, zero-sum game. The "electoral contest would mark the culmination of the process

69. Oppenheim, *Politics in Chile*, 106.

of polarization," as the left consolidated around the UP government while the center parties, most importantly the Christian Democrats, joined with the National Party and the right to create the Democratic Confederation (La Confederación de la Democracia, or CODE).[70] Chile's fluid electoral landscape, which had depended on political centrists to maintain balance, was now polarized into just two coalitions engaged in a furious contest for congressional control. Both sides wanted to increase their representation to a two-thirds majority. For the center-right opposition coalition CODE, this meant it would have the votes needed to overturn presidential vetoes and to impeach President Allende. CODE claimed that the elections were "a final and definitive plebiscite" on the legitimacy of Allende and the Popular Unity government.[71] The UP first and foremost needed to maintain its numbers in Congress. Second, a decisive electoral victory would give it the symbolic political legitimacy and congressional seats needed to push forward with its reforms.

Given the polarized political context and the importance of the election, my analysis focuses on the contest between the two coalitions, rather than analyzing the specific claims of any particular candidate. The creation of the two electoral coalitions and the subsequent degree of coordination in the campaign meant that ads for individual candidates were clearly part of and reflected more general political patterns and strategies. For both the UP and CODE, the election was seen as a debate about the success or failure of Allende and his government. This contest was often fought through competing interpretations of the ideals of the Familial State, as both sides sought to portray the opposition as endangering Chilean families while presenting their coalition as protecting the family. Given this focus, other uses of family discussed in more detail in the previous chapter (e.g., the Patriarchal Leader) are touched on only briefly.[72]

The overall political importance of this election can be seen in the number of ads published by both coalitions. In January and February 1973, the two months leading up to the March election, a total of 2,379 ads were published,

70. Valenzuela, *Breakdown of Democratic Regimes*, 83.
71. Ibid.
72. In addition to being secondary to my argument in this chapter, the number of individual candidates meant that most did not produce enough individual ads to justify a more individualized content analysis. The possible exceptions to this would be a handful of powerful candidates who were long-standing political leaders, including the former president Eduardo Frei; the president of the PN, Sergio Jarpa; the president of the PC, Volodia Teitelboim; and the president of the PS, Carlos Altamirano. It would also be interesting to conduct a more specialized analysis of the campaigns of the women candidates in this election, but this too lies beyond the focus of this chapter.

1,812 in *El Mercurio*, the standard-bearer for the opposition, and 567 in *El Clarín*, the largest of the leftist papers. This number represents a threefold increase over the number of ads in the presidential campaign in 1970 during a similar time period for the same newspapers. Six hundred seven of the ads were in favor of the UP and 1,689 were in support of CODE, clearly demonstrating the greater resources available to the opposition. Two hundred sixty-six of the ads had familial content. As in 1970, this number makes up one of the major categories in my coding scheme. Other types of ads included attacks on communism (77), ads about the personal character of the candidates (296), ads touting successful government programs (51), ads focusing on past successes of CODE candidates (40), ads highlighting the failure of the economy (123), and ads from groups in support of a specific candidate (156). The largest categories were the 377 ads that had no specific issue message but mentioned the name of the candidate or coalition, and the 383 ads announcing campaign rallies, both of which were simple forms of ads without a textual or visual story.[73] Ads with familial content, therefore, represented the second-highest category of the more developed and detailed ads, supplanted only by ads focusing on the candidate's personal character. Within the ads that used familial content, messages fell into the following categories: (1) current economic problems were presented through their effects on the family; (2) the family as currently under threat by either the government or the opposition; (3) the family as the recipient of the success or promised success of government programs; and (4) the family as the entity the UP or CODE sought to protect.

THE FAMILIAL FRAMING OF THE ECONOMIC CRISIS BY CODE

CODE drew heavily on the previous familial critiques to attack Allende and his government. In particular, CODE ads employed the family to shape how the voter should understand two major themes within its campaign propaganda: (1) the economic crisis and (2) increasing political conflict. Within both themes, the political rhetoric of CODE's campaign addressed Chileans through their familial roles, highlighted how the actions of the government interfered with those roles, portrayed the consequences of governmental policy as adversely affecting familial welfare, and argued that Allende and his government were endangering Chilean families.

---

73. Here I am listing those categories with more than fifty ads. There were also a number of ads that did not explicitly support either of the two coalitions.

The worsening economic condition of the country was a major focus in the 1973 congressional campaign. Especially prominent was the invocation of the *colas* in images and text. The scarcity of basic goods, worsened by the ongoing strikes against the government by truckers and small business owners, meant that women often had to spend hours queued in lines to buy basic products such as oil, meat, and vegetables. In CODE ads, the *colas* became a symbol for the lack of respect on the part of the government toward Chilean families and the lack of recognition of their suffering. The *cola* was also presented as an unfair burden that Chilean women were being forced to bear. CODE claimed not only that the government was failing to help women provide for their families, but also that women and their children were the innocent victims of the failed economic policies and ideologies of Allende and the UP. In CODE's campaign, motherhood was the only legitimate role for women, and women were inextricably linked to their familial identities. This symbolism is captured in the following ad (fig. 4.2), featuring a composite image depicting a woman doing housework, women waiting in line, and an inset picture of a child crying. The caption reads, "Please . . . my children need me. Leave me time to care for them!" Below, it states, "*Chilena* . . . married . . . with children . . . works . . . and stands in line!!"[74] In other words, all that the UP government had done for women was to increase their burdens in providing for the basic needs of their families. The implicit message was that if women voted for CODE's candidates, they would once again have time for their children.

Another ad made the attack against the UP even more explicit. Featuring a picture of Chilean women standing in line, the text asks, "Señora, is this what they promised you?" Answering the question below the picture, the ad reads, "They promised abundance. . . . They promised to control inflation. Do not repeat the same mistake!! You need a definite solution now."[75] Here, the *cola* again concretely represented the economic crisis through the burdens it placed on women as wives and mothers. Further, the *cola* symbolized how the UP's economic failures were directly interfering with women's abilities to carry out their familial roles. The CODE propaganda claimed that unlike the Popular Unity, CODE would help women to fulfill these duties. A class subtext existed in these ads, since the women featured clearly are meant to represent the working class. This critique highlighted the failure of the UP to keep its promises to promote "proletariat families."

74. *El Mercurio*, 21 February 1973, 38. This ad was for Sergio Jarpa, president of the rightist National Party, which was a member of CODE.

75. *El Mercurio*, 23 February 1973, 30.

Fig. 4.2 "Please ... my children need me." (*El Mercurio*, 21 February 1973.)

The *cola* was a dominant symbol in the CODE's campaign, and it was directed toward men as well as women. While ads aimed at women emphasized the scarcity of resources and the difficulties that women as wives and mothers confronted, propaganda directed at men targeted their inability to fulfill their familial roles as providers. One ad for a CODE candidate featured a picture of a Chilean man in a hard hat (the typical Chilean "workingman") along with a picture of women waiting in line (fig. 4.3). The caption reads, "*Chileno*, is this the place that your wife deserves?" Underneath the picture the text continues, "She sacrifices herself for you. This cannot continue . . . you have to do something!"[76] Thus the *colas* also threatened Chilean men's masculinity. The *cola* invoked men's fears about not being able to fulfill their masculine familial roles of providing for the material welfare of their family, or of protecting their wives from the indignity of having to stand in long lines in public. Again, the class subtext of the ad makes the attack even more direct. Images of men in hard hats were associated with the left, due to its support of working-class men's labor struggles. Implicitly, CODE argued that the leftist government had betrayed its commitment to these men. Instead of providing the promised jobs and wages, the government emasculated Chilean men by threatening their ability to provide for their wives and children. The visual placement of the pictures dramatizes how Chilean men were forced to watch their wives stand in line to buy basic items. To regain their proper masculine role as familial provider, CODE urged men to vote the UP out of office, and presented its candidates as the only ones "man" enough to stop the abuse.

CODE also mobilized familial ideology in appeals directed at middle-class men. One ad consists of a drawing of a clean-cut young man who is wearing a suit and resting his head on his hand, staring at the assorted papers on a desk in front of him. This man obviously represents not an industrial worker, but rather a typical middle-class, white-collar worker. But the ad's gendered construction of the man's familial duties remains the same. The caption for the ad reads, "Now you do not have work. As a professional, you have seen how the Marxists of the Popular Unity government will not give you any power[;] they have criminally deprived you of the means of supporting yourself and your family."[77] The ad portrays an undertone of class conflict and mistrust among men. It argues that the UP was attacking the economic power of middle-class men—their access to white-collar jobs—and threatening their masculine

76. *El Mercurio*, 24 February 1973, 18.
77. *El Mercurio*, 7 February 1973, 23.

Fig. 4.3 "*Chileno*, is this the place that your wife deserves?" (*El Mercurio*, 24 February 1973.)

identity in both the family and the broader society. In the same vein, another antigovernment ad displays a picture of a man in a suit, sitting on a park bench while holding his head in his hands. The caption reads, "You are without work. The Popular Unity government has taken food from your children and given it to foreign extremists. You feel abandoned, without anyone to help you."[78] Here the government not only threatens the welfare of middle-class families by depriving men of work, but also betrays the national interest. In the ad, the obviously legitimate interests of men in being able to feed their children are illegitimately placed behind the UP's political interests in showing solidarity with other socialist states.

CODE repeatedly appealed to men and women through their familial identities, and the group used a variety of strategies to present the economic crisis as damaging the family. In one ad, a small child was pictured alone and crying (fig. 4.4). The text explained that the child was crying because "his mother is standing in line." Below the picture, the caption continued, "This child cannot wait until 1976! Chilean children need a solution NOW!"[79] The mother is presumably one of the women standing in the *cola* pictured at the top of the ad. The crying child and the rhetoric of the ad create a sense of urgency for the viewer. The ad implicitly asks the viewer to ponder what would happen to Chile's children if the current UP government forced women to stand in line for three more years. The text and images blame Allende and his government for the economic crisis that threatened the ability of fathers and mothers to take care of their children. The only solution the ad presents is for the viewer to vote for CODE candidates in the upcoming election.

CODE depended on specific familial beliefs about both citizens and the state to craft its arguments against the UP. According to the narrative of the ads, the UP government had allowed the economic crisis to interfere with the roles and responsibilities of men and women to their families. In the ads, the *cola* often symbolized for the reader how the economic problems were personally significant. Like the people featured in the ads, many Chileans were having difficulty in finding the basic necessities for their families. In CODE's campaign, *colas* symbolized how the government threatened women's ability to feed their families and take care of their children and men's ability to provide for their families. Further, the economic problems and their effects represented

78. *El Mercurio*, 4 February 1973, 48.
79. *El Mercurio*, 11 February 1973, 36.

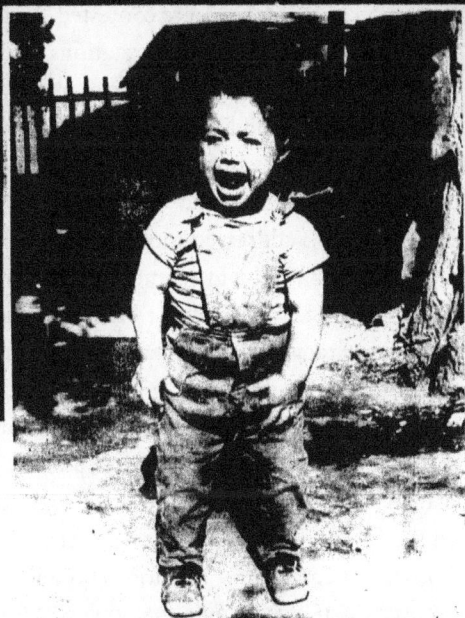

Fig. 4.4 "His mother is standing in line . . ." (*El Mercurio*, 11 February 1973.)

the UP's abdication of a basic responsibility of the Chilean state: promoting familial welfare. For CODE, the economic crisis was a family affair.

VIOLENCE FRAMED AS A THREAT TO THE FAMILY IN CODE'S CAMPAIGN

CODE also turned to familial beliefs to criticize the politicization of everyday life. Many scholars have argued that political and societal polarization, and its accompanying violence, was one cause of the delegitimation suffered by Allende and the Popular Unity government.[80] But as in the case of the economic crisis, both the cause and the effect of violence were contested. During the election, CODE and the UP presented alternative interpretations of current events to try to shape how Chileans understood their political importance. Redeploying critiques associated with the March of the Empty Pots and Pans, CODE employed images of violence against women as a way to dramatize how the UP either promoted or condoned violence that threatened Chilean women and their families. In one ad, CODE addressed mothers directly: "Think on this: Chile is living in a climate of hatred and resentment that lays waste to your future and that of your children. You can contribute to breaking the chain of hatred, strengthening democracy . . . We will help remove prejudice and fear from our Chile, freeing it from foreign ideas."[81] In the ad, the current political situation is framed as rife with violence, fear, resentment, and hatred, all of which threaten the future of women, their children, and the Chilean nation. Women, by voting for CODE, can restore the peace and societal harmony needed to safeguard the future of their families. Like earlier examples, the ad draws on well-established anticommunist rhetoric to present CODE's interpretation of current events. CODE proclaimed that violence, fear, and prejudice were introduced by the UP's "foreign" ideas, here a code word for communism.

Depictions of the violence suffered by women marchers during the March of the Empty Pots and Pans were some of the most potent images in the CODE campaign. These ads allowed CODE to use actual pictures of injured Chilean women, rather than relying on hypothetical claims about the dangers posed by communism or images from other countries. As in the public discourse around the march, it is clear that women's familial identities as wives and mothers are central to the narrative in the ads. Women who supported CODE were again positioned not only as mothers of their individual families, but also

---

80. The best example is Valenzuela, *Breakdown of Democratic Regimes.*
81. *El Mercurio,* 3 February 1973, 30.

metaphorically as the mothers and protectors of the nation. The threat of violence was clearly visible in an ad that features an injured woman sitting on the ground, being helped up by at least two other women and one man (fig. 4.5). The ad accuses the UP government of having failed to keep its promises to "respect women." Instead, women are suffering from "violence, lines, and insults." The ad exhorts the viewer to take action: "Because women deserve respect, this cannot continue."[82]

These ads showed the depths to which CODE claimed the Allende government had sunk. Not only did the UP fail to protect mothers, but it so lacked respect for them that it protected and aided those who attacked them. Another CODE ad with a similar critique featured a poor woman washing her laundry by hand in a tub. Here the text reads, "In your neighborhood[83] the Marxist hordes do not leave you alone to live your life. Under the protection of this government of hate, they attack you with impunity, and in vain you cry to the authorities for help. . . . You feel abandoned and terrified about the future of your children under a Marxist government."[84] The ad paints a bleak picture of the current state of Chile, even for the working class, which was the focus of Allende's government. In the ad, women live under constant threat of attack, the police ignore their obligation to protect citizens from harm, the government turns its back on the people of Chile, and women fear for the future of their children. In the ad, this state of affairs is due to the choice of the government to protect its ideological allies—"the Marxist hordes"—rather than women and children. Ultimately, this type of inflammatory rhetoric questioned the legitimacy of the government by claiming that it had failed in the basic duty of the state to provide security to mothers and their children.

While in the above example women are presented as terrified victims who need protection, CODE ads also argued that Chilean mothers could actively protect their families and the Chilean nation by voting for the opposition. The ads sometimes exhorted women to break out of traditional gender roles that proscribed women's public participation and political involvement. Silvia Pinto, a CODE candidate for the National Party, issued an ad that framed her decision to run for office through her identity as a mother. Pinto argues that the danger posed to her daughter's future drove her to take up the battle against Allende and the UP: "Silvia Pinto says to her daughter, 'One day you will

82. *El Mercurio*, 18 February 1973, 30.
83. The word in the ad is "población." In Chile this refers to a working-class or poor section of the city. It is often translated as "shantytown," which captures its class connotation.
84. *El Mercurio*, 22 February 1973, 32.

Fig. 4.5 "They promised to respect women." (*El Mercurio*, 18 February 1973.)

remember that when I entered into the political battle it was because I was fighting against those who would have snatched from you the freedom to study, to
choose, to grow healthy and strong, to live like a child in a country without
hatred.' Silvia Pinto, symbol of the valiant *Chilena*."[85] In another ad, Silvia Pinto
addresses Chilean men: "Have faith in the women who are fighting alongside
of you against Marxism, which is backwardness, hunger, anguish, uncertainty,
and hatred for Chile. We women are now going into the streets to defend our
homes."[86] In both ads women are forced into politics because of the threats
posed by Allende and his government to their families and homes.

Often similar to the discourse of the anti-Allende women's movement, these
ads understood women's political activism as an outgrowth of their traditional
roles as mothers. But this interpretation did not laud women's increased political activism as a positive development, or one that promoted women's equality. Instead, CODE portrayed women's entry into politics as symbolizing the
political chaos facing the nation. If the current government had not endangered the family, CODE's ads argued, then women would not have had to
leave the safety and security of their homes to protect their families. CODE's
campaign promoted women's political activism and support for its candidates. At the same time, the coalition used women's political activism as proof
of the current government's failure to fulfill its responsibilities to Chilean families. In other words, if not for the economic and political crises facing Chile,
women would be properly devoting their time and attention to their families
and not engaging in political action.

The above examples illustrate that beliefs about family and the state played
a major role in CODE's attacks against Allende and the UP. CODE attacked
the legitimacy of the current government by arguing that the UP had failed to
protect and provide for Chilean families, a basic responsibility of the government. In addition to the economic crisis, the opposition argued that the UP
bore the responsibility for the increasing violence and social polarization that
endangered Chilean families. CODE implicitly argued that when elected, it
would restore the proper respect for men's and women's roles within the family and between the state and the family.[87] CODE turned to beliefs about the

<hr/>

85. *El Mercurio*, 18 February 1973, 31. This ad was for PN deputy candidate Silvia Pinto. In her
ads, she often justified her entrance into politics through referencing her familial identity as a mother.
86. *El Mercurio*, 15 February 1973, 23.
87. This construction moved from the implicit to the explicit under the military government
of Augusto Pinochet, who argued quite clearly that paternal authority needed to be restored. See,
for example, Valenzuela, *La mujer en el Chile militar*.

responsibilities of both the state and political leaders for familial welfare to create a set of criteria that judged the present government as failing in its fundamental responsibilities.

CONTESTING THE FAMILIAL CRITIQUES: THE UP AS THE GOOD PROVIDER

In these ongoing interpretive struggles, the UP once again countered with ads that touted its commitment to the welfare of Chilean families and that presented the opposition as the true threat. The UP urged Chileans to vote for its candidates in order to provide health, education, jobs, and security "for the family and for the patria."[88] To portray their concern for individual Chilean families, candidates representing the Popular Unity government particularly emphasized their concern and caring for Chilean children. Repeating the 1970 presidential campaign slogan, the UP's congressional candidates again proclaimed that in its government "children were the only privileged." The UP contrasted its commitment to children with past governments, which had failed to adequately take care of Chilean children because of their privileging of the capitalist classes.

As concrete examples of this past neglect, the UP often featured ads that referenced Chile's high rates of infant mortality and childhood illnesses.[89] An oft-repeated ad included a picture of a little boy along with the following text: "For every one hundred proletariat children that are born . . . ten die before they turn one. When Chile recognizes that he is the father to all his children . . . equality will begin with the children" (fig. 4.6).[90] Chile's high infant mortality rate had long been an important political issue. The ad assumes that the government has a fundamental responsibility to "father" Chilean children by protecting them from harm. Presenting the 10 percent mortality rate as evidence, the ad implies that previous governments had failed in this basic responsibility of the state. The ad might also have been alluding to a law proposed by Allende to eliminate the distinction between legitimate and illegitimate children when it came to parental support and inheritance rights.[91] Under the UP, the state would no

88. "For the family and for the patria" was a repeated campaign slogan. See the following examples: *El Clarín*, 20 February 1973, 20; *El Clarín*, 23 February 1973, 23; *El Clarín*, 22 February 1973, 9.

89. Throughout the twentieth century, Chile had experienced one of the highest infant mortality rates in Latin America. In 1952, 129 children died for every 1,000 born. Into the 1960s, malnutrition remained a serious problem for a majority of the population. See Collier and Sater, *History of Chile*, 290.

90. *El Clarín*, 8 February 1973, 16; *El Clarín*, 14 February 1973, 15.

91. For a discussion of this issue, see Htun, *Sex and the State*.

De cada cien
niños proletarios
que nacen...
Diez mueren
antes de
cumplir un año.

Cuando Chile sea el padre
de todos sus hijos... la igualdad
comenzará por los niños!

Fig. 4.6   "When Chile recognizes that he is the father to all his children." (*El Clarín*, 8 February 1973.)

longer differentiate between any Chilean children based on their birth or class; all children would be equally entitled to the protection of the state.

The UP's candidates also touted various programs designed to improve the health of Chilean children. For example, a full-page ad for a PS candidate featured a picture of an empty wheelchair along with the following text: "Chilean woman: In 1970, during the government of Frei, there were 205 cases of polio. In 1971, during the government of the Popular Unity, there were 55 cases of polio. In 1972, there were 13 cases of polio. In 1973, there will not be polio in Chile." The ad appeals specifically to women and highlights the concrete improvements in the welfare of children under the UP. Further, the allusion to Frei once again highlights the failure of past governments to dedicate sufficient resources to promoting the welfare of Chilean children.[92]

A centerpiece of the UP's congressional campaign was the government's program to provide a half liter of milk for every child in order to combat malnutrition. The milk provided a concrete symbol of the government's commitment to the well-being of children. Often these ads were directed specifically at the mothers of the children who were benefiting from the program. One ad trumpeting the milk program featured a smiling girl drinking a glass of milk. The ad's text reads, "Chilean woman: The Popular Unity government has delivered a half liter of milk daily to all the children of Chile."[93] Another ad presented

92. *El Clarín*, 22 February 1973, 18.
93. *El Clarín*, 12 February 1973, 12; *El Clarín*, 16 February 1973, 18; *El Clarín*, 22 February 1973, 26.

a profile of a woman looking down at her child. The caption reads, "We will not permit them to take away the half liter of milk for your child. Woman, we will continue to advance."[94] Here the UP campaign asks women to work with the government to protect their children by protecting the milk program. The portrayal of the UP as fighting to protect Chilean families is also the subtext of an ad displaying a picture of a working-class couple. The woman, who is pregnant, addresses the reader, saying, "Thanks to the Popular Unity government, I am assured of a half liter of milk for my children and guaranteed work for my husband. For these reasons we need to destroy the black market and defend our homes from those who wish to destroy them with a civil war."[95] This UP ad was similar to many CODE ads. Women, through their roles as mothers, were called on to fight to defend their homes and families from those who would take away their family's food, work, and security. As the above examples illustrate, to directly confront CODE, the UP highlighted the government programs designed to improve the health and well-being of Chilean children to show its commitment to Chilean families.

The UP also used ads as a way to contest the opposition's claims that the government was at fault for food shortages and *colas*. As in its response to the March of the Empty Pots and Pans, the UP crafted a narrative that placed the blame for the scarcity, the black market, and the lines on the Chilean upper classes, the opposition, and foreign interests. The UP claimed that these groups were motivated by greed and a desire to destroy the UP (because of its defense of Chilean workers and their families). For example, one ad presented two pictures side by side. One picture is a compilation of images showing women standing in lines waiting to buy food. The other shows a variety of sacks of different goods. The caption reads, "At the same time. At the same time that you are standing in line, the greedy opposition organizes the black market and traffics in the products that your home needs. Don't forgive those who have lost their privileges, and for this reason [the loss of their class status] they are getting even by forcing you to stand in line. Defend the security of your home and your children, vote in March . . . [for the UP's candidate]."[96]

The *colas* are portrayed in this ad as a strategic tactic on the part of the upper class both to punish the lower classes for their support of the UP and trick them, especially the women, into voting against the UP. The ad confronts CODE's campaign by arguing that the lines result from the illegal actions of

94. *El Clarín,* 18 February 1973, 14; *El Clarín,* 19 February 1973, 6.
95. *El Clarín,* 2 February 1973, 28; *El Clarín,* 14 February 1973, 20.
96. *El Clarín,* 14 February 1973, 24; *El Clarín,* 11 February 1973, 8.

both international and national elites. The reader can protect her family, children, and home from these attacks by voting for the UP candidates. Other ads defiantly stated that Chilean women were too smart to be tricked by the opposition, and that women knew that the opposition "created the black market . . . [and] the lines."[97] The UP argued that CODE represented the interests of the elites who were profiting at the expense of ordinary Chilean families.

Another ad graphically depicted this argument by creating an image of the "speculator" who is benefiting from the black market. The speculator is a man looking down his nose, smoking, sneering at the reader (fig. 4.7). A distorted close-up exaggerates his nose and eyes. The ad identifies this arrogant figure as a speculator in whose hands "could be the food for your children." Below the image, the text rhetorically asks, "Is there anyone who could be more dangerous? This nefarious character, the toady of the right and its allies, the Christian Democrats, only has one goal: to hoard and speculate with the food that the people need." The voter is addressed as a parent and asked to support the UP's candidates for the sake of Chile's children.[98] In its campaign, the UP attempted to turn the tables on the opposition, arguing that the opposition was at fault for the black market, the lines, and the day-to-day difficulties being faced by Chilean families. These actions benefited the rich while denying basic necessities to poor families.

To combat CODE's claims regarding the recent violence and social disruption, the UP redefined the understanding of security. According to the UP's ads, security meant protection not just from violence but also from economic problems. A good example of the left's broader understanding of security can be seen in an ad for the head of the Communist Party, Senator Volodia Teitelboim, in which he is shown holding his daughter (fig. 4.8). The caption states, "We stand for the security of the family. Volodia and Marina. A father and his daughter. Like them, millions of Chilean families aspire to security. We are all alike in our love for life, for justice, for peace, for dignity. We believe in human values. We fight for them. They are the values that we reaffirm every day. Today is the day to stand up for them. Today is the day to vote for the security of the family."[99]

The ad directly confronts CODE's depiction of the UP as unconcerned about the family and the traditional values of Chilean society. The UP was

---

97. See, for example, *El Clarín*, 22 February 1973, 9; and *El Clarín*, 22 February 1973, 6.
98. *El Clarín*, 2 February 1973, 20.
99. *El Clarín*, 2 March 1973, 15; *El Clarín*, 3 March 1973, 24.

En manos de este especulador puede estar la alimentacion de sus hijos

¿Puede haber alguien más dañino?

Este nefasto personaje, súbdito de la derecha y de sus aliados Demócrata Cristianos tiene una sola meta: acaparar y especular sin medida, ocultar los alimentos que el Pueblo necesita, vender en el Mercado Negro para enriquecerse a costa de los trabajadores que con su esfuerzo mantienen a Chile produciendo.

No dejemos que cumplan con sus siniestros y diabólico propósitos.

No les demos un minuto de respiro hasta que él y sus patrones, los Jarpa y los Frei, traidores de ayer y de hoy, conozcan el amargo gusto de la derrota definitiva.

Que la tortilla se vuelva: Racionamiento para los ricos, abastecimiento para los pobres.

Defiende la Patria con los Socialistas

Fig. 4.7 "In the hands of this speculator could be the food for your children." (*El Clarín*, 2 February 1973.)

working to protect freedom and liberty in order to provide a secure environment in which Chileans could raise their families. The picture depicts the ideal of a loving and close relationship between father and child, thereby countering attacks that claimed the Chilean Communist Party was antifamily. The ad, both visually and textually, depicts the PC leader as just like all other Chilean fathers: he loves his daughter, he is concerned for her future, and he believes in the importance of values, peace, and dignity. Building on this depiction of an ideal father, the ad ends by asking Chileans to vote for Senator Teitelboim to ensure the security of Chilean families. Another Teitelboim ad with the same overall message featured him surrounded by women who "declare ourselves [as supporters] for the security of our families."[100]

Ads for other UP candidates focused on health policies designed to combat infant mortality, polio, and malnutrition as providing true security for Chilean families. Appealing to readers through their roles as parents, one ad presented a young boy, smiling and pointing at the camera. The text tells the reader that this child "needs you" to vote against "infant mortality . . . polio . . . malnutrition . . . ignorance . . . against the right." The current government, by working to assure all these benefits for children, was working, as the slogan proclaims, for the "security for the proletarian family."[101] Thus UP candidates drew on familial beliefs to defend the legitimacy of Allende's government and its political projects.

While Chilean politics was clearly divided along many lines, an examination of the electoral propaganda of both CODE and the UP also reveals areas of consensus. In their battle over how the political and economic crisis should be understood, both sides repeatedly invoked the beliefs of the Familial State, which assigned the state the fundamental responsibility for familial welfare. In their election campaigns, both sides tried to persuade Chileans that their side promoted the family and familial welfare, while the other posed a serious threat to the family. Both sides used claims about familial welfare as an accepted criterion for judging the performance and legitimacy of the government. And the ads of both sides called on Chileans to act because of their familial roles and their concern for familial welfare, thus strengthening the connection between familial identities and citizenship.

In the end, the congressional elections did not give either CODE or the UP

<hr/>

100. *El Clarín*, 23 February 1973, 11; *El Clarín*, 25 February 1973, 8.

101. *El Clarín*, 14 February 1973, 10. This ad was often reproduced and used by different candidates. See also examples in *El Clarín* on the following dates: 24 February 1973, 19; 15 February 1973, 10; and 16 February 1973, 8.

nos pronunciamos por la seguridad de la familia

Volodia y Marina. El Padre y su hija.
Como ellos, millones de familias chilenas
aspiramos a la seguridad.
Nos parecemos en el amor a la vida,
a la justicia, a la paz, a la dignidad.
Creemos en los valores humanos,
luchamos por ellos.
Son valores que reafirmamos todos los
días.
Hoy es día de pronunciarse por ellos.
Hoy es día de votar por la
seguridad de la familia.

se llama
VOLODIA
lo conocemos
votaremos
por él

FRENTE DE INDEPENDIENTES SENADOR VOLODIA TEITELBOIM · BANDERA 121

Fig. 4.8 "We stand for the security of the family."
(*El Clarín*, 2 March 1973.)

the results it wanted. CODE received roughly 55 percent of the vote, and the UP received the remaining 45 percent. The electoral result did not break the political stalemate in the Congress. The UP had actually increased its share of the vote since Allende's election, but the parties on the left were still a minority in Congress and did not have the strength to implement their political agenda. Likewise, CODE had fallen short of the two-thirds majority needed to impeach Allende. Instead of helping to avert crisis, the election hardened the political division of Chile.

Preparing for the Military Coup

From the March elections until the military intervention on 11 September, political polarization tore apart Chilean society. While some moderates continued to search for political compromise, a growing number of partisans from both CODE and the UP saw military intervention as inevitable. At an institutional level, the legislative agenda of Allende's government continued to be stymied by the opposition in Congress. The problems of institutional politics were mirrored by the growing polarization at the societal level. During this time, ongoing attempts to legitimate military intervention against Allende drew heavily on the familial critiques first developed during the March of the Empty Pots and Pans and honed during the elections.

In particular, these critiques were used in the political controversy around Allende's proposal to reform the Chilean educational system, known as the Escuela Nacional Unificada (National Unified School, ENU). The debate over the ENU proposal served as a catalyst for military intervention because it helped sway the Catholic Church and the Chilean armed forces from generally neutral positions onto the side of the opposition. For most of Allende's presidency, the leadership of both institutions had attempted to play a mediating role between the government and the opposition. But the debate over school reform eventually brought both institutions into public conflict with the government. As in the electoral campaigns, the opposition attempted to shape the perception of the proposed reform as another example of Allende's danger to the family.

Allende and his government submitted the educational reform legislation to Congress shortly after the March elections. Placed into an already-polarized political atmosphere, it became one of the most controversial proposals of

Allende's presidency.[102] For the UP, educational reform was fundamental. To promote the needed changes, the legislation was designed to bring the educational system more under the control of the Chilean state. In general, the ENU was an example of the UP's holistic view of the importance of training and education in promoting both the modernization of Chile and the advancement toward a socialist society.[103]

In public statements, Allende and the UP often cast the educational reforms as a duty owed to the families of Chile's workers and peasants. Allende's 1970 platform promised to create both the schools and scholarships necessary to "assure the entrance and survival in the school system of all children of Chile, especially the children of workers and peasants."[104] A system of day-care centers and kindergarten education targeting the poorest sectors was meant to increase the educational gains of poor Chilean families, so that "the children of workers and peasants will be better equipped to enter, remain in, and take advantage of the regular school system."[105] The general emphasis on educational access for all children was carried through into other campaign promises, including "(1) free enrollment, plus free textbooks and school supplies for all children in primary school; (2) free breakfasts in school for all primary children, and free lunches to children in need; (3) a scholarship system at the primary, secondary, and university levels based on academic achievement and family need."[106] Allende also proposed new programs for expanding educational opportunities for Chile's working classes and directed state resources toward rooting out the remaining pockets of adult illiteracy.

The ENU touched a political nerve in Chile. The attempts of the UP and Allende to frame the ENU in terms of the benefits it would provide to Chilean children and their families were overwhelmed by the ferocity of the opposition's attacks. The project mobilized a broad base of opposition, including the Christian Democratic Party and the National Party, El Poder Femenino, associations of teachers and administrators, and the Catholic Church. It threatened the traditional dominance of Catholic private schools for middle- and upper-class Chileans. The ENU seemed to threaten the lifestyle enjoyed by these classes and the traditional roles and responsibilities of parents in the education of their

102. Two excellent sources on the ENU are Farrell, *National Unified School*, and Fischer, *Political Ideology and Educational Reform*.
103. This was part of the UP's party platform. See Farrell's discussion in *National Unified School*, 46–50.
104. Quoted in ibid., 48.
105. Ibid., 49.
106. Ibid., 50.

children. Opposition groups, such as EPF and associations of teachers and school administrators, played on this fear by launching scathing attacks on the UP. They claimed that the government was trying to brainwash Chilean children, usurping the natural duties of parents to their children and undermining the values of familial order and harmony by introducing communist indoctrination to the schools.

Supporters of El Poder Femenino claimed that the ENU posed a threat to their families, and they pledged to "fight to defend the youth and the rights of the parents in the formation of their children, which the state is trying to snatch away."[107] Articles and ads opposing the measure soon appeared in newspapers, such as the ad in *La Tribuna* on 7 April 1973. Featuring a picture of a woman gazing adoringly at her child, it claims that "the always-emotional mother-child link finds itself in grave danger. Between the tender bonds of [mother and child] the state imposes the official will to convert the woman into a simple reproducer and the child into just one more item off the production line."[108] The text and image mimic the earlier attacks of the anticommunist scare campaigns, portraying the ENU proposal as subverting the natural and sacred familial bond between mother and child. According to the opposition, emotional bonds were being destroyed, transforming children into mere "products" and women into "machines."

The EPF also characterized the ENU as an attempt by the government to usurp the rights and responsibilities of parents.[109] ENU opponents argued that the reform weakened parents' control over the education of their children and allowed the government to impose its own political ideology in the schools. Parents' groups such as the Federation of Private School Parents and Guardians (FEDAP) also employed this critique, claiming, "We will not delegate nor give up our right to educate our children."[110] The opposition also incorporated specific anticommunist teachings of the Catholic Church. Conservative members of the clergy, like Archbishop Emilio Tagle Covarrubias, railed against the ENU because it showed a "lack of respect for the conscience of children, and does grave damage to the right of parents to provide the kind of education they desire for their descendants."[111] FEDAP echoed this position, stating, "As parents we are not going to allow ourselves to be considered only as procreators,

107. Morandé, *La guerra*, 118–19.
108. Quoted in Baldez, *Why Women Protest*, 110.
109. See, for example, ibid., 109.
110. Quoted in Farrell, *National Unified School*, 183.
111. Ibid., 192.

and later as productive entities."[112] Again, the ultimate aim of the UP government was to destroy the ability of the family to create emotional bonds. The reforms were seen as implementing a Marxist ideology that dehumanized society by treating parents only in their roles as "procreators" and children as future "productive entities." The arguments against the ENU emphasized that the school reform ultimately threatened the place of the family as the basic nucleus of society. The hierarchy of the Catholic Church was deeply distrustful of the proposed changes on these grounds and came out strongly against the proposal.

The controversy over the ENU also spread to the military. The political scientist Lois Oppenheim argues that even at the beginning of 1973, "military intervention was still not a foregone conclusion," as the military remained divided between those who favored remaining publicly neutral on political affairs and supporting the constitutional order, and those who saw Allende and his government as threatening national security.[113] The opposition used the debate over the ENU to persuade the military to join them in condemning Allende and his government. In this vein, for example, the center-right paper *La Prensa* printed an editorial on 31 May 1973 suggesting that "members of the armed forces, *in their private capacity* as parents," get involved in the debate. According to the paper, nothing "can deprive them of their right as parents to choose the education they want for their children and to protest if that right is violated or not recognized."[114]

This strategy bore fruit in a meeting on 11 April 1973 attended by the minister of education, minister of defense, the commanding officers of the army, navy, and air force, and five hundred officers in their "capacity as parents and grandparents."[115] Admiral Ismael Huerta presented a very detailed critique of the ENU that was widely seen as representing the "official" military position, even though he claimed he was speaking only for himself. In the critique, he echoed earlier worries about the abilities of a politicized educational system to produce the type of young man needed by the armed forces. He framed this critique along familial lines, stating, "There is no reference to education within the family. Nonetheless it is an accepted fact within humanist philosophy that the greatest educational influence occurs within the heart of the family. This is particularly true of the 'military family' where we inculcate the most profound

112. Ibid., 183.
113. Oppenheim, *Politics in Chile*, 79.
114. Quoted in Farrell, *National Unified School*, 207.
115. Ibid., 212.

ideas regarding the norms of authority, discipline, hierarchy, justice, honesty, disinterest, abnegation, sobriety, and good faith, and whose results can be seen. The children of both officers and troops always distinguish themselves . . . which contrasts with the politicized and revolutionary ferment one finds in civilian schools."[116] Admiral Huerta drew a clear distinction between the apolitical, traditional families of military personnel and the politicization of children in public schools. He positioned military families as the bastion of Chile's traditional values. His opposition to the ENU lay in its failure to uphold the importance of the family. According to Admiral Huerta, the politicized atmosphere of schools that would result promoted the opposite of the values most important to the military. This critique was especially damning because it came from one of the institutions that had been seen as apolitical by many Chileans.

These unrelenting attacks forced Allende and his government to postpone the ENU's implementation. The proposal had managed to further alienate many sectors of Chilean society that had not previously supported a military solution. As one scholar has noted, "The most effective propaganda—besides the scarecrow of 'scarcity'— . . . was the 'threat' to their children represented by the ENU. The specter of the ENU frightened very large sectors of the middle classes. Many military men who were sympathetic to the opposition but who had stayed within the limits of legality lost their 'patience' and were radicalized. The ENU was 'proof' for a terrorized middle class that 'Communism' had already begun to endanger the family."[117] The opposition skillfully employed its familial critiques to increase the political mobilization against Allende and to radicalize important sectors of the military and the Catholic Church. Framing the ENU as a threat to the family furthered the breakdown of the political center, which would eventually lead to tragedy.

On 5 September 1973, the EPF, along with other women's opposition groups, organized another march along the lines of the March of the Empty Pots and Pans, which again brought out tens of thousands of protesters.[118] As an announcement for the last women's march before the coup stated, "Chilean Women! Mr. Allende does not deserve to be President of the Republic. Mr. Allende has led the country into a catastrophe. We don't have bread for our children! We don't have medicine for those who are sick! We don't have clothes to wear! We don't have a roof to put over our heads!"[119] This critique was by

116. Quoted in ibid., 213.
117. Bandeira, quoted in ibid., 2.
118. Crummett, "El Poder Femenino," 106.
119. Mattelart, "Chile," 285.

now familiar to the Chilean public. Because of Allende and his policies, mothers were no longer able to feed, clothe, house, or provide medicine for themselves or their children, thus endangering both Chilean families and the Chilean nation. Allende did not deserve to govern because he and the UP government had failed to fulfill their basic responsibilities toward Chilean families. Six days later, early in the morning of 11 September, the military would take to the streets. By the end of the day, the Moneda, a symbol of Chile's democratic traditions, would be bombed, President Salvador Allende would be dead, and the military would be firmly in charge of the Chilean state.

Conclusion

In the political battles over the legitimacy of Allende and the Popular Unity, specific familial beliefs about the state, political leaders, and ordinary citizens provided a powerful discursive framework. While the 1970 election revealed the importance of elite invocations of familial beliefs about politics in defining the expectations and qualities of political leaders and governments, this chapter shows the importance of bottom-up uses of familial beliefs developed within the context of societal mobilization. The March of the Empty Pots and Pans placed familial beliefs at the center of the interpretive struggles over how to judge the political legitimacy of Allende and his government. Starting with the march, Allende's opponents actively transformed the Familial State into a powerful and easily understood criterion by which to judge the legitimacy of Allende and his government. According to this critique, Allende and his government had failed to fulfill their basic duties and responsibilities toward the family and therefore did not deserve to govern. The symbolic impact of the large-scale public actions of women in the March of the Empty Pots and Pans should not be underestimated. The political elite of both the National Party and the Christian Democratic Party increasingly incorporated the women's familial critiques of Allende and the UP into their own political strategies.

Framing the question of Allende's political legitimacy through familial beliefs would be employed again and again during the intense struggles that marked the last two years of his presidency. The interaction between elites and citizens drove the campaigns of the 1973 congressional elections, which drew heavily on familial beliefs about the responsibility of the state and of political leaders. In the debate over school reform, Allende and his government were presented by their opponents as threatening Chilean families, interfering with men's and women's responsibilities to their families, and failing to protect Chilean families from the violence and politicization of everyday life. Thus, from the March of the Empty Pots and Pans in December 1971 to the last march shortly before the coup, Allende and the UP were regularly attacked on specifically familial grounds.

The UP treated these attacks as a serious political threat and vigorously defended its president, its government, and its policies. In its responses, however, it accepted that familial welfare was a legitimate criterion by which to judge governmental performance. Working within a familial framework, Allende and the UP followed two strategies. They presented themselves as the true defenders of Chilean working-class families and criticized their opponents as fundamentally antifamily. But the ongoing political and economic crisis often made it difficult to counter the claims of the opposition, which increasingly depended on current local events. The strong connections between familial welfare and the duties and responsibilities of political leaders invoked in these battles ultimately shaped the political strategies pursued by Pinochet and his military government, which is the subject of the next chapter.

★ FIVE ★

PINOCHET'S CHILEAN FAMILY
Constructing Authoritarian Legitimacy

In March 1974, the military junta, comprising the commanders of the army, air force, navy, and police, published a declaration of principles that outlined its current and future political projects. The statement confirmed the growing suspicions of many Chileans that the junta had no intention of returning to civilian elites the political power it had seized six months earlier. Instead, the junta assigned to itself the "transcendental mission . . . to throw out the outdated party divisions" and to create a "new era in the history of our country."[1] The junta proposed that the Chilean armed forces transform Chilean society. According to the Declaration of Principles, junta members particularly wanted to limit political conflict and promote societal harmony by restoring Chile's traditional values.

To accomplish these goals, the military junta needed to fundamentally change Chilean political practices by destroying the powerful political parties and dramatically limiting citizen participation. Influenced by the U.S. National Security Doctrine and Chilean conservative thought, many in the military hierarchy viewed the current crisis as rooted in the dangerous spread of communist beliefs regarding class conflict.[2] Immediately following the coup, the military targeted the members of the UP's political parties, leftist intellectuals, and political activists associated with labor unions, peasant organizations, and poblador movements. Throughout Chile, UP supporters were rounded up and detained, most infamously in Santiago's Estadio Nacional, where at least seven thousand men and women were held during the months following the coup. Many members of the parties of the UP and leftist activists had voluntarily turned themselves in after their names appeared on public arrest lists, confident that the military would follow legal procedures.[3] But this trust was

1. Gobierno de Chile, *República de Chile*, 136.
2. See Arriagada, *Pinochet*, especially 81–101.
3. See, for example, Stern, *Battling for Hearts and Minds*, xxi–xxii, and Oppenheim, *Politics in Chile*, 117–19.

tragically misplaced. The majority of the approximately three thousand deaths or disappearances attributed to state agents under military rule were committed in the first year following the coup.[4] For those on the left, the military coup and the brutal repression that followed constituted a "psychic shock" that destabilized their belief in the strength of Chile's democratic traditions and respect for the rule of law.

After the first year, while political repression continued, the military government increasingly directed its energies toward creating new institutions and values that would replace the previous political system.[5] Over the course of the next sixteen years, the military government pursued the goal of fundamentally reshaping Chile through its political, economic, and social policies. Regarding politics, the military viewed with deep distrust the steady expansion of political rights that had dramatically increased Chilean suffrage from 11.2 percent of the total population in 1946 to 34.3 percent in 1964. This increase in citizen participation was accompanied by fierce competition between the political parties.[6] Many military leaders viewed this political openness as having nurtured the development of communist ideologies within Chile, which they strongly believed threatened the survival of the Chilean nation. The military government, increasingly under the control of General Augusto Pinochet, railed against political parties and civil society activism and argued that the military needed to strictly control all types of political action in order to curb political excess and reestablish social order.

Segments of the military also deeply distrusted the belief that the state and its institutions could be used to promote development, modernization, and social equity. The growing influence of neoliberal economic ideology within a powerful cadre of University of Chicago–trained Chilean economists—the

4. See http://www.ddhh.gov.cl/estadisticas.html for the most current numbers. The total number killed or disappeared, according to the Chilean government, is 3,195 men and women. Stern argues that the official count is probably much lower than the actual number of victims, given the high standards of proof required by the government and the lingering effects of fear on the families of victims. He conservatively estimates that the number could easily be 4,500. In addition, nearly 30,000 people were tortured and 82,000 were arrested for political reasons (although the arrests number could be as high as 200,000, according to some experts). See Stern, *Remembering Pinochet's Chile*, xxi, 158–60.

5. The United States, following its National Security Doctrine, supported the Chilean junta's national political projects. The National Security Doctrine was designed to prevent the spread of communism. It evolved from the counterinsurgency training the United States initiated in the Latin American region after World War II and saw political activity on issues of social justice as opening the door to communism within countries. After the Cuban Revolution in 1959, the propagation of this doctrine was intensified. See Oppenheim, *Politics in Chile*, 111, and Loveman, *For la Patria*.

6. Stern, *Remembering Pinochet's Chile*, 10.

Chicago Boys—as well as on the international level provided Pinochet with a ready-made argument about the need to limit the state's role in the economy and in the provision of social welfare.[7] The technocratic expertise of the Chicago Boys also allowed Pinochet to implement their neoliberal reforms, thereby transforming the Chilean economy. Finally, Pinochet and the military sought to reestablish respect for a conservative social order grounded in a veneration of family, God, and social hierarchy. The political activism of the 1960s and 1970s had been accompanied by a cultural effervescence that often questioned Chile's traditional social values. The military government actively attacked these changes and promoted traditional social hierarchies (parents above children, men above women, business above labor) in its political and social projects.

To implement these far-ranging political, economic, and social goals, the junta could not simply rely on fear and repression. It needed to legitimate its political control in order to gain, or maintain, the cooperation of important segments of the Chilean populace. As Pamela Lowden has argued, the "Pinochet regime had a particularly strong sense of its own mission and, in keeping with its crusading ethos, was as anxious to win hearts and minds to its cause as it was to silence dissent."[8] Initially, the military government relied on the immediate outpouring of support for military intervention expressed not only by the Chilean right but also by important sectors of the center (including a number of prominent leaders of the Christian Democratic Party) as well as ordinary Chilean citizens. To promote continued cooperation and support after the immediate crisis had passed, the junta began producing and disseminating political discourses that legitimated its control of state power.

In these attempts, the military government turned to existing ideological connections between the familial and the political. The concrete invocations of familial beliefs by Pinochet and his government followed three general patterns. First, Pinochet justified the actions of the military by framing those actions as necessary to protect Chilean families. The military argued that threats to Chilean families legitimated both the original intervention and the continued military control of political power. Second, Pinochet sought to justify the military's political power by providing for the welfare of Chilean families. Improvements to familial welfare were used to symbolize the economic and social progress the military government claimed to be making. In government propaganda,

7. For a detailed discussion of the importance of the Chicago Boys to the economic policies of the military government and its political legitimacy, see Huneeus, *Pinochet Regime*, chapter 8, and Arriagada, *Pinochet*, 40–49.
8. Lowden, *Moral Opposition*, 7.

the family was presented as the true beneficiary of government programs. Within this general strategy, the military government adeptly invoked the Familial State, justifying its political power by upholding a belief in the state's fundamental duty to protect and promote familial welfare. Pinochet also deployed the ideals of the Patriarchal Leader, casting himself as the protector of the Chilean family, a strong patriarch ready to defend the family from any and all threats.[9] Finally, the military also relied heavily on the family as a metaphor for the Chilean nation (Familial Nation). Indeed, the family and the nation were often intertwined in government rhetoric. The ideals of the Familial Nation supported the uses of the two other categories and helped the military to justify ongoing state repression. Throughout their years of political rule, Pinochet and his military government would consistently turn to these familial beliefs in their attempts to justify their political power.

The Family Endangered: Communism and Other Threats

Brian Loveman argues that the possibility for military intervention exists in almost all political systems. In Latin America specifically, political culture and military training assign to the armed forces the duty to protect the patria. Indeed, he notes, "The military acts when the judgment is made that governments have put the patria at risk."[10] What is the patria, and how does the military know that it is at risk? In Chile, this decision was shaped by the intense political battles of Allende's presidency. As I showed in the previous chapter, these conflicts were often fought on and through specific understandings of the relationships among the family, the state, and citizens. To argue that Allende and the ideology of the Popular Unity threatened the survival of the patria, and therefore that the armed forces had no choice but to act, the Chilean military often turned to this nexus of beliefs.

The connection between the military regime's strategy and previous struggles becomes evident when examining how the leaders of the junta incorporated the mobilization of anti-Allende women and their arguments about how Allende had endangered Chilean families. Anti-Allende women's groups had publicly and repeatedly called for military intervention. Margaret Power argues that after the stalemated 1973 election, women's groups and other right-wing

---

9. For a discussion of the patriarchal dimensions of Pinochet's rule and how his government related to women, see Valenzuela, *La mujer en el Chile militar.*

10. Loveman, *For la Patria,* xiv.

organizations began to "actively call for Allende's removal" and hoped "to create a climate among the general public that made military intervention acceptable . . . and to encourage the military to stage a coup."[11]

In pursuit of this goal, El Poder Femenino launched a number of campaigns designed to publicly shame the military into action. On 21 August 1973, somewhere between three hundred and fifteen hundred women, mainly military wives, protested in front of the home of the commander in chief of the army, General Prats. The demonstration, and the lack of support among military officers that their wives' presence signaled, proved to be the last straw for General Prats and he resigned his post. General Prats was widely seen as opposed to military intervention in civilian politics and loyal to Allende as the elected president. On the recommendation of General Prats, General Augusto Pinochet was appointed as his successor.[12] EPF also targeted the military rank and file, staging a series of actions designed to question the courage and masculinity of male soldiers. In this campaign, women threw chicken feed in front of military barracks, presented feathers to the police and military officials during military parades, and sang a popular Chilean children's song about chickens in the presence of soldiers and police.[13] According to Officer Ernesto Torres, these actions told soldiers that "they were not capable of defending their mothers, their wives, their daughters, or their families. They lacked the courage and intellectual capacity to defend them. They were chicken."[14] These actions, spearheaded by EPF, framed the choice for the military: intervene in politics and protect the women's families, or be considered a coward.

Women's public actions helped make a military coup against the civilian government "thinkable."[15] In explaining the reason behind the coup, the military junta claimed that Chilean women, as mothers, had shown them "that it was the patria that was in danger and that—demonstrated by the ineffectiveness of political action—only in the armed forces . . . existed the hope for the

---

11. Power, *Right-Wing Women*, 222.

12. Ibid., 227. As Power discusses, Prats had been hounded by the opposition since June, when he had been involved in a scandal concerning an altercation with Alejandrina Cox. On 27 June, Mrs. Cox had found herself stopped in traffic alongside General Prats. She claimed that with no planning on her part, and driven by her frustration with the current situation in Chile, she stuck her tongue out at him. Thinking Mrs. Cox was a man because of her short hair and dark glasses, General Prats drew his pistol, fired at her car, and demanded she get out. When she did, and he realized that Mrs. Cox was a woman, he was very upset. The opposition quickly exploited the incident, replaying the arguments that the UP did not respect women and instead endangered them. See Power, *Right-Wing Women*, 222–28, for an in-depth treatment of the incident and its outcomes.

13. Ibid., 228–30.

14. Quoted in ibid., 228.

15. Schatzberg, *Political Legitimacy*.

salvation of Chile. . . . Your voice was for us the voice of the patria that called us to save her."[16] In his first presidential message after the coup, General Pinochet praised the Chilean women who "risked their lives and abandoned the tranquility of their homes to implore the intervention of the military institutions."[17] Indeed, prominent members of the military publicly stated that it was the call of Chilean mothers that had spurred them into action.[18]

El Poder Femenino and the broader conservative women's movement against Allende also provided the military with "a public and supposedly apolitical face to the call for military intervention" and "allowed the armed forces to claim legitimacy for their illegal seizure of power."[19] Conservative women's groups had used their identities as mothers to criticize Allende and his government as a danger to their families. The military turned to the familial arguments developed within these groups to make the case that the Chilean nation was in danger and that the military had been called in to fulfill its duty to protect Chilean families. As one ad proclaimed shortly after the coup, "Woman: today you can dream. Now the sacrifice is justified. The patria has a place for your children" (fig. 5.1).[20] The military's action had restored tranquility and hope to women. While the actual decision on the part of the military commanders to overthrow Allende probably did not depend on these appeals, women's actions helped create a political climate in which military intervention was seen as an acceptable solution and provided the military with a ready-made argument justifying their overthrow of Allende.

Pinochet and the military government also justified their action by invoking a fundamental duty to protect the family from communism. In doing so, they drew on the established anticommunist rhetoric used by Allende's opposition. The series of legal decrees, known as Constitutional Acts, passed by the military government starting in 1974 enshrined the government's duty to protect the family. This duty was then used to justify state repression. Article 2, which made it illegal for any individual to threaten the "established regime," stated that "any act of individuals or groups directed at disseminating doctrines which threaten the family, or which promote violence or the concept of a society based on class struggle, . . . is illicit and in violation of the institutional organization of the Republic."[21] The military government linked the family, the

16. Gobierno de Chile, *República de Chile*, 194.
17. Pinochet, "Mensaje presidencial 11 septiembre 1973–11 septiembre 1974," 2.
18. Crummett, "El Poder Femenino"; Power, *Right-Wing Women*, 244–46.
19. Power, *Right-Wing Women*, 232.
20. *El Mercurio*, 27 October 1973, 29.
21. Quoted in Loveman, *Chile*, 271.

Fig. 5.1 "Woman: today you can dream." (*El Mercurio*, 27 October 1973.)

larger Chilean society, and the government and argued that to threaten one was to threaten the others. Article 2 particularly singled out the Chilean Communist Party and the various socialist parties because of the threat that Marxist-inspired ideologies represented to the family.

Portraying the family as under threat was a staple of Pinochet's pronouncements. In June 1978, an editorial in the state-sponsored women's magazine *Amiga* reminded readers of the terrors of the past in order to shore up support for the current government. The editorial stated, "We cannot forget that this was our constant feeling of this epoch: insecurity about daily life, insecurity about employment, insecurity about the future, insecurity about the education of the children, insecurity . . . about the survival of the family."[22] The editors argued that Pinochet and his government deserved the support of the reader because he had brought security to the family. Pinochet continually presented the threat communism posed to the family as a way to legitimate his political power. In 1980, for example, he stated, "Marxism constitutes an enemy that in a deliberate form foments and promotes the disintegration of the family, principally during the formation of the infancy and the youth. Destruction of this basic nucleus of the society results inevitably in the creation of a totalitarian system."[23] Subsecretary General Jovino Novoa repeated these sentiments in an interview in 1980, arguing that "there are certain ideologies or tendencies, fundamentally Marxist doctrines, that have as one of their principal objectives the destruction of the nuclear family, because this [destruction] facilitates their separate actions at every level. For us, who know firsthand what a Marxist regime can do, it is fundamental that our society is cemented in the basic nucleus that is the family."[24] Communism, by tearing the morals of the family asunder, "threatened the integrity of the nation."[25] The military government's overall message was clear: if the family falls apart, then the whole society is threatened. The threat to the family, and thus to the Chilean nation, posed by communism became a justification for military intervention and its continued control of political power.

One of the clearest examples of the ideological importance of familial arguments appeared in a pamphlet titled *Valores patrios y valores familiares* (Patriotic values and familial values), published in 1982 by the National Secretariat

22. "Lección de la violencia," *Amiga*, June 1978, 3.
23. *Amiga*, November 1980, 5.
24. "La necesidad de defender a la familia," *Amiga*, March 1980, 9.
25. Gobierno de Chile, *República de Chile*, 109.

of Women (Secretaría Nacional de la Mujer, SNM; more on this group below).[26] The connection between the family and the nation was clearly stated at the beginning of the pamphlet: "The terms patria and patriotism come from the Latin *pater*, which means father. This indicates . . . a filial relation with the nation of origin, equivalent to a concept of filiation and familial paternity."[27] Bringing this familial logic to its logical conclusion, the pamphlet asserted, "The patria is the true reflection of the home . . . [and] familial solidarity will be the primary foundation of true patriotism."[28] Indeed, "The family is . . . a thermometer of the collective life that a nation should always take care of if it aspires to have a future."[29] For the military government, a strong nation depended on a family that was bound together through bonds of filial loyalty. To protect the nation, the military government had to protect the family. Chilean families were endangered: "Movements, which seriously attack the integrity of the family, can have their origins in wrong positions, human conflicts, and conceptual errors; but—in our epoch—[they] have been instrumentalized by Marxism as a medium to destroy Western society, attacking its base, the unity of the family."[30] As Minister Sergio Badiola further argued, a fundamental duty of the state should be to protect the family, because "without the protection owed to the institution of the family, the people would remain without protection, exposed to whatever totalitarian threat. . . . For this reason, Marxism first corrodes the bases of the family so that later, with easy pressure, it can take over the people."[31] So too, Pinochet justified the ongoing need for military rule to restore order because Marxism promoted "all types of disorder. Material disorder through street demonstrations. Economic disorder through demagogic and inflationary pressures. Social disorder through constant strikes. Moral disorder by encouraging drugs, pornography, family division. Spiritual disorder through systematic class hatred."[32]

The previous democratic system was particularly at fault for having allowed the dominance of the Socialist and Communist parties, which represented

26. This pamphlet was one of nine published by the SNM; in 1983 it was estimated to have thirty-five thousand copies in print. See Secretaría Nacional de la Mujer, *Diez años de voluntariado*. A discussion of the mission of the SNM, as well as the other civil organizations created by the military government, can be found in any of the presidential messages from 1974 to 1987.

27. Secretaría Nacional de la Mujer, *Valores patrios y valores familiares*, 6. *Patrios* means the duty or love one feels toward one's country.

28. Ibid., 11.

29. Ibid., 21.

30. Ibid., 23.

31. "La fuerza del voluntariado," *Amiga*, April 1980, 7.

32. Quoted in Arriagada, *Pinochet*, 24.

the greatest threat to the foundational values and traditions of Chilean society. Officials of the military government also argued that the previous government had failed because it had been transformed into a system of electoral favors based on bribes, personal ambitions, and benefits, and consequently the family had been forgotten.[33] According to the military government, the chaos and problems of the UP years were the ultimate aim of communist ideology. The continual portrayal of communism as having infiltrated Chilean society in ways that endangered both individual families and the larger national family provided Pinochet and his government with justification for their continued control of the Chilean state.

As the 1980s progressed, other social problems were increasingly presented as endangering the family and used to justify the military's continued political control. Pinochet argued as early as 1979 that Chilean families faced "the worldwide occurrence of a gigantic campaign directed . . . at the destruction of the family. . . . Drugs, pornography, and delinquency are only part of the sinister arsenal of . . . a desperate attempt of the enemies of order, justice, liberty, and faith." But Pinochet and his government protected Chilean families against these threats, because "the family, honored friends, is the principal and preferential preoccupation of the government and . . . to protect it from the threats that surround it constitutes for us a sacred duty that we are disposed to assume with maximum energy and decisiveness."[34] Protecting the family became a kind of spiritual calling that justified all means employed by the government toward that end.

Pinochet as Chile's Benevolent Provider

In addition to invoking threats to the family to justify his rule, Pinochet disseminated positive portrayals of himself and his government in familial terms. In government publications and in press coverage of government programs, Pinochet cultivated an image of himself as a benefactor of Chilean families, one committed to upholding the ideal that the "state should direct a preferential attention to achieve [the goal] that the family will be constituted in a harmonious form."[35] Pinochet and the military government also contrasted

33. Pinochet, *Política, politiquería, y demagogia*, 7, 9.
34. "Conceptos sobre familia," *Amiga*, November 1979, 5–6.
35. "La necesidad de defender a la familia," *Amiga*, March 1980, 9.

their fundamental commitment to the ideals of the Familial State with the failure of previous democratic governments to secure familial welfare.

Within this overall strategy, Pinochet and his government recognized the symbolic power of maintaining the support—or at least the appearance of the support—of Chilean women. To maintain this rapport, Pinochet created a web of state-sponsored women's organizations. The central women's organizations were the SNM and CEMA-Chile (Centros de Madres–Chile, or Mothers' Centers), both headed by his wife, Lucía Hiriart de Pinochet. These two institutions served a dual purpose: to foster women's support of the government, and to portray that support as proof of Pinochet's dedication to the welfare of Chilean families. The SNM was created on 17 October 1973, barely a month after the military coup. According to the law, SNM was established to "propagate patriotic and familial values," "coordinate the labor entrusted by the President of the Republic," "collaborate in the programs that contribute to the formation and development of Chile in the familial context," and serve as a channel of connection between Chileans and their government.[36] The underlying purpose of the SNM was to create and promote ideological justifications for the military regime directed specifically at women.

CEMA-Chile, on the other hand, was designed to create an organized social space to provide material benefits and foster exchange between government supporters and poor Chileans. While the leadership and the volunteers of these two organizations were mostly military or upper-class wives, the women they served were often from the lower classes. The mission and function of CEMA-Chile under Pinochet's government in many ways continued previous political uses of the Mothers' Centers to incorporate women into politics. These centers had existed as an organized state institution since the late 1940s, but they had greatly expanded under President Frei (1964–70). He increased the funding for and the number of centers, providing women—particularly in rural areas—with a new public space in which to gather, socialize, and participate in his government's political projects. Allende also turned to the Mothers' Centers to incorporate women into Popular Unity projects, continuing the expansion begun by Frei. By the end of his presidency in 1970, "nine thousand CEMAs existed nationwide, with a total CEMA membership of 450,000 women."[37] While the Mothers' Centers' programs under Frei and Allende addressed women mostly as wives and mothers, they did offer limited space for

36. Secretaría Nacional de la Mujer, *Objectivos y programas*, 7.
37. Tinsman, *Partners in Conflict*, 147.

discussions of women's equality.[38] During Pinochet's rule, CEMA-Chile continued to envision women through their familial roles, and its diverse social programs targeted women as mothers. CEMA-Chile's stated mission was to "achieve the integral development of the Chilean woman . . . and with her the well-being of her family." The centers were to "contribute to the well-being of . . . the family" by providing women with opportunities to "work daily for the uplift of the woman, the family, and the patria."[39]

Given the general cutbacks in government services and two economic recessions, CEMA-Chile programs represented a source of material support for many poor women as they struggled to provide for their families in the 1970s and 1980s.[40] For example, CEMA-Chile funded the development and staffing of Homes of the Campesina Mother, which provided a place for pregnant rural women to live that was closer to a hospital. In 1987, CEMA-Chile claimed that 5,974 healthy babies had been born to the mothers who had stayed in the ninety-one homes spread throughout the country.[41] Volunteers from Mothers' Centers also staffed and funded twenty-nine homes for adolescent girls in "irregular" condition (those who had been orphaned or abandoned) or "moral danger" (those who had been victims of abuse and incest). In 1983, in response to the popular protests in the shantytowns of Santiago, CEMA-Chile began an affordable housing program. Indeed, not only were members to be the recipients of these houses built with government money, but their male family members could also be chosen to receive training and be hired to build these houses. CEMA-Chile also participated in the production of school uniforms, which provided members with jobs and discounts on the items themselves. Other endeavors that could generate material benefits for women included courses on traditional arts and crafts, in which members sold their own goods in special stores staffed by CEMA-Chile volunteers. CEMA-Chile propaganda claimed that these programs were designed to benefit the entire family.[42]

Within a context of the general withdrawal of state resources from social welfare, the existence of these programs helped to keep CEMA-Chile's membership

---

38. For a discussion of the importance of Mothers' Centers in the Christian Democrats' incorporation of women, see Power, *Right-Wing Women*, 111–18; and Tinsman, *Partners in Conflict*, 146–56. For a discussion of the experiences of Chilean women who participated in the program under Pinochet, see Valdés and Weinstein, *Mujeres que sueñan*.

39. CEMA-Chile, *Edición aniversario*, 8.

40. Valdés and Weinstein, *Mujeres que sueñan*, 87–128.

41. CEMA-Chile, *Edición aniversario*, 34.

42. Ibid., 44.

levels high and generated support for Pinochet and his government. In 1987, CEMA-Chile claimed 215,321 adult women members, as well as 9,412 adolescent female members associated with the Centros Cemitas, organizations developed by the government for the daughters of CEMA-Chile members.[43] Almost a quarter of a million women and girls belonged to CEMA-Chile, and they were served by 5,249 volunteers, mostly upper-class women and the wives of military officers, in the ten thousand centers spread throughout the country.[44] The women who ran and volunteered at Mothers' Centers were seen as being completely loyal to Pinochet and his political projects. But the affiliations of the women who participated in CEMA-Chile were more ambiguous. Certainly many women who belonged to Mothers' Centers were strong supporters of Pinochet and saw him as the stalwart defender and generous provider portrayed in government propaganda. Other poor women, however, had a more instrumental relationship with the Mothers' Centers, taking advantage of the material resources and programs associated with them while not necessarily supporting the larger political project of the government.[45]

But the purpose of these women's organizations was not only to engender citizen support for the military government but also to present the members and volunteers to the rest of society as symbols of Chilean women's unwavering support for Pinochet. Just as military leaders had used the mobilization of women against Allende to help justify military intervention, continuing public commitment on the part of women volunteers was used as a sign of Pinochet's dedication to familial welfare. In public parades commemorating Chile's independence and military victories, volunteers from SNM, CEMA-Chile, and the other charitable organizations marched in their multicolored uniforms alongside members of the four branches of the armed forces. The Chilean feminist scholar Ximena Bunster argues that these public demonstrations presented the women volunteers to "the public eye [as] a 'living affirmation,' a tacit approval of the oppressive junta regime."[46] The women's organizations helped the government continue to claim that the representatives of Chilean families remained committed to the projects of the military government.

43. Valdés and Weinstein, *Mujeres que sueñan*, 89.
44. CEMA-Chile, *Edición aniversario*, 6.
45. Valdés and Weinstein recognize the importance of any help given to women and their families, though they also discuss the price paid for these resources in terms of the control of the participants exacted by the organizations. See *Mujeres que sueñan*, 87–128. Patricia Richards also notes that a few women she interviewed joined only to allay their neighbors' suspicions about their opposition to Pinochet. See "*Pobladoras*," "*Indígenas*," and the *State*, 37.
46. Bunster, "Watch Out for the Little Nazi Man," 490.

Women's symbolic support also played a role in promoting the patriarchal family as a template for the type of society the military government wanted to create. In her analysis of the gender politics of the military government, the Chilean sociologist María Elena Valenzuela argued that the country was presented as a home in which "Pinochet is the father-governor-head of the household, while the civilian population fulfills the role of the spouse and children."[47] Publicly, Pinochet venerated the traditional nuclear family, which was clearly led by the man as husband, father, and provider.

The propaganda disseminated by the state-sponsored women's organizations presented Pinochet and other military leaders as fathers/husbands to the Chilean nation, with women volunteers often appearing as metaphorical wives and mothers. For example, an editorial in *Amiga* praised the work of both Pinochet and his wife in promoting the "fundamental values of the national soul" and noted that "today, this head of the household is the head of the great Chilean family, and has succeeded in transmitting these same principles" to the nation.[48] Many of the government's programs that addressed familial welfare were placed in the hands of military wives and overseen by women's organizations. Men were in charge of the political and public functions of the government, while their wives and other women took responsibility for the family. Subsecretary General Mario Ríos Tobar explicitly stated this connection, arguing that the aim of programs developed by the SNM and CEMA-Chile was "to demonstrate once again that the action of the public men is intimately connected to the actions that their wives realize. Further, this experience of the National Secretariat of Women is an experience of the government. This has been the first government that has integrated the entire family in general to work in public labors."[49] The women's organizations provided a gendered symmetry to government policies and the symbolic construction of the military state. Pinochet (and his government) was the husband/provider, while Lucía Hiriart, along with the SNM and the Mothers' Centers, was the wife/nurturer, both for the Chilean nation and for actual Chilean families. This metaphorical marriage and family were modeled on the actual marriage between Lucía Hiriart and Augusto Pinochet. Publicly, Lucía Hiriart always gave unconditional support to her husband and served as the head of the most important of the

47. Valenzuela, *La mujer en el Chile militar*, 87. For similar analyses of patriarchal ideology providing political justifications for the military regime, see Bunster, "Watch Out for the Little Nazi Man"; Kirkwood, *Ser política in Chile*; and Munizaga, *El discurso público*.
48. "Presidente Pinochet: Patria y nacionalidad," *Amiga*, September 1976, 6.
49. "La impotancia de un seminario," *Amiga*, August 1978, 44.

women's organizations, CEMA-Chile and SNM. In this role, she traveled throughout Chile and the rest of the world describing the care and concern that Pinochet had for Chilean families. Pinochet used the women's organizations to present himself as a successful Patriarchal Leader and to showcase how the military government was fulfilling the responsibilities of the Familial State.

Providing Nutrition and Housing to Chilean Families

Pinochet's self-presentation as a benevolent provider for Chilean families was not limited to programs designed exclusively to generate support among women. Similar arguments were mobilized around general programs, particularly those directed toward the continuing problems of housing and nutrition. These issues had figured prominently in previous democratic governments' social welfare programs, and many Chileans continued to expect the current military government to dedicate time and resources to addressing these problems. In fact, more Chilean families than ever were living in precarious conditions, due to the economic policies pursued by the military government. Despite this, Pinochet reversed the long-term trend of increasing support for social welfare programs in the twentieth century. In 1986, for example, the per capita level of "national social expenditures" was still less than the 1969–70 average. Conservative estimates argue that by 1986, 30 percent of Chileans were living in conditions of extreme poverty, as opposed to 10 percent in 1970.[50] At the level of propaganda, however, the military government touted their programs' benefits for Chilean families. This strategy is apparent in the government's portrayals of its child and maternal nutrition and housing programs.[51] In government advertising around these issues, Pinochet was cast as the provider and protector of Chilean families. In its public discourse, the military government sought to legitimate its rule by demonstrating a fundamental concern for Chilean families.

Chile's high rates of infant mortality had been a perennial area of focus for governments throughout the twentieth century.[52] In pledging to decrease infant

---

50. These statistics, as well as a very extensive discussion of the overall economic effects of Pinochet's neoliberal policies, can be found in Oxhorn, *Organizing Civil Society*, 68–75.

51. See my discussion in chapters 3 and 4 on the importance of these issues in the Popular Unity government.

52. For a discussion of the importance of this issue in the first wave of the women's movement in Chile, see Lavrin, *Women, Feminism, and Social Change.*

mortality, Pinochet and his government could claim to be following in the footsteps of previous Chilean governments.[53] In order to advance its legitimacy, Pinochet's government turned to well-established beliefs about the importance of maternal and infant care as a matter of fundamental concern for the state. Indeed, government-produced propaganda argued that Pinochet was actually more committed than were past governments to the health of Chile's mothers and children and that he had achieved better results. This commitment meant that even though the military government decreased the state's overall health care expenditures, Pinochet actually expanded government-run and -financed programs dedicated to "impoverished infants and pregnant mothers," such as infant immunization and nutrition programs.[54] Placing Dr. Fernando Monckeberg, a well-known spokesperson on issues of malnutrition, maternal health and child welfare, in charge cemented the appearance of continuity between Pinochet's concern for mothers and children and that of previous governments.[55] In a special supplement in *El Mercurio* about health and nutrition in December 1977, Dr. Monckeberg touted the success of the current programs by citing a drop in the overall rate of malnutrition. He claimed that in 1967, "67 percent of children below the age of ten presented some grade of malnutrition. Today, this number has been diminished to 16 percent. In 1972, the infant mortality rate was 71 per 1,000. In 1976, it has decreased to 55 per 1,000. . . . In 1972, the preschool (1–4) mortality was 3.5 per 1,000. In 1976, it was 2 per 1,000."[56] As Dr. Monckeberg stated in 1978 at the dedication of a center for maternal and infant health in Temuco, "I do not know of any country in the world that is making an effort like this. . . . Ten years ago, . . . Chile had the highest rate of infant mortality in Latin America. Today . . . [malnutrition] has been reduced to a bit more that 12 percent, and infant mortality . . . is the lowest in Latin America."[57]

Pinochet's commitment to the nutritional health of Chile's older children was also heralded in press reports. One newspaper headline trumpeted the

53. See my discussion in chapter 3 of Allende's use of his milk program and how he portrayed it as part of his deep concern for Chilean families.

54. For a critical discussion of Pinochet's health policies, see Collins and Lear, *Chile's Free-Market Miracle*, especially chapter 8. While noting the improved infant mortality rates, the authors also show the general decrease of health among the Chilean poor. Further, even in children between the ages of one and four, the rate of illness and mortality rose during the military government. This rise was often caused by accidents and poisonings due to the increasingly unsafe and dangerous living conditions of poor families.

55. "Subalimentación en Chile?" *Qué Pasa*, 18 May 1976, 28–31.

56. *El Mercurio*, 13–14 December 1977, 4–5.

57. *Amiga*, June 1978, 22.

news that "CONPAN [Corporación Nacional de Pan, National Bread Board] is fighting . . . an exceptional battle" against childhood malnutrition. The editorial claimed that approximately 580,000 children between the ages of six and sixteen were the victims of extreme poverty, and it went on to urge readers to support the government's programs designed to decrease the rate of malnutrition.[58] Other articles focused on CONPAN's commitment to improving the system of milk distribution, especially in rural areas.[59]

Often, the portrayals of the current military government's successes were contrasted with claims about how past democratically elected governments had failed to solve these fundamental familial problems even while spending larger amounts of money. The present government, through its greater dedication to the welfare of Chilean families and the removal of self-interested politicians, had placed these problems into the hands of world-class experts who were focusing on the totality of the problem.[60] The dominance of technocrats and the lack of political participation in Pinochet's government were justified by the increased familial welfare.

By the 1970s, helping provide housing for Chilean families had also become an accepted state responsibility. Both Presidents Frei and Allende had expanded state-sponsored housing developments to try to ameliorate the housing deficit in Santiago (caused by the rural-to-urban migration of the 1950s and 1960s). Because of this past political history, housing had come to be seen as an important government program that benefited Chilean families. Newspaper reports and government statements presented the Chilean family as the primary beneficiary of the government's polices. An article in *Amiga* in October 1978 provides an excellent example of this pattern. Titled "A Large Aspiration Was Made a Reality," the article begins, "Many families lived a different September. They had heard that others—of scarce resources like themselves—had been relocated from their unhealthy housing [and] moved to a new residence. But [the move represented] much more [than a house], more accurately a new reality."[61] It continues by detailing how on 9 September 1978 "the President of the Republic and the First Lady . . . presented four hundred families the keys to their new homes in Nueva Matucana." Prominently featured in the article was a picture of a grateful woman thanking Pinochet and a grateful man thanking Lucía Hiriart (fig. 5.2). In both pictures, the presidential couple is placed slightly

58. *El Mercurio*, 1 September 1976, 3.
59. *Qué Pasa*, 18 May 1976, 30.
60. Ibid., 29.
61. *Amiga*, October 1978, 10.

Fig. 5.2 "The President and the First Lady present the keys to the *pobladores*." (*Amiga*, October 1978.)

higher up so that the pobladores are gazing up into the eyes of Pinochet and Lucía Hiriart. This visual placement highlights the social, class, and political hierarchy between the two couples. The images also dramatize a narrative of who was providing the house and who was receiving it as a gift.[62] The article

62. Ibid., 8.

ends with the personal testimony of some of the new home owners, including Silvia Poblete, a mother of six children. In talking about her new house, she told *Amiga*, "You know that before everything was promised and nothing was done. Now, no . . . because all that [Pinochet] said, he did and he kept his promise."[63]

This was the sentiment that Pinochet wanted disseminated more broadly: that he, unlike earlier presidents, kept his promises to Chilean families. In these organized acts, housing was presented not as a right of citizenship and a fundamental responsibility of the state, but as a gift from Pinochet that demonstrated his personal concern and caring for Chilean families. The minister of housing and urbanism, Miguel Angel Poduje, explicitly stated this argument in an interview in *El Mercurio* on 18 November 1985. According to Minister Poduje, "Housing has an economic, financial, social effect, as well as effects on health, education, and morality. The difference between a person who lives in a house and one who lives in a temporary shelter, [is the difference between] a family in an ordered form, or one [that promotes] promiscuity, delinquency."[64] Thus, providing housing promoted orderly families and a moral society. Through its housing policies, the government protected especially poor families from a host of dangerous threats, and it demonstrated Pinochet's dedication to protecting and providing for those families.

This underlying message was repeated in the press coverage of these ceremonies held to tout the successes of the military government's policies. The overall message of articles about the government's housing policies was that the government was working hard and helping many Chilean families find housing. Headlines such as "Presentation of Title to Thirty-Seven Thousand Families in the National Stadium: Massive Operation to Grant Titles to Pobladores"[65] and "Testimony of a Poblador: At Last I Will Have My Own House"[66] were common. In these public ceremonies, Pinochet would present titles of ownership for land that had been occupied and developed in the early 1970s, before the military coup. These events provided powerful images of families receiving titles to their homes while requiring very little expenditure of governmental resources. These staged ceremonies were designed to promote the perception that Pinochet was helping a large number of Chilean families, and to counter growing criticisms about the continuing housing deficits, a central

---

63. Ibid., 10.
64. *El Mercurio*, 18 November 1985.
65. *El Mercurio*, 26 September 1979, C1.
66. *El Mercurio*, 6 September 1981, A1. The families receiving their titles were part of a total of 164,000 for the year. The project was part of a law passed by the government to recognize and register the titles of long-term occupants.

cause of social protest by pobladores throughout the 1980s.[67] A typical example of this strategy can be seen in an article in *El Mercurio* from September 1981, which claims that the National Stadium had been filled with "thousands and thousands of renters, *allegados*,[68] and families that have been waiting for ten to twenty years for a document that gave them definite ownership of their living space." The article went on to feature the personal testimonies of poor Chileans thanking the current government for their houses.[69]

Housing policies were also highlighted in the political propaganda campaign launched by the government to drum up support for its new constitution, which was being voted on in 1980. Using the theme "Solid Bases for a Great Nation," the government featured major successes of the past seven years, such as the extension of potable water and the increase of forestry exports. The ad featuring the housing policies read, "A Just Housing Subsidy. Orientation of the subsidies. 1973: favored the sectors with the highest income. 1979: favors the most dispossessed sectors. Until 1973 the families with the highest income, who only represented 15 percent of Chileans, received 28.3 percent of the state's housing subsidies. The modest sectors, which represented 55 percent of Chilean families, drew scarcely 40.5 percent of these subsidies. Today 55 percent of the most modest families draw 60 percent of state subsidies. This is true social justice, because [the government] gives more to those who have less" (fig. 5.3).[70] As with nutrition, Pinochet presented his policies as more efficient and fair in protecting poor families than were the policies of previous governments. The statistics used in the ad, however, are carefully chosen to avoid discussing his overall cuts in state funding.[71] But the text is less important than the visual story presented. The majority of space is dedicated to the visual representation of happy families and modern houses: loving couples embrace each other and their children, while other children play both inside and outside the different types of houses provided through government programs. The pictures again bring home the government's message that through their housing subsidies they were providing for Chilean families.

---

67. I examine the importance of housing in generating resistance to Pinochet in chapter 6. For more detailed accounts of the general rise of the "shantytown" protests, see Schneider, *Shantytown Protest*, and Oxhorn, *Organizing Civil Society*.

68. *Allegado* can be translated as "guest." Given the housing shortage in Santiago, especially among the poor, it was not uncommon for Chilean families to have friends, distant relatives, or even paying strangers living in the same house.

69. *El Mercurio*, 6 September 1981, A1.

70. *El Mercurio*, 23 September 1979, D7.

71. Schneider, *Shantytown Protest*, 99.

Fig. 5.3 "Solid Bases for a Great Nation." (*El Mercurio*, 23 September 1979.)

The text of this ad reflects a tension within the military government's housing policy. Throughout its seventeen-year rule, the military government publicly vowed to help more Chilean families find housing. But it rejected arguments that housing represented a basic right of Chilean families, instead embracing a more fluid concept of "security of residence" that could be met through either renting or owning.[72] While previous governments had discussed housing in terms of poor families' fundamental right to lead a dignified life, under Pinochet housing was presented as an issue of personal consumption and dependent on individual and familial efforts. This shift in understanding reveals the basic neoliberal economic approach of Pinochet's government, which emphasized the importance of decreasing the role of the state, privatizing social welfare provisions, and focusing on Chileans not as citizens but as consumers. The growing dominance of a neoliberal discourse, however, could not completely supplant earlier understandings about the duties of the state toward

---

72. *Qué Pasa*, 25 January 1974, 18.

families, even though it created new tensions within those older understand-ings.[73] The shift away from a discourse of citizenship to a discourse of con-sumption fit well within Pinochet's presentation of himself as the benevolent provider. If housing was not actually a right of citizens, then the efforts on the part of Pinochet and his government were more clearly a sign of his personal compassion and dedication to the welfare of Chilean families.

Bringing Families Together: Government Propaganda and "Somos Millones"

The importance of arguments about familial welfare within ongoing attempts by Pinochet to justify his rule can also be seen in the general publicity cam-paigns that extolled the successes of the military government. One of Pinochet's most well-produced publicity campaigns for television was "Somos Millones" (We are millions). Its goal was to present Pinochet and his government in the most favorable light possible in the lead-up to the 1988 plebiscite on his rule.[74] The spots designed for "Somos Millones" touted the successes of the military government during the previous fifteen years. Under military rule, Chilean television stations had been "strictly controlled and . . . [their] program con-tents carefully censored by the authorities."[75] Pinochet recognized the power of television as a form of communication between the government and ordi-nary Chileans, and he sought to control its content and to use it to promote his political agenda. The Chilean media scholar David Hojman contends that between 1973 and 1988, "No expression of dissidence, no matter how small, was allowed. By contrast, television advertisements by official agencies, part of several publicity campaigns by government organisms, . . . were often shown at peak viewing times, and repeated again and again up to the point of reaching

73. Neoliberal economic policies not only affect the arrangement of material programs but also influence cultural values and norms. Many scholars argue that this broader influence of neolib-eral ideology represents a legacy of Pinochet's government, one that continues to limit the quality of Chile's current democracy. For a discussion of the ways in which neoliberalism was both integrated and resisted, particularly by Chilean pobladores and women, see Paley, *Marketing Democracy*, and Schild, "New Subjects of Rights?"

74. The campaign slogan referred to the millions of Chileans, but also to the millions of people who supported the ideological and political views of Pinochet. I discovered this point from David Hojman's "YES or NO to Pinochet," 172, 194n3. During my time in Chile, I was able to obtain a video-tape of nineteen spots produced for the "Somos Millones" campaign. I do not have the exact dates for when the ads appeared or how often they played. As explained below, Hojman contends that such spots were repeated constantly on both the state- and university-owned television channels.

75. Hojman, "YES or NO," 172.

saturation levels."[76] This was certainly the case for the "Somos Millones" campaign, which aired on the national television station and the private stations controlled by the Catholic University and the University of Chile.

"Somos Millones," both textually and visually, justified Pinochet's political control by showing how Chilean families had benefited from his government. "Somos Millones" was replete with images of happy and successful traditional families who represented the geographical and industrial diversity of Chile. At the beginning of each spot, written across the scene and read by a male narrator with a deep voice, was a statistical presentation of what Chile had been like in the 1970s. The presentation of the past was designed to highlight how far Chile had come under Pinochet, as expressed through carefully chosen evidence and issues. Of the nineteen different thirty- to forty-five-second spots I viewed, fourteen portrayed the economic and social progress of the Pinochet years through images of familial welfare and progress. In discussing the economic successes of the military government, for example, the spots portrayed the increase in traditional agriculture, the growth of new export agricultural sectors, the increase of copper production, the development of the fishery and forestry sectors, and the rise of Chile as a major import/export power in Latin America. Regarding social programs, the spots featured housing programs, increased access to preschool and high school for Chilean children, better care for "undervalued" children, the increased number of rural medical posts and therefore access to health care, the decrease in infant mortality, the diminishing level of alcoholism, and the maintenance of general social peace. The remaining spots featured general symbols of Chile's progress and modernization, including the building of the Austral Highway, which opened up the southern part of the country, the better maintenance of the road system, the increase in the number of houses with television sets, and the better provision of potable water.

Using familial welfare as a measure of legitimacy, the spots claimed that Pinochet and his government had more than fulfilled the basic duties of the Chilean state. The visual text of the ads dramatizes how Pinochet's policies benefited families. Ads dealing with social issues presented the family as the direct recipient of the government's programs. Interestingly, the spots also often framed the less-obvious benefits of economic policies (e.g., increased trade) in terms of how they ultimately improved the welfare of Chilean families.

76. Ibid.

One of the best examples of these familial strategies was the spot that high-lighted the number of rural health clinics built by the government. The ad started with the statistics that in 1970 there were only 776 clinics in rural Chile, and it went on to claim that now, in 1987, there were 2,770. Further, the current clinics were modern and staffed by qualified people. What this policy had meant to actual people played out through the visual narrative. It began with a campesino family comprising a father, a son, and a very pregnant mother. The scenery, with its trees and fields, lets the viewer know that the family lives in a rural area of southern Chile. The family is of very modest means, since they take their horse and wagon to travel to the government health clinic. In the clinic, equipped with modern technology, a smiling male doctor examines the pregnant wife while her happy, healthy son watches. The spot contrasts the traditional lifestyle of the poor campesino family with the modern neonatal care received in the government's clinic. The message of the ad was that thanks to Pinochet and his government, rural families were living a better life. The emphasis on familial progress was further emphasized by the focus on neo-natal care, an area of medicine devoted to mothers and their children, the future citizens of Chile. By beginning the spot with a presentation of statistics from 1970, the ad also argued that this government, in contrast to earlier gov-ernments, had truly improved the welfare of Chilean families.

In another ad, Pinochet took credit for Chile's decreased rates of infant mortality. The ad begins with the statistic that "in 1970, for every 1,000 babies born, 83 died before their first birthday. Now, 982 babies live," which means that only 18 babies per 1,000 died before reaching the age of one. The accom-panying images tell the story of the birth of a child. A young man is shown waiting in the hall of the hospital. A male doctor comes out and tells the new father about the birth of his child. The father then joins his wife in her room just as a female nurse hands the newborn baby back to the mother. The spot ends with the image of the mother and the father gazing adoringly at their child. The visual narrative implies that the happiness and joy being felt by the new family was made possible by the government's commitment to the welfare of Chilean mothers and their children. Without Pinochet's dedication, this baby might have been one of the Chilean children tragically lost at birth.

A similar strategy was apparent in the spots featuring the government's housing policies. Throughout the 1970s and 1980s, a growing number of peo-ple lacked housing in Chile. In 1973, there had been an estimated deficit of four hundred thousand housing units. By 1990, this number had grown to 1.1 million, which meant that "39 percent of all Chilean families lacked adequate housing."[77] Given this reality, the spot carefully featured statistics on the improvement in the quality of homes, stating that in 1970, "50 percent of the housing in the country was considered to be in bad repair. Today, 85 of every 100 houses are in good condition," and that "every day more and more families are proprietors of a house where they live dignified lives." What the spot is really designed to communicate, however, is found again in the visual story. Through the images shown, having a house symbolizes having the ideal family life. To start, the camera focuses on a little girl playing with her teddy bear in the front yard of a modest duplex while her mother works in the garden. The picture cuts away to scenes of a coming storm, and then returns to the mother and daughter, who are now standing at the window, watching the rain fall. A bus pulls up and a man runs to the front door, where he is greeted by the wife and daughter. The spot ends with a cozy picture of the wife drying the husband's hair while the daughter talks to her parents. The modern home provided through government programs is presented as a warm haven from a dark and rainy world. The home is a refuge to which the father gratefully returns after a hard day's work, where his wife and daughter wait in comfort and security. Thus the true outcome of the government's policies was not the statistics presented at the beginning of the ad, but rather how they promoted happy, traditional families.

This visual narrative was repeated in a spot on the growth of the number of homes with televisions. In this spot, the increase in television ownership from 335,000 to 2,000,000 households symbolizes the general economic progress and the increased access to consumer goods routinely touted by the government as an outcome of its neoliberal economic policies. The spot claims that televisions were now even found in the most remote areas of the country, such as the featured small town in the north of Chile, replete with dusty, unpaved streets and whitewashed buildings. As the ad opens, a young boy is sitting outside his house, looking bored, while his mother hangs laundry behind him. The setting makes it easy to see why having a television to "inform, educate, and entertain" (as the spot claims) would be a marked improvement in their quality of life. The image then shifts to the father coming home from work, sitting down in the living room with his son, and turning on the television to watch a soccer game. The last image is of a father and son bonding over the national pastime, united with other Chileans through their love of soccer. This romanticized view of family unity was made possible, according to the

---

77. Collins and Lear, *Chile's Free-Market Miracle*, 156, 161.

spot, by the consumer goods brought to Chile by the present government's policies.

"Somos Millones" also portrayed the government as committed to protecting the family from current social problems that might threaten its welfare. This theme was developed in an ad about programs dedicated to decreasing alcoholism. The spot features the story of a father and a son walking home in the evening. The dramatic tension in the narrative rises when the father steps into a convenience store that sells liquor. The danger facing the family is clear to the viewer in the angry and worried look on the face of the son, as well as his clenched hands. The rage and powerlessness felt by the child are evident, and the viewer is encouraged to imagine what type of problems might beset the family if the father succumbs to the temptation of alcohol. The father returns with a brown paper bag, notices the look on his son's face, and pulls out the bread he has just purchased. The tension lifts, the father claps his son on the back, and they walk down the street. Meanwhile, the narrator states that in 1970 more than 400,000 Chileans were trapped by alcohol, whereas today 280,000 are recovering from alcoholism. Of course, these two carefully chosen statistics don't necessarily measure the same thing. But what was clearly presented to the viewers was that the present government more fully realized the danger posed to the family by alcoholism and had reacted to protect familial welfare.

An implicit portrayal of Pinochet as the metaphorical father to Chilean children was part of the spot about the greater emphasis the current government placed on "undervalued children," those who were orphaned, abandoned, or removed from their homes because of abuse. The narrator emphasizes that the previous government had provided for only nine thousand children, whereas Pinochet' government had given fifteen thousand children a safe home. Visually, an empty swing swaying in the wind represents the prior neglect. Under Pinochet's government, however, happy children play in a park at a birthday party. Completing the picture, the birthday boy is overjoyed with his surprise gift of a puppy. The institutional homes provided by the military government for Chile's "undervalued" children are presented as utopias complete with caring, qualified staff that provide a warm and loving setting.

In the previous spots, the uses of familial images were easily connected to the actual goals of the featured policy initiatives. But the family was also used to portray the benefits of policies that promoted economic and technological progress. These spots followed the same template of contrasting the past with the present and highlighting the amount of development and growth promoted by Pinochet and his government. For example, one ad about the fishing industry tells the story of growth through the relationship between a father and son. While the narrator says that fishing now brings in more than six hundred million dollars a year, what that really means is seen through the images of the father and son walking to the harbor together in the morning. The son waves good-bye as the father sets out to reap the bounty of the sea; later in the day, he brings in a good catch on a large, modern seine boat. In other words, the growth of the fishing industry under Pinochet meant that this Chilean man could provide for his family. Another ad focusing on the growth of exports follows the same story line. The visual narrative features a port busy with barges being loaded and unloaded. While the father works with heavy machinery on the docks, his son is shown at home playing with toy cranes. This dual story implies not only that the father has a good job, but also that the son will follow his father into the same type of employment. The ad ends with an image of the ideal nuclear family sitting down to breakfast on their patio, with the busy port visible in the background. The family is the ultimate beneficiary of the economic progress and security of Pinochet's government.

Probably the most idyllic depiction of the "ideal" Chilean family life promoted by the government's economic policies was presented in the spot that touted the growing efficiency of the agricultural sector. Rather than depicting how most agriculture goods were being produced in Chile in the 1980s—on large factory farms with many workers—the spot features a prosperous family vineyard in the country's central valley. The father and the son are walking through a field, which is laden with grapevines ready to be harvested. Meanwhile, the mother is in the kitchen making *pan amasado*, a Chilean delicacy infused with nostalgia about home, hearth, and traditional rural life. When the bread is done, the mother rings the dinner bell and the happy family sits down to a bountiful meal provided by their farm. The message was that thanks to the government, Chilean agriculture now provides bountiful produce to feed Chilean families. According to all three spots, Pinochet and his policies provide fathers with work and promising futures for their sons.

There are a number of obvious similarities among all the ads. First, the ultimate goals of economic progress and development were presented as improvements in the welfare of Chilean families. It was not individuals who benefited, but rather entire families. Meanwhile, the visual subtext of many of the spots was that Pinochet's policies had strengthened the traditional family by providing good jobs for Chilean men, thereby enabling them to fulfill their roles as heads of households in taking care of their wives and children. The increased prosperity also meant that Chilean women were able and content to stay at home, maintaining the house as a refuge for their husbands and nurturing the development of their children. Children were protected at birth and able to take advantage of new opportunities. By often featuring sons, the ads also made an implicit promise about how a continuation of Pinochet's rule would mean a bright future for the breadwinners of tomorrow's traditional families. Overall, the military government's claims about Chile's current economic prosperity, its increasing levels of modernization, and its social progress were symbolized through invocations of the improvements in the welfare of Chilean families.

Conclusion

Pinochet and his government drew on cultural understandings of the Familial State and the Patriarchal Leader in their attempts to justify and legitimate their usurpation and retention of political power. In particular, Pinochet used cultural understanding about the responsibility of the state to protect and provide for families as a reason for Chileans to support his rule. In these attempts, the government also called on the ideals of the Familial Nation, depicting the nation as a family and arguing that the traditional nuclear family was the base of Chilean society. As the valiant protectors of Chilean families, Pinochet and the military government had answered the call of Chilean mothers by saving Chilean families from the moral and material dangers posed by Marxist ideology, excessive politicization, and the government of Salvador Allende. But Pinochet did not act just as the defender of Chilean families. The government's depictions of women's organizations, policies around housing and nutrition, and explicit propaganda campaigns like "Somos Millones" were all designed to showcase Pinochet's commitment to providing for the material welfare of Chilean families.

A focus on familial claims reveals the ongoing attempts by Pinochet and the military government to justify their control of political power. The military government crafted strategies that drew on existing cultural understandings and previous political events to create popular support, rather than relying only on repression to maintain power. By focusing on how Pinochet turned to ideals of Familial State and Patriarchal Leader in framing his legitimation strategies, we also gain a new appreciation for the power of familial understandings of politics. Through his uses of familial beliefs, Pinochet attempted to demonstrate his government's fulfillment of what was considered a basic duty of the state, the protection and provision of Chilean families. In so doing, the family became a key resource in his attempts to maintain political support for his regime. But Pinochet's use of familial beliefs in his pursuit of political legitimacy did not go uncontested. The next chapter examines the multiple ways that familial beliefs were used by the social movements that organized against Pinochet, protested the military government, and demanded a return to democracy.

★ SIX ★

MOBILIZING FAMILIES
Justifying Political Dissent Under Pinochet

On 14 December 1985, after four dramatic years of widespread protest, pobladores, pastoral agents, and professionals met at a working conference convened
by the archbishopric of Santiago around the theme "Pobladores por una vida
digna" (Pobladores for a dignified life). In the letter addressed to the "Government of Chile" produced in the conference, the pobladores described the current problems besetting their communities, which included "matrimonial and
familial crisis; educational desertion, alcoholism, drug addiction, child prostitution, vagrancy, delinquency." The pobladores placed the ultimate blame
for these problems on the present government, writing, "We consider the
[entity] directly responsible the regime that has governed the country."[1] By
organizing the conference and publishing the conference proceedings, the participants were taking a stand against the military government and fighting to
save their communities.

The massive protests by pobladores between 1983 and 1986 represented one
part of a broad-based opposition that mobilized against the military government. To consolidate his rule, Pinochet had attempted to depoliticize Chilean
society by banning and repressing long-standing institutions of political participation, particularly political parties, peasant organizations, and labor unions.
This strategy was only partly successful. Even with repression, the political
parties of the left (PC, PS) and center (PDC, PRD) as well as labor and peasant
unions continued to generate spaces for resistance. More dramatically, new
actors mobilized to protest the effects of Pinochet's political and economic
projects. The massive human rights violations of the military government—
which included detentions, torture, imprisonment, and disappearances of political opponents—generated opposition in both civil society and religious institutions. Pinochet's social and economic policies, which increased poverty

1. Vicaría de la Solidaridad, *1985 Encuentro*.

and exacerbated the unequal distribution of wealth, also sparked protests, particularly in the *poblaciones* surrounding Santiago. More and more Chilean women mobilized against the extremely conservative gender ideologies of the government. These diverse groups and organizations pursued a variety of strategies in resisting the military dictatorship, including massive public protests, strikes, the publication of written materials in magazines, pamphlets, conference proceedings, and academic papers, symbolic protests and hunger strikes, and the organization of international protests and solidarity networks.

Familial beliefs emerged as a key resource for opposition groups in legitimizing alternative definitions of citizenship and political participation. In particular, beliefs about the duties and responsibilities of the Chilean state to families, as well as the duties and responsibilities of family members to one another, were the basis for many groups' attempts to delegitimize the military government. Opposition groups turned to familial beliefs to both criticize Pinochet and justify their resistance. Their actions directly contested Pinochet's ongoing attempts, explored in the last chapter, to use the ideals of the Familial State and Patriarchal Leader to justify his political rule. Opposition groups sought to turn Pinochet's own use of familial beliefs against him, pointing out the myriad ways in which the current military government was failing to live up to its responsibilities to protect Chilean families. As with the earlier protest against Salvador Allende organized by the right, failing to protect Chilean families became grounds to argue for political change. Like the earlier mobilization of El Poder Femenino, groups opposing Pinochet turned to the ideals of Militant Families to organize political participation, to justify their right to speak publicly against the current government, and to reveal the illegitimacy of the military government.

To explore the importance of familial beliefs in the political struggles against Pinochet, I analyze the public discourse of three major sectors of the opposition: the human rights movement, the poblador movement, and the women's movement. For the human rights movement, I examine specifically the Agrupación de Familiares de Detenidos Desaparecidos (Association of Relatives of the Detained Disappeared, AFDD), one of the oldest and most well-known groups in the field. For the poblador movement, which is incredibly diverse, I focus on the Sin Casa (or homeless) movement. Finally, for the women's movement, I analyze both the public discourse of the popular women's group Movimiento de Mujeres Pobladoras (Movement of Popular Women, MOMUPO) and the writings produced by explicitly feminist activists within the women's movement.

The Missing Family Member:
The Agrupación de Familiares de Detenidos Desaparecidos

Fundamentally distrustful of the exuberant, chaotic, and participatory nature of the Chilean polis under Allende, Pinochet sought to radically depoliticize Chilean society by attacking the institutional framework of Chilean democracy: closing Congress, banning first the parties of the Popular Unity and then all political parties, and declaring illegal myriad civil society groups (neighborhood associations, peasant groups, student groups, women's groups, etc.) that had both created and funneled Chilean political expression. Widespread purges of administrative and bureaucratic personnel were conducted, and "virtually all important national institutions (including the soccer federation) were assigned to generals or admirals, colonels or captains."[2] The most repressive and brutal of the attempts to remake Chilean politics and society were directed at the supporters of the Popular Unity government. In the weeks following the coup, the military detained thousands of Chileans, and many of the most active supporters of the UP were disappeared and killed.[3] Others were imprisoned or forced to flee Chile as political exiles.

Human rights groups, including the AFDD, began to form shortly after the coup in response to these abuses. Chileans, not yet understanding the horror of state-sponsored disappearances, went searching for information about their loved ones who had been taken into custody by the police or armed forces. The new military regime, however, refused to provide information or to follow the standard procedures of Chilean judicial processes. The judicial system also failed to act to protect the disappeared person, as "judges typically accepted at face value the word of government officials that the 'disappeared' were not in custody."[4]

In the face of bureaucratic stonewalling by the new military government and continuing repression, many Chileans turned to their churches for help. Religious organizations, particularly the Catholic Church, represented some of the few remaining institutions outside military control. The Catholic Church, working with the Lutheran, Methodist, and Jewish communities, as well as the ecumenical World Council of Churches, provided an umbrella of protection and institutional support for many of the family members searching for loved ones. Organized only a month after the coup, the Committee for Cooperation

2. Collier and Sater, *History of Chile*, 359.
3. Ibid., 360.
4. Loveman, *Chile*, 263.

for Peace labored to help families find their relatives and demanded that the military inform the families of the status and conditions of those detained.[5] Pinochet and the military government fiercely resisted the committee and forced it to disband in 1975. But Cardinal Raúl Silva Henríquez quickly reorganized the group as the Vicaría de la Solidaridad under the auspices of the archbishopric of Santiago. This placed the organization completely within the Catholic Church, thereby partly shielding it from government repression. From 1976 on, the Vicaría "provided legal defense and tirelessly filed habeas corpus actions on behalf of family members."[6] Many hoped that these actions would force the government to publicly acknowledge whether a person was in government custody, what the charges were, and where the person was being held.[7]

Alongside the Vicaría, the family members of those detained or disappeared began to organize. Formed in 1974, the AFDD was one of the first organizations that condemned Pinochet and his government for violating the human rights of Chileans. Family ties and familial identities were at the heart of the AFDD. According to the group's public statements, the ties of love and caring that bound families together gave them the strength to search for their missing loved ones despite the continuing repression and danger. The AFDD turned to familial roles to explain why its members had mobilized. This dominant narrative can be seen in a 1983 illustrated pamphlet designed to explain to the general public what the AFDD was, why it had organized, and why it protested the government. Titled *Asi lo hemos vivido* (This was how we lived), the pamphlet explained political repression through its familial effects. Following the disappearance of a person, "everything was painful, desperate, the families did not know what to do. The only thing that was clear was that they must look for them and find them as soon as possible." The drawings accompanying the text show women searching for their husbands, sons, or brothers. One woman, holding her baby in her arms, says, "He is not in the clinic or in prison. Where is he?" Another woman, who appears pregnant, says, "I have been looking for him for so long. Will he ever get to see our child?" Standing in front of a government office, one woman tells another woman, "My son is gone," and then asks, "Who do you have disappeared?" (fig. 6.1).[8]

5. Ensalaco, *Chile Under Pinochet*, 58–62.
6. Ibid., 61.
7. Loveman, *Chile*, 263.
8. AFDD, *Asi lo hemos vivido*, 31. I thank the Fundación de Documentación y Archivo de la Vicaría de la Solidaridad for granting me permission to reproduce the images from *Asi lo hemos vivido* and the magazine *Solidaridad*. Their extensive archive of documents relating to the activities of

Fig. 6.1   "What happened?" (AFDD, *Asi lo hemos vivido.*)

Other drawings depicted the persistence of the searchers and hinted at the number of people affected by the disappearances. For example, under the caption "In the search we found each other," a drawing shows the various places where the families had met: in front of the National Stadium, the morgue, the hospital, the jail, the Supreme Court, the Vicaría, in the streets of Santiago, and other locations across the country (fig. 6.2). In front stands a line of men, women, and children, with either masks over their eyes or with their backs to the reader. The question marks appearing on many of the figures designate them as missing, evoking the central question that organized the AFDD: "Where are they?" The words and the pictures work together to project the sense of anguish felt by the families as they fruitlessly searched for their loved ones.[9] The organization did not claim that its genesis was located in a political cause or ideology, but rather in the easily understood actions of family members, most often mothers and wives. As stated by a member of the AFDD, "Starting from our desperate search, with our pain and anguish to know about our children, parents, spouses and brothers, we got to know each other."[10] Familial

---

human rights and poblador groups, as well as opposition publications, was an invaluable resource for this project. Most of the sources relating to the activities of the AFDD and around the issue of housing are part of the Vicaría's collection.

9. Ibid., 43.

10. AFDD de Región V, *Report*, 27 January 1979, 2.

Fig. 6.2 "In the search we found each other." (AFDD, *Asi lo hemos vivido.*)

identities were central to how AFDD members understood the reasons behind their actions, and they drew courage and conviction from those identities and ties. The search by the family members, and thus the formation of the AFDD, was presented not as explicitly political, but rather as rooted in the feelings and duties that bound families together. In a context where overt political actions were easily repressed, a familial narrative provided political benefits. The AFDD turned to family identities and a discourse of familial relationships to open a space for their claims against a military government that was attempting to eliminate all public criticism.

The AFDD further argued that the military government, by refusing to acknowledge and respond to the legitimate request of the families, had in fact driven the family members to form the organization. The AFDD described its interactions with the military government in the following way: "The families presented appeals on the grounds of unconstitutionality = 'They were rejected.' The families presented actions and denunciations = 'The records have been filed.' The families wrote letters to the generals = 'There was no response.' The families asked the ministers of the interior, justice, and defense for interviews = 'There were no audiences.' All of the authorities have said, 'There are no detained. There is no information.' At the end = Silence."[11] As suggested by these equations of the state with a lack of action, the military government was unwilling to help the families find their loved ones or to provide any information about missing persons, leaving the families no choice but "to organize, to fight together and confront united the lies and the intent to hide and silence the truth."[12] As dramatized in figure 6.1, a government official tells a woman, "[His name] does not appear in the list of the detained. Don't look anymore!"[13] Given this reception, the AFFD had to organize "to save the lives of our family members detained and sequestered by the security apparatus of this military government."[14] The AFDD used the family to carve out a space to speak out against the Pinochet regime. It was as family members that they had gone searching; it was as family members that they had organized the AFDD; and it was as family members that they had approached the government and the public.

In employing the family to mobilize its members and frame its critiques of the government, the AFDD also directly confronted the political narrative of Pinochet and his government. Instead of protecting and caring for them, AFDD members claimed that Pinochet had destroyed their families and their homes through his policies. These sentiments were visually depicted in the *Asi lo hemos vivido* pamphlet. One drawing, titled "Como afecta a la familia" (How it affects the family), conveys its point through before and after pictures (fig. 6.3). Before, the family comprises a couple, their two young children, and a grandmother, and all of them are smiling and standing before a healthy, fruit-bearing tree. The after picture presents a cutout of the man with a question mark placed on his face, signifying that he had been disappeared. The grief of the remaining family members is shown through the frowns on their faces, while behind them the family tree has lost all its leaves and fruit. Thus the disappearance of the husband/father/son symbolically destroys the family, even if some individual members survive.[15]

A similar claim, that the political repression of Pinochet had destroyed Chilean families, was depicted through another image in the pamphlet (fig. 6.4). This time, the picture showed a house torn apart by the policies of exile (*exilio*) and repression (*represion*), which causes misery (*miseria*), loneliness (*soledad*), fear (*miedo*), and flight (*huida*).[16]

11. AFDD, *Asi lo hemos vivido*, 32.
12. AFDD de Región V, *Report*, 27 January 1979, 2.
13. AFDD, *Asi lo hemos vivido*, 31.
14. AFDD de Región V, *Report*, 27 January 1979, 2.
15. AFDD, *Asi lo hemos vivido*, 85.
16. Ibid., 89.

Fig. 6.3 "How it affects the family." (AFDD, *Asi lo hemos vivido.*)

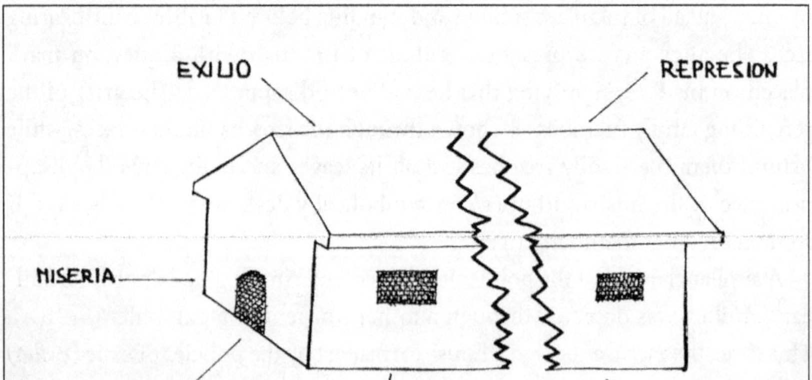

Fig. 6.4 "Exile, repression." (AFDD, *Asi lo hemos vivido.*)

In its public actions, the AFDD often drew on women's familial roles in particular, presenting its members as the grieving mothers, sisters, wives, and daughters of the disappeared. The protesting women wore on their chests black-and-white pictures of their missing loved ones, and they often carried placards bearing an enlarged photo of the missing person with the person's name, the date disappeared, and the question "Donde están?" (Where are they?).[17] The picture identifies the woman as not just an individual but also as the mother, wife, sister, or daughter of the missing person. As Marjorie Agosín noted, "Photographs have become the talismans, the symbols of mothers looking for their missing children. . . . The photograph says, 'Here it is, that's what he looks like, he exists.'"[18]

Such symbolic evocation of relational identities was epitomized in a form of protest that the AFDD developed in 1978. The Conjunto Folclórico (Folkloric Group) added to the repertoire of protest action the rhythms and visuals of the *cueca*, a traditional Chilean dance. Traditionally, the *cueca* is performed by a couple and represents romantic courtship. Danced at *peñas*—gatherings where Chileans get together to sing and dance, drink wine, and eat empanadas to celebrate the independence of Chile or other festivities—the *cueca* evokes fond memories for many Chileans. The Conjunto transformed the traditional *cueca* from a dance celebrating love to a dance through which the wife mourns the absence of her missing husband and plaintively asks, "Where is he? Who has forced me to dance alone?" As Marjorie Agosín has argued, the *cueca sola* became a way for the women "to denounce the government's actions in a public space."[19] It is important to note that the women claimed this right to public space through drawing on their familial roles and identities. The Conjunto also performed in street demonstrations, at the Caupolicán Theater in a program celebrating International Women's Day, and in front of delegations from the United Nations.[20] The importance of the *cueca sola* as a symbol of the human rights movements was carried over into international popular culture when Sting wrote and recorded his 1987 hit "They Dance Alone" to publicize the plight of the disappeared in Chile and Argentina.

17. Like the Madres de Plaza de Mayo, this is the iconic image of the AFDD and continues to be used today in protests. A good source of such images is AFDD, *Un camino de imágenes*. Drawings made by AFDD members are featured in *Asi lo hemos vivido*. This image of the women is also reproduced in *arpilleras* (hand-sewn tapestries made by Chilean women, often from burlap and yarn), which can be found in Agosín, *Scraps of Life*, and Agosín, *Tapestries of Hope*.

18. Agosín, *Scraps of Life*, 85–86.

19. Agosín, *Tapestries of Hope*, 34.

20. Descriptions and pictures of the protests can be found in AFDD, *Un camino de imágenes*.

The Conjunto also changed the traditional love songs of the *cueca* into songs about the disappearance of a family member. Often the Conjunto would create new songs to commemorate the ongoing actions of the AFDD, such as the *cueca* they wrote and performed at the Lonquén mine in memory of the secret grave discovered there in 1979. The text highlights the familial relations of the women and explains the nature of the *cueca sola*:

Soy madre, soy esposa,	I am a mother, I am a wife,
soy hija, soy hermana.	I am a daughter, I am a sister.
Yo me llamo Pisagua[21]	I am called Pisagua and I dance
y bailo *cueca*.	the *cueca*.
Yo bailo para ti.	I dance for you.
Yo bailo *la cueca* y bailo sola.	I dance the *cueca* and I dance alone.[22]

Multiple uses of the family are present in this *cueca*. First, it is through the family that the place of the speaker is legitimized. She is the female relative of the missing person; she feels and knows the pain caused by the disappearance of her loved one. The singer also invites the audience to relate to this pain through their shared familial identities and to support the AFDD in demanding answers from the military government. Thus familial relations serve to create legitimacy for the speaker and her actions as well as to evoke empathy and support for her cause.

The public demonstrations of the AFDD members, armed with their pictures of disappeared family members, dramatically represented the violence and suffering experienced by Chilean families because of the repressive policies of Pinochet and the military government. Women, who were often the public face of the AFDD, contested Pinochet's claims that his actions were designed to protect Chilean mothers and their children. Images of grieving women were a staple in magazines critical of the government, such as *Solidaridad* and *Apsi*. A typical depiction appeared on the cover of *Solidaridad* in September 1979, featuring a picture of four women crying at the memorial mass given in honor of the remains found in Lonquén. The black-and-white pictures pinned to their coats clearly identify the women as members of the AFDD.

Often, the reporting of the AFDD's public events by opposition magazines explicitly contrasted the present government's rhetorical commitment to families

21. Pisagua is the name of an old nitrate port city in northern Chile that served as a detention center after the military coup and from which many prisoners disappeared.
22. AFDD, *Un camino de imágenes*, 31.

with the lived experiences of the mothers of the disappeared. An excellent example was an article in *Solidaridad* about an AFDD demonstration on Mother's Day, which directly contrasted the pro-family, pro-mother rhetoric of the government with the reality of the mothers of the disappeared:

> It was the middle of the day on Thursday the tenth of May, Mother's Day. Earlier, the wife of the head of state had sent her greetings to Chilean mothers, wishing them a happy celebration with their children. A few hours later, the pedestrian passage of Ahumada Street witnessed the shocking and anguished call of dozens of mothers carrying their small children in their arms and holding signs written with unsure letters. [They were] crying out to know the whereabouts of their children and husbands: "For my child, Señor! Since Tuesday I have not seen him. They assaulted me at my home! I want my child! Please . . . I cannot find him anywhere!"

In addition to focusing on the pain of mothers grieving over their disappeared children, the article described in great detail the actions of the police, who arrested the women after confiscating their placards. The article stressed that even mothers carrying their children were arrested. It claimed that this lack of respect for the mothers elicited a strong reaction from the public audience in front of the Metropolitan Cathedral in the Plaza de Armas, the central plaza of downtown Santiago.[23] The article highlighted the hypocrisy of a government that on the one hand wished mothers a happy Mother's Day, and on the other hand destroyed families and arrested mothers.

In a culture so steeped in the traditions of the Catholic Church, the image of the grieving mother symbolically invokes the Virgin Mary and her grief over the death of her son. In statements supporting the work of the AFDD, the Catholic Church often invoked images of mothers, sisters, or daughters grieving for the lost son, husband, father, and child. In the mass given for the victims of Lonquén, Cristían Precht, the vicar to the Vicaría de la Solidaridad, made the grieving daughter the central motif of his sermon. The discourse exemplified how supportive members of the Catholic Church sought to transform personal tragedy into a call for political change:

> Today, in this place of Lonquén, we have encountered the cries of the

23. "Derechos humanos: Con avances y retrocesos," *Solidaridad*, 18–31 May 1984, 5.

daughter of our people, and the question arises in us when we see these women crying: For whom do you cry, daughter of my people? The first answer is that the daughter of my people cries because her children have been killed; because her children were taken from their home and found in the abandoned mine of Lonquén. For this reason cries the daughter of my people.

The daughter of my people also cries because here are other women; wives, mothers, daughters, friends of others that have been detained and disappeared, and for them also cries the daughter of my people. . . . They cry because in the Patria they have lost the sense of life . . .

The daughter of my people does not only cry. She is also capable of fighting . . .

We want to make a patria in which, like a family, we can have distinct ideas, distinct projects, distinct ideals, and put them in common, as they do in the table of the home, in the neighborhood, or in the community. . . . This is the way that we all understand the fight of the Agrupación de Familiares de Detenidos Desaparecidos. They are fighting for their life. Yes! But they are also fighting for the patria. They are fighting so that other children will not suffer this disgrace; they are fighting so that other mothers will not have to protest by weeping.[24]

The repeated use of familial metaphors positions the listeners as symbolically related to those in the AFDD. The mourning members of the AFDD are the daughters of the patria, presented as an ideal family that deals with its differences around a table and without violence. The speaker, Father Precht, constructs the grieving women within their familial relationships, as daughters, mothers, and wives. Through these relationships, others are asked to understand their grief and to join them. But their sorrow is not only for their children but also for anyone living in a country that allowed this type of grief to be visited on women. The sermon ends with a call to support the work of the AFDD. The AFDD members are positioned as fighting not for just their own particular families but for other Chilean families and the metaphoric family of the nation. In addition, an idealized vision of family, where differences are handled without violence, is presented as an example of what has been destroyed by the actions of the current government. The AFDD is fighting for a return of a government that protects its children, so that "other mothers" will not have to

24. Homily given by Cristián B. Precht, 25 February 1979, available at the Centro de Documentación de Vicaría de la Solidaridad.

grieve. The sermon recognizes the public grief of women as a form of protest. By publicly weeping, by sharing their sorrows, mothers, daughters, and wives fight against a government that had brought death to the Chilean nation.

What did the AFDD gain through these uses of family? First, beliefs about family helped members to create a space from which to criticize the government. Given that the group, at least at the beginning, had the practical aim of trying to find the missing person and then secure the release of that person, members needed to craft a discourse that could be recognized as legitimate by the military government and by the general Chilean society. The ongoing repression of explicitly political activities, and the attempts on the part of the military government to portray any opposition as driven by a desire to destroy the Chilean nation, meant that activism that could be framed as familial, and thus presumably apolitical, was afforded some protection. In its presentation of human rights violations, the AFDD asked Chileans to consider whether the government had the right to deny families information about the fate of their loved ones. Familial identities also provided a bridge between AFDD members and the wider public. AFDD members asked their fellow Chileans to identify the group's actions as driven by familial ties, not political conviction. Any mother, father, wife, daughter, or son would do the same. Finally, the importance of the Catholic Church in providing both material and symbolic support to the AFDD cannot be overlooked. The belief in the sanctity of the family and of familial bonds provided one basis for the ongoing relationship between the AFDD and the Catholic Church. The AFDD astutely turned to the ideals of Militant Families to pursue its goals.

The Family Exposed: The Housing Movement

The AFDD was not the only opposition group to turn to the nexus of beliefs about the relationships among the state, citizens, and the family in its struggles against Pinochet. Similar uses can be found throughout the myriad groups that began organizing in the late 1970s and 1980s in the poblaciones around economic issues. These groups used familial identities to organize and familial beliefs to justify their political actions. As with the AFDD, organizing around family welfare (and based on familial identities) often reflected how people understood the concrete effects of Pinochet's economic policies. As was also the case with the AFDD, the family provided specific political benefits for these groups as they engaged in political struggles against the government.

One major issue around which mobilization took place was the continued lack of adequate housing for the poor in Santiago. The housing crisis was rooted in the ongoing rural-to-urban migration. By the early 1950s, rural migration had "exceeded industrial growth, rendering the city impotent in the face of the growing demand for housing and forcing over 45 percent of Santiago's population to seek shelter in substandard or unsanitary housing."[25] In 1957, the first organized *toma* (illegal land occupation) took place in the neighborhood of La Victoria. Involving three thousand families and "organized by the Communist Party's Committee of the Homeless," this action would set a pattern for future poblador attempts to deal with the problems of housing deficits.[26]

The other political parties of the center and left, always searching for new issues and voters, soon embraced the call for more governmental involvement. In the late 1960s, the Frei government began addressing the lack of affordable housing. His government created a Ministry of Housing, funded the Popular Savings Plan (in which the government underwrote loans through private banks for the construction and improvement of homes), and instituted Operación Sitio (Operation Place), "self-help housing projects" in which the government provided the land and some technical assistance for poor families to build their own homes.[27] Frei's housing policies mostly benefited poor families that already had some resources. Those not receiving the benefits—and unhappy with the pace of reform—often decided to continue to occupy land around Santiago.[28]

The successes and failures of Frei's housing policies were a matter of great debate during the 1970 presidential campaign. Tomic, Frei's PDC successor, promised to deepen and accelerate Frei's housing policies, with the aim to provide a house for every Chilean family. Allende stressed his commitment to housing as a right of all Chilean families, and he promoted state programs designed to help Chile's working-class families secure dignified living spaces.[29] After winning the election, Allende focused his housing policies on building "popular" housing that could be purchased by Chilean families based on a percentage of their income.[30] But the pobladores living in the urban shantytowns often felt that the reforms were moving too slowly and took matters into their

25. Schneider, *Shantytown Protest*, 41.
26. Ibid., 43.
27. Loveman, *Chile*, 239.
28. Schneider's *Shantytown Protest* explores the important role played by the Communist Party in organizing the *tomas* as well as its relationship to the families that composed the new shantytowns.
29. See chapter 2.
30. Sergio Marras, "Las casas en que nos vivimos," *Apsi*, August 1980, 2.

own hands. Often led by more radical groups within the Popular Unity coalition, "illegal urban land seizures rose tenfold and accounted for one-quarter of the growth in the shantytown population of Santiago" during the Allende years.[31]

After the military coup, the lack of adequate housing continued to be a major issue. By 1980, Pinochet's policies had exacerbated the housing crisis in Santiago, increasing the housing deficit to 699,000 houses, which affected 31 percent of the population.[32] Throughout the 1980s, the lived reality of more and more Chilean families was a lack of housing options, homelessness, and being forced to live as *allegados* in the homes of friends or other family members. The pobladores continued to organize around housing. Even amid heavy government repression, a new wave of *tomas* by homeless families began in 1979.[33]

Ongoing activism on the part of shantytown residents, often connected to the now-banned political parties, drew on their previous struggles and past government actions to define housing as a problem that primarily affected families, as opposed to workers, peasants, students, and so forth. As a family issue, housing represented a legitimate demand that even the military government had to recognize. Press reports on the growing number of *tomas* reinforced the familial framing. In interviews, the *toma* participants stressed that they had been driven to their actions because of the precarious situation of their families. For example, when the participants of the first *tomas* in 1979 were interviewed, they stressed their lack of options as a family and their desperation to fulfill their roles as mothers and fathers. Ghislaine Kruiget, identified in the report as married, age twenty-five, and mother of four children, claimed that her family's recent eviction left them no choice but to take part in the *toma*: "I have four children and my husband is unemployed; therefore, we had to do something. It is true that we took this site, but without bothering anybody; if we were given a solution, we would leave without any problem."[34] For Kruiget, she and her husband had been driven to participate in order to provide housing for their children, not necessarily to protest the government. Implicitly, however, the lack of other options is laid at the feet of the current government. Even Chilean newspapers, which were both censored and ideologically supportive

31. Schneider, *Shantytown Protest*, 68.
32. According to a study by the Centro de Investigaciones Socioeconómicas, cited in Marras, "Las casas," 2.
33. See, for example, "Diez detenidos en la 'toma' de sitio Eriazo," *La Tercera*, 8 November 1979, and "Tomas de sitios en La Cisterna," *Las Ultimas Notícias*, 19 November 1979.
34. "Tomas de sitios en La Cisterna," *Las Ultimas Notícias*, 19 November 1979.

of Pinochet, wrote generally sympathetic stories that highlighted the familial identities of the participants, characterizing them as young "couples with two or three children, who lived as *allegados* with their parents or other relatives."[35] The stories about the ongoing *tomas* claimed that these families were willing to brave possible repression just to escape their constrained existence and to own their own homes.

The military government was clearly unhappy with the renewed occupations and the sympathetic press reporting of the young families. Determined to end the new round of popular mobilization around housing, the government turned to more repressive measures. On 1 April 1980 a policy promulgated by the Ministry of Housing stated that people that had been involved in illegal occupations "would remain unable to be assigned public housing," a punitive measure designed to increase the cost to poblador families for participating in future *tomas*.[36] Pinochet and his government also attacked the public presentation of the participants as poor Chilean families who were simply searching for a better place to live. The general argued that the *tomas* were actually the work of political subversives using the families as a way to shield their political actions. The governor of Santiago, General Rolando Garay Cinfuentes, for example, issued a public statement to the media in which he noted, "One can lament that the pobladores were tricked by false expectations, by those who induced them to take this type of illegal action." Here the families are presented as naïve victims of subversive elements. General Garay stressed that *tomas* were not permitted in any circumstance under current law. He further called on the pobladores to return to their previous dwellings, because they were interfering with the orderly eradication of the shantytowns by the government. The general indicated that if the families left, the authorities would help them to find alternative sites, but that if they did not, they would be evicted.[37]

General Garay also stressed that he wanted to make it very clear that "this type of pressure will not be accepted by the government. . . . [The families] have committed a grave error." Garay again stressed the belief of the government that the trouble had been caused by "people interested in creating problems," who had tricked innocent families into joining the takeover. Ignoring the poverty and unemployment that constrained the ability of the pobladores

---

35. "Deben abandonar sitios tomados," *El Mercurio*, 15 March 1980.
36. "No somos usurpadores," *Las Ultimas Noticias*, 9 April 1980.
37. "Los pobladores del campamento Nuevo Amanecer serán ubicados en otro lugar," *La Tercera*, 19 March 1980.

to obtain housing, he framed the issues through the government's neoliberal belief that housing was not a right, and that those families "that desire a house or a legal site can obtain [these goods] with work, with force, with the sacrifice of everyone of the family group."[38] Following the government's lead, *La Nación*, a pro-government paper, featured a half-page picture of women and children crowded together, accompanied by a caption that speculated that the "illegal occupants" had possibly used the children "to stop police action." The caption continues, "There were children everywhere in La Bandera. The illegal occupants gathered the little ones, perhaps to chill police action. Everything was planned."[39] In other words, the families involved could not claim innocence if they had been willing to place their children in harm's way in order to make a political point against the government. The pobladores taking part in the *tomas* were positioned as "bad" or "failed" families. Pinochet and his government sought to undermine the familial presentation of the pobladores as a way of responding to the implicit critique that the military government was failing these Chilean families.

While the government might have hoped to control the actions and public perception of the pobladores, the *tomas* continued to grow throughout the 1980s. Indeed, the *tomas* represented the first large-scale protests against government policies within the poblaciones. As the movement grew, the detrimental effects of the housing crisis on familial welfare became the basis for a pointed critique of Pinochet and his policies. For example, in April 1980, eight thousand families without homes in the western areas of Santiago sent a letter to the minister of housing asking for solutions to the housing problem. The letter justified the actions of the pobladores by stressing the enormous amount of suffering caused by homelessness within Chilean families, particularly to the children. A leader of the Committee of the Homeless, a key group in the broader poblador movement, estimated that a "total of almost twenty-four thousand children live in subhuman conditions," and that in the summer children suffered with "constant diarrhea, sickness, and infection. And in the winter there is the problem of the communal colds, bronchitis, and so forth."[40] The poblador families engaged in the *tomas* attempted to mitigate government repression by stressing the familial nature of their actions, stating, "We only want the authorities to remember that we are poblador families, and we do not have

38. Ibid.
39. "Toma en población La Bandera," *La Nación*, 23 July 1980. See also reports in the *La Nación* on 24 July 1980 and in *El Mercurio* on 25 July 1980.
40. Radio Cooperativa, *Programa El Diario*, 1 April 1980.

any arms other than our convictions that we are acting fairly."[41] In other words, government repression would be directed against unarmed families, not armed, subversive political groups. Thus the public statements from the Committees of the Homeless sought to contest the government's claims that the families involved had been tricked into illegal action, were fronts for the actions of banned political groups, or simply were greedy individuals who wanted a house without the necessary familial sacrifices. The pobladores created a counter-narrative through the testimony of many of the participants, who again and again referenced their families' legitimate needs, their lack of options in meeting them, and the responsibility of the government to provide help in meeting those needs.[42] The persuasiveness of the pobladores' argument rested on broader beliefs about the importance of family and the responsibilities of the government.

As with the AFDD, the actions of the Committees of the Homeless were supported by the Catholic Church. Following the lead of the pobladores, the Catholic Church also portrayed housing as an issue that affected the family and around which families had a right to organize. The church "had come to the conclusion that the problem is tremendously dramatic. It concerns families that belong to the sectors most marginalized in society. The majority of them do not have work. . . . The most numerous cases correspond to families with children that live as *allegados* with relatives or friends before adopting their determination to occupy the land."[43] The Catholic Church also directly contested the government's portrayal of the families as political agitators; instead, it stressed the pobladores' actions as being a necessary and logical response of families. For the church, as for the pobladores, housing was an issue that directly affected familial welfare. The Catholic Church held the position that poblador families had a legitimate reason to organize and demand governmental action to solve the problem. As Archbishop Silva, the highest Catholic official in Chile, had affirmed in his visit with the participants of the *toma* at La Granja in 1980, theirs were "just demands" and deserved governmental support, not repression.[44]

In November 1980, the Vicaría de la Solidaridad organized a conference on "Popular Family and Housing," which brought together pobladores involved in the Committees of the Homeless, priests and laity who worked in the

41. "Toma en población La Bandera," *La Nación*, 23 July 1980.
42. "El gobierno no acepta 'tomas,'" *Las Ultimas Noticias*, 14 March 1980.
43. "Cardenal Silva lloró al visitar refugio en población La Bandera," *La Tercera*, 24 July 1980.
44. Ibid.

poblaciones, and housing professionals. This meeting strengthened the familial arguments used by the participants of the *tomas* and illustrates the dominant framework for using the housing crisis to criticize the military government during the next ten years. First, the lack of housing was portrayed as a problem affecting families. Second, housing was presented as a right and not as a consumer good. Finally, the participants argued that a government that failed to provide for Chilean families did not deserve to rule.

For housing activists, the family, not individuals, was the ultimate victim of the lack of adequate housing in Chile. This was explicitly stated in the letter sent by the Vicaría announcing the conference: "It is known to everyone the extremely grave problem that exists in the areas of housing and that affects the integral life of the nation and in a special way the popular family. . . . There are hundreds of thousands of families that lack the indispensable and sufficient means to exercise their right to have a dignified habitation." Indeed, the lack of housing interfered with proper family life. This meant that "the humane and social virtues cannot develop in a normal form," which leaves the family vulnerable to drug addiction, alcoholism, prostitution, delinquency, traumatization of children, and overall health problems.[45] The pobladores also argued that the lack of healthy familial living caused "family disintegration . . . problems in the relationships within the family and within the *población*, problems in the formation of children, [and] . . . having to choose between paying the rent or feeding the family."[46] The overall health of family members suffered from sicknesses caused by the lack of hygiene, as well as alcoholism and drug addiction.[47] Further, homeless families lacked the ability to provide an adequate education to their children in these circumstances. The housing and social professionals in attendance rounded off the consensus. In their reports, they emphasized the disruptive nature of housing problems for families. Effects such as disintegration, aggression, neurosis, and impermanence were all discussed.[48] The three groups involved—pobladores, pastoral agents, and professionals—agreed on the types of familial problems created by the lack of housing, and they also agreed that having a house would help solve these problems.[49]

In addition to portraying the family as the ultimate victim of the housing

45. Vicaría de la Solidaridad, "Seminario de la familia popular," 11.
46. Ibid., 8–9.
47. Ibid., 9.
48. Ibid., 14.
49. In presenting home ownership as a panacea for other social ills, the participants could draw on the housing campaigns of Frei and Allende, both of whom had constructed home ownership along the same lines. See my discussion in chapter 3.

crisis, the conference participants claimed that families had a right to demand adequate housing from the government. Their reports argued that all Chilean families had "the right to housing [that] is more than a site and a roof: it is the right to a dignified space that permits the integral development of the human, the family, and the community."[50] The magnitude of the problem meant that there were "hundreds of thousands of Chilean families that cannot count on the minimum elements to exercise their right to a dignified house." Participants strongly criticized "the actual housing policy," which "conceives of housing as an individual good that is commercialized in accordance to the laws of the market, and one that must be achieved through one's own means."[51] This opposition discourse being developed around housing by the church, the pobladores, and the professionals vehemently argued that adequate housing was the right of every Chilean family. As the base for society, the family had the right to adequate housing and could legitimately demand the satisfaction of that right from the government. This right was founded on the belief that the well-being of the family was integral to the proper development of the "common good," which was the proper aim of political society.[52] Further, this well-being could not be achieved without a "house," understood as a space for the development of family life. The military government's own public discourse on the family recognized and reaffirmed the basic position of the family in society and justified a wide array of government actions by invoking the need to protect Chilean families. The pobladores, therefore, could draw on the government's own discourse to justify their demands for housing.

After having established the detrimental effects of the housing crisis on the family and the right of families to housing, the blame for the current crisis clearly belonged with Pinochet and his government. In particular, the conference participants blamed the lack of adequate resources directed toward housing, combined with the general political-economic policies of the government, for the suffering and the misery of Chilean families. These overall economic policies had impoverished poblador families through promoting unemployment, underemployment, and low salaries. Pinochet's housing policies, according to the pobladores, not only lacked adequate funding but also were disproportionately directed toward middle- and upper-class families, who could already afford housing. In pursuing policies that failed to address the housing crisis,

50. Vicaría de la Solidaridad, "Seminario de la familia popular," 7.

51. Ibid.

52. Vicaría de la Solidaridad, "Convocatoria" (opening statement) by Father Reyes for the "Seminario de la familia popular."

the participants claimed that Pinochet and his government had reneged on their responsibility to help poor Chilean families survive and prosper.[53] The system created by the military "developed a logic that preferred only the sector with the highest incomes," favored individualism over community cohesion, and did not have "channels through which to approach the authorities."[54] They argued that the "habitational problems of the popular sectors demanded a massive response," and they decried the fact that the "right to housing" was being consigned to individual efforts.[55] Church and poblador organizations like the Committees of the Homeless directly attacked the neoliberal positioning of housing as simply another "good" that could be purchased in a market and that depended on the individual efforts of people to be secured. Again and again, housing was presented not as an issue of individuals, but rather of families, communities, and the nation. By positioning housing as one of the crucial components needed by the family, providing housing became a duty and responsibility of the government, and not simply a question of individual effort or discretionary largesse on the part of Pinochet. Conference participants argued that if the government failed to provide better solutions to the housing problem, it was failing to provide for Chilean families and did not deserve to rule.

Over the next ten years, the opposition continued to use the family to frame the ongoing housing crisis by focusing on these three points. Housing issues were a prominent topic in *Solidaridad*, *Apsi*, and statements by the Catholic Church. These two publications often positioned the family as the ultimate victim of Pinochet's housing policies, as can be seen from the June 1982 *Solidaridad* cover shown in figure 6.5. Families continued to suffer from "family disintegration, overcrowding, lack of hygiene, humiliation, infections, alcoholism, drug addiction, low scholarly performance, school desertion."[56] Ongoing critiques compared the lack of current government action with the policies of the past democratic governments, which had recognized the right of Chilean families to housing. For example, an article in *Apsi* argued that previously "the state always, through diverse programs, directed important resources to help those who could not count on dignified housing. . . . Today, housing is not considered to be a 'social good.'" The article further claimed that poor families were ignored and estimated that of the 627,000 homeless families in

53. Vicaría de la Solidaridad, "Seminario de la familia popular," 9–10.
54. Ibid., 12.
55. Ibid., 13.
56. "Sin casa, sin esperanza," *Apsi*, 10–23 February 1981, 7.

Fig. 6.5 "The homeless in search of a home." (*Solidaridad*, June 1982.)

1983, only 46,000 had applied for the housing subsidies established in 1978.[57] Another study estimated that even in the expanded programs, dedicated supposedly to helping poor families, only 11.4 percent of the 210,368 families that applied had received benefits.[58]

Throughout the 1980s, the lack of adequate solutions to the persistent housing crisis continued to generate opposition to Pinochet. The declaration by the United Nations establishing 1987 as the International Year of Shelter for the Homeless reinvigorated the opposition movement on this issue. To culminate the year of action, the archbishopric of Santiago along with the UN-supported Comisión Económica para América Latina y el Caribe (Economic Commission for Latin America and the Caribbean) sponsored a conference on "Family and Housing," which reinforced the themes developed in the 1980 conference. Once again, participants testified about the myriad problems suffered by Chilean families, and the community at large, because of the lack of housing. As the conference participants declared, "The family cannot fulfill its mission if it does not have a house."[59] Opposition magazines like *Solidaridad, Apsi,* and *Mensaje* argued that the government had marginalized its role in constructing low-cost housing, handing off its duty to a private sector more interested in building houses for the middle and upper class. At the end of seventeen years of rule by Pinochet, the housing statistics featured in multiple articles presented a bleak picture. More than 1.2 million families—or one in three—did not have their own housing.[60] While Pinochet pledged to build 70,000 houses in 1987, by that date many experts believed that at least 845,000 houses would be required to meet the housing needs of Chilean families.[61] Multiple articles in *Solidaridad* featured the now-common pictures of families trying to make a home for themselves in the flimsy, one-room shelters constructed in the shantytowns, which continued to lack access to running water, sewers, and electricity.[62]

In the last few years of the Pinochet government, the opposition continually used the housing crisis to criticize Pinochet. Housing came to symbolize the lack of commitment on the part of Pinochet and his government to the problems facing many Chilean families. To combat the opposition's charges, Pinochet

57. Ibid.

58. *Solidaridad,* 15–30 June 1982, 16.

59. "Familia y vivienda," *Mensaje,* December 1987.

60. "Encuentro familia y vivienda: Compromiso con los sin hogar," *Solidaridad,* 20 November–4 December 1987, 10.

61. "La pobreza aloja con nosotros," *Solidaridad,* 13–26 June 1987, 16.

62. See, for example, *Solidaridad* 15–29 May, 30 May–12 June, 13–26 June, 17 September–1 October, 9–22 October, and 20 November–4 December 1987.

launched a propaganda campaign in 1987 called "Chile: One House . . . One Family," which implied a governmental commitment to a house for every family and symbolically cast the Chilean nation as one family.[63] The government directed substantial resources (estimated by *Apsi* to be ninety-eight million pesos) to a publicity campaign filled with images of Chilean families being presented with houses by the government. But the opposition attacked both the truthfulness and efficacy of the military government's housing policy. These groups argued that Pinochet's government had built far less housing than had the governments of Allende, Frei, and Alessandri. The opposition also contended that instead of spending money on housing, the military government spent money on lying about both the number of houses it was building and its commitment to making sure Chilean families had access to adequate homes. Whether Chilean families had access to adequate housing became a criterion by which to judge the government's commitment to Chilean families. The dramatic coverage of the housing crisis in Chile, and the construction of this crisis as a particularly familial problem, provided unique advantages to the opposition in the struggle over whether Pinochet and his government were fulfilling the responsibilities of the Familial State.

A New Democratic Family for Chile: The Women's Movement

The growth and tremendous scope of women's activism was a hallmark of social movements in Latin America during the 1970s and 1980s.[64] Indeed, the Chilean scholar Clarisa Hardy argued that not only did women compose the majority of participants in the popular movements in Chile, but they also were the driving force behind these movements.[65] Besides being the backbone of the human rights and popular movements, many women mobilized around their gender identities. Women's groups began analyzing how the problems facing Chilean society specifically affected women's lives. In this section, I analyze how two different strands within the women's movement evoked the family in their political struggles against Pinochet and his government. The first

---

63. "El gobierno y su campaña por la vivienda: Chile: Una casa, una mentira," *Apsi*, 8–14 June 1987.

64. For Chile, see Baldez, *Why Women Protest*; Chuchryk, "Feminist Anti-authoritarian Politics"; Dandavati, *Women's Movement*; Franceschet, *Women and Politics in Chile*, Frohman and Valdés, "Democracy in the Country"; and Gaviola, Largo, and Palestro, *Una historia necesaria*. For Latin America in general, see Jaquette, *Women's Movement* (1989/1994), and Radcliffe and Westwood, "*ViVa.*"

65. Hardy, *Organizarse para vivir*, 129–31.

strand focuses on popular feminism, which developed within the "struggle for women's rights among poor women." According to the political scientist Lisa Baldez, popular feminism "joins the everyday, survival-oriented concerns of *pobladoras* with an awareness of the larger causes of problems specific to women."[66] I focus particularly on the critiques developed by the Movimiento de Mujeres Pobladoras (MOMUPO), one of the most important popular feminist groups and the only one not directly affiliated with one of the political parties. Its actions and discourse represent many of the ways in which the broader women's movement drew on the nexus of beliefs between the Familial State, Patriarchal Leader, *and* Militant Families in its opposition to Pinochet. The second strand I examine is the explicitly feminist movement centered in a number of groups comprising professional and intellectual middle-class women.[67] Here, I focus on the development of a wide-ranging analysis and criticism of the connection between the patriarchal social structure of the family and the policies of the military government. In their arguments against the military government, feminist activists created a vision of democracy based on gender equality within the family.

THE MOVEMENT OF POPULAR WOMEN

MOMUPO's mobilization around familial beliefs strongly resembled the patterns found in both the human rights and housing movements. Once again, the family was used to mobilize members and to justify their right to protest, and as a criterion to judge the legitimacy of the military government. In 1979, a group of women who had been involved in the Catholic Action movement in the 1960s began to meet to discuss their experiences as women and as pobladoras.[68] MOMUPO began in these meetings. By the end of the 1980s, the group had become one of the most important popular women's organizations in Santiago. MOMUPO's members were dedicated to fostering the participation of women who either had not been politically active before the coup or had originally supported the military government and Pinochet. They sought to provide a space for women other than the government-run Mothers' Centers, which promoted conservative gender ideologies. To contest Pinochet's claims, they contrasted the quotidian experiences of Chilean families (in which men

---

66. Baldez, *Why Women Protest*, 137.
67. These groups included Centro de Estudios de la Mujer (Center for the Study of Women), La Morada, and Mujeres por la Vida (Women for Life), among a number of others.
68. Valdés and Weinstein, *Mujeres que sueñan*, 133; Baldez, *Why Women Protest*, 138.

were often unemployed and women were increasingly the sole providers) with the idealized families (which were economically secure and reflected traditional gender roles) featured in government propaganda. Chile's actual families were barely surviving on the combination of the limited welfare programs provided by the government, charitable organizations, the church, and community organizations such as the *ollas comunes*.[69]

MOMUPO's organizing strategies were rooted in the practice of consciousness-raising, which sought to transform women's understanding of the daily problems faced by their families as stemming not from personal, individual failings but from the larger political-economic system. As explained by Marina Valdés, one of the group's founders, MOMUPO wanted to help "the housewife, the ordinary woman" understand why "her family was splitting apart, her husband didn't have work, . . . she had to go to work, . . . her unemployed husband began to drink, . . . her children took drugs and . . . her husband, sitting at home, resented her going to work."[70] In other words, MOMUPO attempted to reach women through their identities as mothers and wives to help them understand how the problems facing their families were ultimately a symptom of the inequities promoted and defended by the military government.

In this process, MOMUPO placed women's concerns about their families at the center of its political arguments. MOMUPO claimed that it was women's familial identities and concern over their families' welfare that led women into politics. According to MOMUPO, in Chile "politics was the preferential area of men, and today, because of the fact of living in this situation of misery in their houses, it has taken a lot [for women] to open this space, to go out with other women to resolve their basic necessities."[71] MOMUPO framed women's political participation and demands by invoking women's concerns as wives and mothers for their families' welfare. Women's familial identities provided an accepted and powerful way to appeal to women of all political persuasions. The anti-Allende women's groups had used this tactic, as had earlier women's organizations in Chile.[72]

69. *Ollas comunes* translates as the "common pots." The name was used to designate community programs in which a neighborhood group would pool resources to produce a meal that would be shared with the community members. These *ollas comunes* were a common strategy for combating hunger and malnutrition in shantytown neighborhoods during the economic crisis, in Chile and elsewhere in Latin America.

70. Quoted in Baldez, *Why Women Protest*, 139.

71. MOMUPO, *Inquietudes de la lucha . . .* , September 1985.

72. For the use of this claim by anti-Allende women's groups, see Power, *Right-Wing Women*; Baldez, *Why Women Protest*; and chapter 4 of this work. For earlier uses, see Lavrin, *Women, Feminism, and Social Change*.

How MOMUPO stated its support for the National Accord provides an excellent example of this justification. Developed under the auspices of the Catholic Church and signed in 1985, the National Accord called for a transition to full democracy by recognizing the need for free elections, the "reestablishment of the rule of law," and a return to state responsibility for providing the basic necessities for a dignified familial life.[73] MOMUPO's statement in support of this measure read as follows: "We, the women, are those who give life, therefore, we will always defend life. For popular women these years of dictatorship have been years of DEATH. Unemployment is death. Hunger is death. Repression is death. The lack of a future for the youth is death."[74] The group's reasons for opposing the present regime could not be more forcefully stated. As mothers who give life, women must be opposed to a government that promotes policies that cause both the symbolic and the real death of their families.

The belief that women as wives and mothers acted to protect their families' welfare also framed MOMUPO's statements about the problems in health care, employment, housing, nutrition, the provision of water, sewers, and electricity, and the effects of political repression. For example, in one bulletin dedicated to discussing health care problems, MOMUPO argued, "We have the right to health. . . . We understand health as living spaces that are clean, hygienic, spacious, with light from the sun and green spaces, where our children can breathe clean air, where we can watch them run without the danger of a canal, of a drug dealer, without violence, nor repression. . . . The state should guarantee that I, you, our children, our families" have health. For MOMUPO, a healthy society could not be constructed with "malnourished children, with anguished and neurotic women, with frustrated and alcoholic men, with a youth that evades its lack of a future with drugs, alcohol, and prostitution."[75] According to MOMUPO, hunger and malnutrition "are every day more pronounced in our families." This familial reality led MOMUPO to "initiate campaigns against the hunger and the misery," which included practical actions such as the creation and maintenance of soup kitchens and the consciousness-raising of members about the causes of the situation. These women claimed that the basic cause of hunger was the government's lack of concern for the economic well-being of Chilean families, as evidenced by its refusal to control

---

73. Collier and Sater, *History of Chile*, 378.
74. MOMUPO, *Inquietudes de la lucha . . .* , September 1985.
75. MOMUPO, *Inquietudes de la lucha . . .* , August 1985.

prices for basic food items.[76] MOMUPO thus framed women's daily struggles as wives and mothers as a reason to mobilize. In particular, they blamed the problems of Chilean families on the government's policies and its failure to provide a situation in which Chilean families could flourish. Pinochet had reneged on the state's commitments to the health of Chilean families. The banging of pots and pans would again ring out in the evening hours in Santiago, now symbolizing the rejection of the military government's political and economic projects.

Further, MOMUPO argued that the lack of work was particularly harmful to the family because of its effects on men. Denied the opportunity to provide for their families, men who before had "worked every day putting their hands in service to a faith in having a more dignified life, for themselves and their families," were now drowning their difficulties in "bottles of wine so as to not confront the fact that they feel marginalized by a brutal and loathsome system."[77] This group's rhetoric argued that the precarious economic system, which caused feelings of failure and alcoholism in men, threatened the ability of poor Chilean families to survive. While MOMUPO created a space for women to develop a critique of the oppression they faced as women, it also "prioritized their working-class identity" and sought to include men in their struggle.[78] MOMUPO's holistic view of the popular family was captured in the image that graced its publications (fig. 6.6). In the front stands the man/husband/father, fist raised and holding a Chilean flag. Beside and a bit behind him is the woman/wife/mother, one arm around the man, the other around her daughter. A small boy is holding on to her back, while a third child is positioned in front of his father, fist raised in the same manner. In the image, the whole family joins the struggle, and the struggle unites the family.[79] This image captures not only MOMUPO's vision but also a longer tradition within parts of the left of promoting a view of the working-class family as based on the equal participation of men and women in the struggle. Nonetheless, men and women retain distinct roles and positions within the family, with men taking the lead and women watching the children.

MOMUPO's critique of the legitimacy of the military government echoed the critiques advanced by El Poder Femenino against Allende. Both groups

76. MOMUPO, *Inquietudes de la lucha* . . . , July 1985.
77. MOMUPO, *Inquietudes de la lucha* . . . , May 1985.
78. Mooney, *Politics of Motherhood*, 158.
79. A representation of the poblador family found on the cover of MOMUPO, *Inquietudes de la lucha* . . . , September 1985.

Fig. 6.6 "Concerns of the struggle." (MOMUPO, *Inquietudes de la lucha*, September 1985.)

demanded similar benefits from the state and questioned the legitimacy of the government for failing in its responsibilities to families. The similarities between these two groups reveal the underlying importance of familial welfare as a way to conceptualize the rights, obligations, and responsibilities of the state. But the type of "politicized motherhood" crafted by MOMUPO was much more explicitly political. MOMUPO's vision was not only that women participated in moments of crisis. The group also embraced a broader goal of women's participation as raising women's consciousness about the specifically gendered effects of the country's political and social problems. MOMUPO sought to make explicit the connections between the familial and the political and to use those connections to critique the legitimacy of Pinochet and his government.

THE FEMINIST CRITIQUE

While working with MOMUPO and other women's groups, feminist activists and scholars also launched their own scathing critique of Pinochet's government. Their analysis exposed how Pinochet and the military government were using the authoritarian and patriarchal beliefs of Chilean society to justify their rule. Their criticism was unusual within the broader democratization movement in that they challenged the prevailing gendered assumptions about the family. In particular, feminists attacked Pinochet's presentation of himself as the Patriarchal Leader. The military government's overt and explicit manipulation of the ideologies of motherhood and the family to garner political support "only made visible an authoritarianism embedded in Chilean social structure . . . that the family is authoritarian, that the socialization of children is authoritarian."[80] Indeed, the slogan of the feminist women's movement in Chile was "Democracy in the Country and the Home."[81] This phrase and what it symbolized—that without democracy in the home, political democracy was impossible—eventually spread throughout the larger women's movement.

Feminists used public events, meetings, and publications to attempt to raise awareness about the military's uses of gender ideology to justify its rule. For example, in 1986 María Elena Valenzuela and María Teresa Marshall, two well-known feminist scholars, produced a pamphlet titled *La mujer y el gobierno militar* (The woman and the military government), which analyzed how the

---

80. Chuchryk, "From Dictatorship," 81.
81. Julieta Kirkwood, a Chilean feminist and scholar, is widely recognized as having produced some of the most sustained and detailed analysis around this issue. See *Ser política en Chile*. For an excellent synopsis of her writings and influence, see Chuchryk, "From Dictatorship."

uses of motherhood and the family helped keep the authoritarian government in power. Written in easy-to-understand language and illustrated with drawings, it was clearly produced as a tool for consciousness-raising. Each section began with a quote from the government, designed to highlight how its politics depended on a patriarchal gender ideology. The pamphlet then proceeded to point out the hypocrisy of the government's ideologies in light of its actions.

The section titled "Large Families," for example, begins with a quote from Pinochet about the need for population growth. The authors' analysis stressed that "for the military government, the woman-mother should put her sexuality in service to procreation, and therefore have as many children as possible." The authors argued that not only did this policy limit women's worth to their reproductive capabilities, but the military government wanted children without providing Chilean families with the resources needed to raise those children: "The campaign of population increase designed by the government does not consider what a large family means in term of the economic capacity needed for its maintenance and the demands of time and dedication to raise it. Above all else, the government has never thought to increase the community and social support infrastructure."[82] Instead, they argued, the military government simply shifted the burden of raising families to women. Pinochet and his government had sought to achieve their ends by limiting the access of women and couples to family-planning resources and technologies, rather than creating the social systems that would promote and sustain large families, including a rethinking of the roles of men and women within the family.

This pattern of pointing to the repressive nature of the government's gendered demands on women was continued throughout the pamphlet. Other arguments included a critique of the government's emphasis on women remaining within the home, since staying home reinforced the marginalization of women in society, their feelings of isolation, and their abilities to understand the social nature of their problems. Instead of involving women in the public world, the government promoted the belief that women should dedicate themselves unthinkingly to the maintenance of Pinochet's regime. According to the authors, it was "in this form [that] the government has manipulated the sentiments of the woman, allocating to women the work to make [the regime] a reality. [The government] locates the woman as the base of sustenance for the regime and assigns her the work of 'serving, understanding, and supporting it,' the same subjugated relationship that it expects of the woman to her

82. Valenzuela and Marshall, *La mujer*, 3.

husband."[83] The pamphlet highlighted how the military government purposely used patriarchal images of the family to build support for itself. Patriarchy, the authors argued, could be found in "all the corners of our society and reconstitutes itself through beliefs, habits, and values shared by the majority of people." The "cultural and symbolic" dominance of patriarchy had been "utilized by the military government to prevent political mobilizations against it."[84] In their writings, feminist activists illuminated how the military government was able to use Chileans' unexamined patriarchal beliefs to justify its rule and garner societal support. Simply protesting the military government without examining the larger gendered belief system would not return Chile to democracy.

Feminist critiques also attacked the basis of Pinochet's use of the Patriarchal Leader by showing how he relied on the connections between familial and political authority to justify his political projects. Throughout the 1980s, feminists engaged in a variety of public actions designed to protest Pinochet's government and demand a return to democracy. In these actions, both popular and feminist women's groups pointed out the hypocrisy of a regime that, on the one hand, officially portrayed the woman as the "defender of the family, the patria, and that puts emphasis on order and security," while in reality the family was "threatened by the lack of possibilities to develop," and "the country is in danger because of the institutionalized violence" promoted by the regime.[85]

Feminist groups understood and contested the symbolic importance of the patriarchal family as a political resource for the government. Instead of the traditional image of the family, they argued for a more democratic model of the family as a new base for the nation. This family removed women and children from patriarchal control, just as democracy would remove Chile from the control of Pinochet and his authoritarian dictatorship. The fact that the government's legitimacy rested in part on patriarchal social relations meant that "democracy in the home for the military government [is] highly dangerous."[86] Therefore, feminists urged Chileans to change their own familial structure as a way to help bring about democracy in the larger society. True democratization required changes in the position of women both in the family and in the government.

83. Ibid., 5.
84. Ibid., 6.
85. Quote by Graciela Bórquez, vice president of the Women's Department of the Christian Democrat Party, in "Mujeres: Vamos a andar," *Solidaridad*, 13–26 January 1986, 25.
86. Valenzuela and Marshall, *La mujer*, 6.

Feminist groups sought to change how the relationships between women, men, families, and the state was conceptualized by arguing for gender equality, both in public and in private. The explicitly feminist women's groups exposed the connections between the authoritarian nature of Chilean politics and the authoritarian and patriarchal nature of Chilean families. They contested the imagery of the Chilean nation as a traditional Chilean family that prospered under the control of the benevolent but strict patriarch. Indeed, given the gendered power relations that had governed the lives of Chilean women, some Chilean feminists argued that women had never experienced true democracy.[87] For feminists, redemocratizing Chile meant a radical commitment to democratizing the private world of the family, especially the familial relationships between men and women. The defeat of Pinochet in the 1988 plebiscite and the eventual return to democracy were certainly the result, in part, of the women's movements' creative and sustained critiques of Pinochet and his political legitimacy.

Conclusion

Faced with the political repression of the traditional Chilean institutions and mechanisms of democratic rule, opposition groups recreated political participation and justified political dissent by invoking the complex interrelationships between the state, citizens, and the family. Familial identities became the basis from which to justify opposition against the political, social, and economic policies of Pinochet. Mobilizing through the ideals of Militant Families, both men and women claimed to be driven to search for their disappeared loved ones because of their familial ties. The suffering of their families also drove participants in the housing and popular women's movements, while a hope for more egalitarian families and political structures spurred feminist action. In his drive to depoliticize Chilean society and remain in power, Pinochet heavily repressed the traditional political identities of Chileans: those of worker, union member, and political party activist.

During the military government, strongly held beliefs about the roles of men and women within the family became the basis for political participation, for justifying political demands, and for questioning the legitimacy of the government. The usefulness of familial identities as a way to mobilize political action

87. For a more detailed discussion of the impact of the women's movement, see Chuchryk, "From Dictatorship," and Valdés and Weinstein, *Mujeres que sueñan.*

and to create a public space also presented particular advantages for women. As Jane Jaquette argues, "within political cultures where motherhood is sacred," the "rhetoric of political motherhood is thus rational and powerful for women."[88] More skilled in this area because of the long tradition of women mobilizing around familial identities, women played particularly important roles in the opposition movements.[89] The women of the AFDD evoked the image of the grieving mother to attack Pinochet for having destroyed their families through his repressive policies. MOMUPO members presented themselves as poor mothers trying to feed their families and raise their children in a healthy environment. The military government attempted to undercut the familial presentation of the opposition, labeling them not as authentic Chileans but rather as foreign agitators, the dupes of political activists, or even prostitutes. But the government found it difficult to repress familial identities, which were valued by the wider society, the Catholic Church, and the government's own rhetoric.

The democratic opposition turned the military's own familial discourse into the basis of their own critiques. Drawing on the long-standing belief that the Chilean state is responsible for the welfare of Chilean families—a belief reaffirmed in Pinochet's own pro-family propaganda and rhetoric—human rights, women's, and popular groups argued that Pinochet's government was failing in the duties of the Familial State. The AFDD asked how the military government could claim to be protecting Chilean families when it had destroyed their families by disappearing family members. Activists in the housing movement blamed Pinochet for failing in his basic responsibility to provide adequate housing for Chilean families. The women's movements pointed out the hypocrisy of a regime that on the one hand lauded the family but on the other hand did not provide the jobs, housing, health care, education, or safety that those families needed. The feminist movement exposed the ways that the Pinochet government was manipulating patriarchal familial beliefs for its own political ends. They attacked the construction of Pinochet as the Patriarchal Leader and revealed the connection between men's power within patriarchal families and Pinochet's dictatorship. They argued for a radical reimagining of social and political relationships in Chile based on equality. Both the family and the nation needed democratization. Thus opposition groups employed familial beliefs with great skill in their political projects and critiqued the manipulation of those beliefs by the military government.

88. Jaquette, *Women's Movement* (1994), 227–28.
89. See, for example, Jaquette, *Women's Movement* (1994), 223–28. For a more global perspective, see Jetter, Orleck, and Taylor, *Politics of Motherhood*.

★ SEVEN ★

RECONCILING THE FAMILY
Legitimizing the Transition to Democracy

In 1988, Chileans prepared to take part in a plebiscite on the continued rule of General Augusto Pinochet. As outlined in the 1980 Constitution written by the military government, Chileans would be asked to vote either SI (yes) to continue the present government for eight more years, or NO, signaling their discontent with the current regime and triggering presidential and congressional elections in 1989. The 1988 plebiscite presented both opportunities and risks for Pinochet as well as for the diverse democratic opposition. Confident in his ability to win and remain in power, Pinochet wanted the added legitimacy that an electoral contest represented. Opposition groups, after witnessing the inability of either the large-scale societal mobilizations or the economic crisis of the 1980s to oust Pinochet, saw the plebiscite as their best opportunity to bring back democratic governance. The varied strands of the democratic opposition coalesced around the reemerging political parties to form the coalition known as the Concertación de Partidos por el NO (Coalition of Parties for NO), or simply the Concertación.

The plebiscite quickly emerged as a clearly defined contest between the competing visions of Chile's future offered by Pinochet and his opposition. As such, the plebiscite provides a unique opportunity to analyze the mobilization of familial beliefs. The electoral strategies of Pinochet and the Concertación distilled the political uses of familial beliefs developed and employed by both parties during the preceding fifteen years. In the plebiscite, opposing portrayals of the family and its welfare reflected the larger debates around the responsibilities of the state and the relationships between the state and ordinary citizens. Both sides sought to portray themselves as defending Chilean families and their opponents as a threat to these families. In essence, both sides asked Chileans to vote either SI or NO for the sake of their families. These strategies reveal the centrality of the beliefs about the family in the political struggles surrounding the end of Pinochet's military government and the transition back to democratic rule.

Preparing for the Plebiscite

In an anticlimactic announcement on 30 August 1988, the military junta declared that Pinochet was the sole candidate in the upcoming plebiscite. With his nomination, the final preparations for the plebiscite began. For many Chileans, the real question was whether Pinochet would conduct an election that could legitimately claim to meet minimal conditions of freedom and fairness, since these standards had not been reached in the two previous votes conducted by the regime, the 1978 consultation and the 1980 vote on the new constitution.[1] Probably the best guarantee for a fair election was Pinochet's confidence in his ability to win the plebiscite without the overt election tampering that would put the legitimacy of the results in question.[2]

This confidence, however, did not mean that Pinochet considered his victory as a foregone conclusion. In preparation for the 1988 vote, Pinochet consolidated his hold on political power by increasing government spending on social welfare programs, producing endless propaganda campaigns that touted governmental successes, and unleashing a new wave of political repression. To shore up support among members of the poor and working class, he drastically increased the number of low-cost housing units being built. These new programs were also an attempt to deflect criticisms about his failure to address the lack of adequate housing, one of the most serious social problems facing Chile. Aided by two hundred million dollars in foreign loans, "presidential campaign stops were often coordinated with ribbon-cutting ceremonies for low-income developments."[3] The military government was also banking on taking advantage of Chile's growing economy and burgeoning international trade ties.

Pinochet also devoted an immense amount of resources to his propaganda campaigns that preceded the plebiscite, including "Somos Millones"[4] (We are

1. In 1978, Pinochet organized a referendum to show popular support for his regime in response to a UN resolution condemning human rights abuses in Chile. No organized opposition was allowed and Pinochet spared no expense or effort in guaranteeing a positive vote. Huneeus, *Pinochet Regime*, 86–87.
2. Constable and Valenzuela, *Nation of Enemies*, 304.
3. Ibid., 298.
4. "Somos Millones" was discussed in depth in chapter 5. María Eugenia Hirmas, a Chilean sociologist and media scholar, argued that since 1973, "there exists a coherence in the propaganda of the military regime that has been maintained in its overall line. [The propaganda] is designed to reinforce the discourse of Pinochet and the politics of the government." See María Eugenia Hirmas, "Propaganda de gobierno en television: Mayo, Informe no. 1," personal papers of María Hirmas, May 1988. I thank María Eugenia Hirmas for providing me with copies of the media analysis she produced about the plebiscite and media portrayals of the Concertación.

millions), "Democracia, SI" (Democracy, YES), "SI, Somos Millones" (YES, we are millions), and "SI, Usted Decide" (YES, you decide). The Chilean sociologist María Eugenia Hirmas estimated that between January and August of 1988, the nine months preceding the official start of the campaign, the government ran 7,302 spots that lasted for a total of 108 hours and 53 minutes and cost 1.8 billion pesos, an immense sum.[5] During the same time, the opposition was banned from making television advertisements, and the usual heavy censorship of political events and news on television continued.[6] In addition to the social spending and the increased propaganda campaigns, the government also attempted to silence its critics through a new wave of repression. The Vicaría reported that between January and June of 1988, during the height of the campaign to register voters and reconstitute Chilean political parties, Pinochet's government made 1,780 political arrests.[7]

Confident that these policies had consolidated his position, Pinochet granted a number of concessions to the opposition that liberalized the political process and provided legitimacy to the election. These changes included ending the state of exception, which permitted most political exiles to return to Chile,[8] and appointing the Constitutional Tribunal mandated by the 1980 Constitution. This tribunal made a number of crucial rulings that helped assure a more free and fair contest, such as allowing for independent observers at polling stations, mandating free and equal airtime on television stations for both sides, and constituting an independent electoral tribunal to oversee the plebiscite. These actions were surprising given that the tribunal's members had been appointed by the Chilean Supreme Court (generally pro-regime), the military junta, the National Security Council, and Pinochet himself. These decisions, and the ability of the opposition to exploit the political opening they created, demonstrate how even elections designed to be noncompetitive "generate tensions . . . and create a situation that is hard for the authorities to control."[9]

Opposition social groups and political parties were initially divided over how to approach the plebiscite. Past experiences had proven that the military government was quite capable of rigging elections. A number of factors eventually convinced most opposition actors to participate in a unified and organized

5. These figures are a summation of those presented in María Eugenia Hirmas, "Propaganda de gobierno en TV: Mayo–agosto de 1988, Informe no. 2," personal papers of María Hirmas, September 1988.

6. Constable and Valenzuela, *Nation of Enemies*, 297.

7. Ibid., 302.

8. Loveman, *Chile*, 304.

9. Huneeus, *Pinochet Regime*, 397–98.

way. First, the leaders of the parties of the center and the left had gone through an intensive period of political learning and soul searching about the causes of the coup, and this laid the groundwork for their eventual cooperation. Earlier cooperation in the Constitutional Study Group (1978), the Democratic Alliance (1983), and the Committee for Free Elections (1987) all promoted a willingness on the part of opposition political elites to create coalitions.[10] In addition, movement activists pressured the parties to participate; in particular, the women's movements called publicly for political unity among the parties, and opposition intellectuals provided political and technical advice.[11] Finally, over the course of 1987 it became increasingly apparent that Pinochet's government was preparing for the plebiscite, and that calls for free elections for all political offices, without the plebiscite, were not being heeded. In November 1987 the Christian Democrats announced that they would participate. By 2 February 1988 more than fifteen parties and groups that opposed Pinochet had officially formed the Concertación de Partidos por el NO, and they called on Chileans to register to vote and then to vote NO.[12] The Concertación included the Christian Democrats, the Radical Party, and the moderate factions of the Socialist Party, which had organized the Party for Democracy (PPD) because of Pinochet's continued exclusion of "all Marxist and 'anti-family' parties."[13] Eventually, the more radical socialist factions joined the Concertación as well.[14]

The relaxation of the censorship and government control of the media, particularly televised propaganda, played a decisive role in guaranteeing a competitive process. Both sides were granted equal access to the airwaves for fifteen minutes a day for twenty-seven days, beginning on 5 September and ending on 1 October, four days before the vote. The television board, however, hedged its bets by trying to limit the importance and impact of the electoral television

---

10. For a general discussion of the process, see ibid., chapter 11. For a discussion of the role of political learning among the party elite of the left, see Hite, *When the Romance Ended*.

11. For the importance of the women's movements in the creation of the Concertación, see Baldez, *Why Women Protest*, and Franceschet, *Women and Politics in Chile*. For a thorough accounting of the role of intellectuals in opposing the military government, see Puryear, *Thinking Politics*.

12. Collier and Sater, *History of Chile*, 379.

13. Constable and Valenzuela, *Nation of Enemies*, 311. While initially formed as way to allow socialist participation, the Party for Democracy took on a life of its own when the Socialist Party reformed in 1989 after this law was changed.

14. Of the major political parties opposed to Pinochet, only the Communist Party, maintaining the illegitimacy of a process that resulted from the imposition of the military government's rule, did not join. Nonetheless, the party eventually supported a NO vote for its partisans. See Constable and Valenzuela, *Nation of Enemies*, 302.

propaganda (*franja*).[15] First, the fifteen minutes given to each side had to be used as a block of time and could not be spread throughout the day to target particular audience segments.[16] Second, the board set the start time for the franja as 10:45 on weeknights and noon on weekends, times that usually did not draw a substantial viewing audience.[17] The SI and NO franjas were aired back to back, creating a thirty-minute block of campaign propaganda. The opening fifteen minutes alternated between the two campaigns. Finally, while the NO campaign was strictly limited, the government continued to show propaganda throughout the day by claiming that the ads supplied information about governmental programs. According to a study by the leadership of the NO campaign, "1,156 spots of government propaganda" were shown in the month of September on television outside the sanctioned fifteen minutes.[18]

These attempts by Pinochet to limit the impact of television access backfired. The Chilean public viewed the franja from the two sides as a dueling television program rather than mere campaign spots, and judged them accordingly. The franja soon became the most watched program on TV, reaching an estimated 65.3 percent of the viewing audience during the four weeks they were shown.[19] Postelection surveys revealed that more than 90 percent of voters had watched the franja.[20] For the two sides, the franja functioned as a way to "reinforce their supporters, provide their supporters with arguments and sentiments to support their positions, and to win adherents within the undecided."[21] The importance of the franja as a source of debate and contestation was augmented by the fact that the spots were subsequently analyzed in the newspapers and dominated many everyday conversations. The newspaper coverage strengthened the perception that the ads represented a battle between the SI and the NO campaigns in terms of quality and creativeness, with the NO campaign often the victor. Instead of ignoring the late-night broadcasts, Chileans were glued to their television sets.

Initially, Pinochet and his campaign considered the franja a "secondary element," because they enjoyed greater access to and control over television programming outside the mandated time, and because of their more extensive ad

15. In Spanish, *franja* literally means a "stripe, band, or fringe." The word "franja" came to mean the program "strips" produced by the NO and SI campaigns. The word is still used in Chile to designate the official televised campaign advertisements.

16. Hirmas, "La franja," 116–17.

17. Ibid., 114–17.

18. Quoted in ibid., 114–15.

19. Hirmas, "La franja," 117.

20. Huneeus, *Pinochet Regime*, 419.

21. Hirmas, "La franja," 121.

campaign in other media outlets, specifically newspapers. The low priority of the TV spots was reflected in the poor quality of the first few days of the SI franja, which were prepared before it became clear that the franja were becoming the defining spectacle of the plebiscite.[22] On the NO side, their franja was the opposition's only access to television. Instead of squabbling over how to divide the time among its various members, the Concertación produced a coherent fifteen-minute program tied together by the respected journalist Patricio Bañados and the theme song "Chile, la alegría ya viene" (Chile, happiness is coming). In addition, the aesthetic quality was quite high, as artists and technicians who had suffered censorship under Pinochet's government lent their skills to the production.[23] In the following analysis, the franja represent the central source for the NO campaign, while an analysis of the SI campaign focuses on both the franja and other forms of propaganda.[24]

SI: The Family Endangered and Protected

PINOCHET: THE FAMILY'S PROTECTOR

The SI campaign presented the plebiscite as a stark choice between the order, security, development, and prosperity that were the result of Pinochet's rule versus the chaos, disorder, violence, and scarcity that would be the outcome of his defeat. Reiterating many of the themes that had dominated government propaganda for years, Pinochet was cast once again as the defender of and provider for Chilean families. Pinochet continuously claimed that a vote for the NO coalition was simply a vote to return to the policies and problems of the Popular Unity years. In addition to these negative aspects, Pinochet also promised a plethora of new government programs that would increase the wealth and prosperity of Chilean families. Like countless other politicians, he embraced women, kissed babies, and staged photo opportunities with smiling, happy families.

22. Ibid., 110.

23. For a discussion of these aspects, see *La campaña del NO* and Hirmas, "La franja."

24. I was able to find a tape of only the first twelve episodes of the SI franja. The lack of a media archive accessible to researchers was one of the greatest limitations I faced. María Eugenia Hirmas was kind enough to provide me access to the SI franja she had, and I am thankful to Ximena Velasco for providing me with a tape of the NO franja, which I believe was complete except for the last episode. The NO franja was a personal recording, however, and I am not confident in assigning dates to them, unless dates were mentioned somewhere within the spots themselves. All the following references to the SI and NO franjas are from these two sources.

Pinochet's campaign relied on dramatic images to represent the choice be-tween Pinochet and the opposition. Of the propaganda analyzed, this pairing of the negative and positive was best captured in a comic book–style pamphlet titled *¿Por dónde ir?* (Which way to go?). The pamphlet presents eighteen con-trasting scenes. On the left page of each pair, in black-and-white, is the fate of Chile if the NO vote wins. On the other side, in bright colors, is the future for Chile under Pinochet. The cover image of a family standing at a crossroads makes it clear that the future of the Chilean family is at stake in this election (fig. 7.1). The mother, father, son, and daughter in the picture can take either a left or a right turn. The left leads them toward the NO banner, surrounded by a barren landscape, devoid of almost any vegetation and populated by two small shacks. The road is rough and unpaved, and boulders are strewn about. If they take a right, toward SI, they travel on a paved road, with a cloverleaf interchange in the background. Passing under a clean, shiny sign reading "Votar SI" (Vote YES), they are surrounded by straight rows of vegetation and are headed toward a modern city full of skyscrapers. In case of any lingering

Fig. 7.1   "Votar SI, votar NO." (Campaña por SI, *¿Por dónde ir?*)

Fig. 7.2 "NO . . . SI." (Campaña por SI, *¿Por dónde ir?*)

doubts, the back cover features the same family at the crossroads, except now the NO road is overrun with snakes, lizards, skeletons, and monsters, while the SI road winds over rolling hills to a lake (fig. 7.2). Given these images, the question of "which way to go?" is clearly rhetorical.[25]

The two scenarios that deal with housing and security capture perfectly how the choice between SI and NO was framed by invoking familial welfare. The choice is between voting NO and endangering the family, or voting SI and protecting the family. Playing on the fears of economic crises and rising crime, the SI propaganda features two scenarios. In the NO narrative, a Chilean family with few resources is forced to try to find a home in a bad neighborhood (fig. 7.3). A poorly dressed, thin, and worried-looking couple is fearfully opening the door to a house that has a "For Rent" sign on it. Clearly upset, their gaunt daughter watches her parents. Behind the family, there is a run-down street, a woman getting water from a fire hydrant, and a man being held up by another man holding a knife. The scene is one of urban blight. The caption

25. Campaña por el SI, *¿Por dónde ir?* Figures 7.1–7.7 are from this same source. There are no page numbers in the pamphlet.

Votar "NO" es vivir en lo ajeno, como allegado o arrendatario, o sin título de dominio.

Fig. 7.3 "To vote NO is to live without your own home." (Campaña por SI, *¿Por dónde ir?*)

reads, "To vote NO is to live without your own home, as a guest[26] or a renter, without a deed."

Opposed to this portrait of insecurity, the SI scenario features a clean and tidy neighborhood of individual houses on their own lots (fig. 7.4). Here the couple is presented as more economically successful. They stand with smiles on their faces as a man hands them the deed to a house. Behind the couple, children play and two other couples walk arm in arm. The caption reads, "To vote SI is to achieve well-being and improve the quality of life." The insets feature three men holding deeds to houses, representing the middle class, the worker (with a hard hat), and a man dressed in the traditional garb of Chilean campesinos. In addition to promising homes to Chilean families, the picture presents home ownership as connected to masculinity and men's ability to provide for their families.

Decent housing as a symbol for family prosperity is also featured in the scenario dealing with class conflict and solidarity. Below the caption "To vote NO is to foment class conflict," three young men with angry looks on their

26. The term "guest," *allegado* in Spanish, in this context refers to the practice among poor Chilean families of living in the household of relatives or friends. For more on this phenomenon, please see chapters 5 and 6.

Fig. 7.4   "To vote SI is to achieve well-being." (Campaña por SI, *¿Por dónde ir?*)

faces are throwing rocks. Behind them, standing on the "free" rock pile, is an older man dressed in a suit, exhorting the youths to throw more rocks. The man in the suit represents the party politicians Pinochet continually denounced as demagogues, whose pursuit of their own interests had led Chile toward Marxism and class conflict. Voting SI, on the other hand, will "end extreme poverty" and to put the voter in "solidarity with those who have less." This social solidarity and the end of poverty are depicted through the services provided for a poor family (fig. 7.5). Two construction workers are making improvements to the family's humble home, while a doctor examines the couple's son, and a woman with a clipboard, perhaps a social worker or a volunteer from CEMA, offers advice. The narrative of the SI propaganda thus used the family to represent the benefits of the government's programs. According to the ad, Pinochet and his government have provided and will continue to provide Chilean families with better housing, a more secure environment, and social harmony. Voting for SI also means greater feelings of solidarity across class divisions and an increased willingness on the part of well-off individuals to help others.

The pamphlet also captured many of the strategies developed by the SI campaign to create an environment of fear and anxiety about a future without Pinochet. Often these attempts were directed specifically at women. One

Fig. 7.5 "To vote SI is to end extreme poverty." (Campaña por SI, *¿Por dónde ir?*)

strategy used throughout the campaign was to portray a NO vote as creating an environment that endangered the family. For example, in one scenario a housewife is standing by her front door, staring worriedly up at the clock (fig. 7.6). Clearly, the woman is waiting for her family and anxious about why they have not yet returned home. The picture tells us that this is the fate of mothers if NO wins. The caption reads, "To vote NO is to live in fear of an insecure society." Notice that it is not just the housewife who lives with this anxiety; incredibly, the woman in the framed picture on the wall frowns, as does the vase on the end table. The opposing picture for the SI side features the family returning home (fig. 7.7). The mother is smiling and happy, patting the head of her young son, who grins at her and points toward the door, through which his sister is running toward them with open arms. The father is standing behind his daughter looking pleased, while the woman in the picture and the vase sport wide smiles. The caption reads, "To vote SI is to continue in peace; it is to walk in safety; it is to live better."

Along with a sense of general anxiety, the specific threat of economic insecurity was evoked by images of the *colas* and the scarcity of consumer goods associated with the Allende years. The pamphlet included images of long lines of women waiting to go into a shop, a woman with an empty shopping cart worriedly looking at the bare shelves in a supermarket, and two women in

Fig. 7.6 "To vote NO is to live in fear of an insecure society." (Campaña por SI, *¿Por dónde ir?*)

Fig. 7.7 "To vote SI is to continue in peace." (Campaña por SI, *¿Por dónde ir?*)

front of desks bearing signs that read "Without JAP,[27] there is absolutely nothing. With JAP, there is only chicken." These signs reinvoke the charge that under the Popular Unity, it was only through supporting the government that one gained access to the limited consumer goods available. Women could avoid the fate of long lines by voting SI, which would guarantee supermarkets with packed shelves and full shopping carts, as depicted on the opposing page.

This focus on family suffering caused by scarcity was repeated in two newspaper campaigns, "Since Fifteen Years Ago" and "Memories from Fifteen Years Ago." Presenting the time before the military government as one of chaos, violence, scarcity, and economic insecurity, the ads argued that this was Chile's future if Pinochet lost. The "Memories" campaign featured regular Chileans talking about their memories and experiences of the Popular Unity period. For example, one ad features the testimony of Elena Tagle Katalinic, a housewife, who recalls that "during the Popular Unity, they tried to obligate the housewives to enroll in the . . . political organizations that controlled the distribution of consumer goods," and that there was "a great scarcity of goods. I am referring to the articles of prime necessity, essential for the ability to maintain a family."[28] This ad charges that political parties had endangered Chilean families by basing their access to necessities on party membership and loyalty. Ads featuring other personal testimonies stressed how the scarcity of goods placed extra burdens on women, forcing them to stand in long lines for basic items instead of remaining at home and preparing meals for their families. Another woman, Señora Martínez, states, "The UP was one unending line for bread."[29] The connection between scarcity, lines, and violence was also evoked in a number of ads that showed pictures from the past of women fighting while standing in line. The reason for this uncharacteristic display of violence by Chilean mothers and housewives was the "exasperation" caused by the dire economic conditions. The ads emphasized that the "atmosphere of violence and resentment" fostered by the UP had pushed even mothers to the brink.[30]

Many ads also played on Chilean men's concern about their ability to protect and provide for their families. The personal testimonies of Carlos Carrasco Prieto, a teacher and father of three, and Juan Escobar Galaz, a master bricklayer

27. JAP refers to Juntas de Abastecimiento y Precio, neighborhood groups that formed consumer cooperatives to help people gain access to basic goods at the official prices during the truckers' strikes under Allende. For more on this, see chapter 4.

28. *El Mercurio*, 21 September 1988, C2.

29. *El Mercurio*, 16 September 1988, C2; 24 September 1988, C2. For similar themes, see *El Mercurio*, 23 September 1988, C2.

30. *El Mercurio*, 11 September 1988, C3; 1 September 1988, C3.

and father of seven, focused on how they had worried about their inability to provide for their families during the time of the UP. Señor Carrasco notes, "I remember in a way so detailed and clear, when we had to go out asking if please could someone sell us some type of food to bring home. One could not find anything simply because there was nothing. A sad experience, and a personal one because I had three children. . . . In the winter the situation was even more drastic. There was no oil for the stoves. . . . It was truly sad and lamentable and one felt impotent. . . . [I remember] the permanent worry for your own security and the security of your family."[31] The feelings of impotence and the conditions that made providing for a family almost impossible were repeated in the testimony of Señor Escobar, who emphasized how he feared not being able to find enough food to feed his seven children. He tells the reader, "Recently we were remembering all of the suffering that we endured in order to get food for our children. . . . I had to sacrifice myself for my family. At that time, I had seven children . . . the oldest was eleven and from there down. Imagine . . . I had to do whatever manner of things to find milk." Señor Escobar continues, "One sent a child to stand in line and you did not know if [the child] would return. . . . I suffered much, all of us, my wife and my children, suffered much during the time of the UP."[32] The two men's testimonies center around the pain they felt in not being able to fulfill their masculine familial roles in a time of economic crisis. The lack of basic consumer goods meant that they had been unable to provide for their wives and children, even with the immense sacrifices they made. They worried over the safety of their children forced to wait in line in the street. These ads argued that a NO victory would once again make it difficult for women to feed and take care of their families, and for men to provide economic and personal security for their wives and children. Indeed, a NO victory would even threaten men's virility, making them "impotent."

The television franja also repeated this theme that a NO vote endangered families and men's and women's abilities to fulfill their familial roles. One spot depicts a mother and her children fleeing from a group of protesters. The protesters, wearing hard hats on their heads and bandannas over their faces, resembled the pictures of violent UP supporters that had been a regular feature of newspaper propaganda during the last fifteen years. The mother and her children rush desperately past people lying hurt on the streets and through burning

---

31. *El Mercurio*, 15 September 1988, C2.
32. *El Mercurio*, 12 September 1988, C3; 14 September 1988, C2.

barricades to get to their car. The narrator claims that a country of NO is a country of violence, and that the first innocent victim of NO might be someone from your family. Women are invited to identify with the woman in the spot and to fear for their own safety as well as the safety of their children. Male viewers can imagine their wives and children being threatened in such a fashion. The ad was directed toward women and men of the middle and upper classes, who were more likely to own a car. The spot was designed to invoke fear of class struggle that would endanger their families by giving lower-class hoodlums free rein if Pinochet were defeated and leftist political parties took over.

Later on, a SI spot picked up the story of what might have happened if the mother and child had reached the safety of their car. Produced on grainy, black-and-white film, the mother, with her child in the backseat, drives down a street lined with broken streetlights. Makeshift barricades of burning tires and lumber litter the street. The urban scene is dark, and violence lurks in the shadows. The ad shows the mother's perspective; the viewer sees her clenched hands on the steering wheel, hears her nervous breathing, and watches as she searches for danger on the street. Suddenly a group of men carrying sticks appears and begins to hit the car. As the driver's side window is smashed, the viewer hears the screams of the woman and her child before the image goes dark. The narrator tells the viewer that in a country of NO, fear is found on the streets. The voice exhorts Chileans to remember "that the first innocent victim might be someone in your family." Once again, the SI campaign connects the danger and violence imagined in the spot with the possible fate of any Chilean family if the NO campaign wins. These two spots were some of the most extreme uses of the family.

The SI franja also featured several spots designed to highlight acts of violence perpetrated by leftist radicals during Pinochet's rule. These ads moved the threat of violence from a fictional projection to real events. One spot of this type featured footage of Pinochet after the failed attempt on his life in 1986.[33] Pinochet talks about how the country is still endangered by extremists. The spot then switches to the present, where the widow of one of the police officers killed in the assassination attempt speaks about Chileans' rejection of

33. The assassination attempt was carried out by the Manuel Rodríguez Patriotic Front (Frente Patriótico Manuel Rodríguez, FPMR), a clandestine group dedicated to armed resistance and linked to the Communist Party. On 7 September 1986, a highly trained group of FPMR operatives attempted to ambush Pinochet's motorcade as he returned to Santiago from his weekend retreat in the mountains. Five bodyguards were killed in the attack, but Pinochet managed to escape. Ensalaco credits the assassination attempt with weakening moderate opposition leaders' support for direct action and street protests. See *Chile Under Pinochet*, 150–55.

violence and claims that terrorist attacks, such as the one that killed her husband, could be controlled only by a SI victory. Pinochet's campaign argued that the real consequences of voting for NO included the death of loved ones, the destruction of families, and a lack of respect for law and order. Viewers, particularly women, were asked to identify with the young widow and to imagine their own families being destroyed by violence.

The SI campaign also directly appealed to mothers to vote SI in order to protect their children from this violence. Employing the anticommunist rhetoric of the conservative women's mobilization against Allende, an ad placed in *El Mercurio* on 1 October calls on "Chilean mothers" to protect their children from the increasing threat of communism, claiming that "the declarations formulated by communists . . . and their allies called for violence and subversion." The ad issues "an alert to Chilean mothers so that they would redouble the protection of their children in the days prior to and following 5 October." It continues, "It seems to us unacceptable that our children will be the first victims of the violence proposed by the communists. . . . Mothers of Chile! The children, to whom with immense love you have given your life, now require more than ever, our protection and our love. The worst pain that a mother could suffer is having a child be a victim of terrorism. . . . Mother! . . . You can give to your child a future of protection for your family and your nation. Think, Reflect, Protect Them."[34] The explicit argument of the ad is that voting for SI was a way that Chilean mothers could protect both their children and their country. Once again, any move away from Pinochet and his government would allow communism, violence, and terrorism to again dominate Chile and to endanger Chilean families.

PINOCHET AS THE GOOD PROVIDER

As the second major component of its overall strategy, the SI campaign featured positive portrayals of the benefits of Pinochet's government. In this part of the campaign, the family represented both the ultimate beneficiary of existing government programs and the entity toward which future benefits would be directed. The implicit argument was that Pinochet was a successful and legitimate leader because Chilean families had flourished under his government. Pinochet combined appeals to the ideals of the Familial State (his government had fulfilled its duties vis-à-vis Chilean families) and the Patriarchal Leader (his own personal success as Chile's symbolic father).

34. *El Mercurio*, 1 October 1988, C4.

One of the most repeated images used to promote this argument was, again, the government's provision of housing to poor Chilean families. On the second day of the franja, a spot featured images from the inauguration of a new housing development built by the government. Pinochet is shown talking to the family in their house and walking through the new development greeting his supporters, who are wearing big SI buttons. It ends with a shot of a couple standing in front of their house, soon to be the home of their new family, as the woman is pregnant. The viewer is left with a sense that the couple's unborn child will have a better future thanks to Pinochet. According to the spot, Pinochet and his government had been providing houses for the past fifteen years, a commitment to poor Chilean families not taken seriously by previous governments. The spot ends with the statement, "One house, one family, one goal motivated the government to solve the problems of past governments, the immediate need for thousands of houses."

The past success of his housing programs and the promise of more houses after a SI victory were repeated in newspaper campaign ads. For example, one features SI spelled out using drawings of houses (fig. 7.8). The ad declares, "SI. It is an irrefutable truth that never before has a government constructed so many houses as this one. Nor has anyone given so many deeds. But beyond the statistics are the hopeful smiles of hundreds of thousands of families who with these houses have exchanged marginality for dignity, and the darkness of a yesterday without horizons for a good present and a better future. More about the family than the house . . . Chile, a Winning Country."[35] In this and other ads, Pinochet portrayed his housing policies as a central part of his strategy for improving the lives of Chilean families. The rhetoric of this campaign, linking owning a house to progress, harked back to rhetoric of the Christian Democrats in the 1970 election.

The portrayal of Pinochet as a successful Patriarchal Leader was central to a series of ads that detailed his promises to different social groups. Some of the most touted promises featured the family as the ultimate beneficiary of government programs. Indeed, Pinochet promised to defend "the well-being and the security of every family, because it represents the essential nucleus of the society." He extended his housing campaign by claiming that seventy thousand more families would be provided with a solution to their housing needs. The government also promised to provide ample consumer goods so that "every home could count on the necessities," to keep inflation low, and to

---

35. *El Mercurio*, 6 September 1988, C14.

Si. Es una verdad indesmentible que nunca antes un gobierno construyó tantas casas como ésta. Ni ninguno entregó tantos títulos de dominio. Pero más allá de las cifras están las sonrisas esperanzadas de cientos de miles de familias que con estas casas han cambiado la marginalidad por dignidad, y la oscuridad de un ayer sin horizontes por un buen presente y un mejor futuro.

MAS POR LA FAMILIA QUE POR LAS CASAS...

Chile, Un País Ganador.

Fig. 7.8   "More about the family than the house." (*El Mercurio*, 6 September 1988.)

constantly improve "the quality of lives of Chilean homes, with a vision of solidarity, justice, and equity." Many of the promises to other groups repeated the one made to the family or presented new ones with the family as the ultimate beneficiary. Pinochet promised the Chilean woman that "the social net of our government always will protect your basic necessities, supplying nutrition, health, and education to your children, with adequate professional attention to the pregnancy of every Chilean woman, decreasing infant mortality to minimum levels, more possibilities [of access] to higher education, unemployment benefits . . . and a housing program that will give a dignified house to every Chilean family that needs it."[36] Many of the same promises were repeated for the workers.

SI propaganda frequently featured Pinochet surrounded by mothers and their children to portray him as a paternal figure. Pinochet's concern for the welfare of children in particular was emphasized in an ad that featured him kissing a baby. In this ad Pinochet promises "to definitively end infant mortality" (fig. 7.9).[37] In another ad, Pinochet is hugging two children, a young girl and a young boy. The caption reads, "Our promise: To defend the family as the essential nucleus of the society."[38] Pinochet, the ads imply, is dedicated

36. *El Mercurio*, 2 October 1988, D8.
37. *El Mercurio*, 8 September 1988, A8.
38. *El Mercurio*, 9 September 1988, A12.

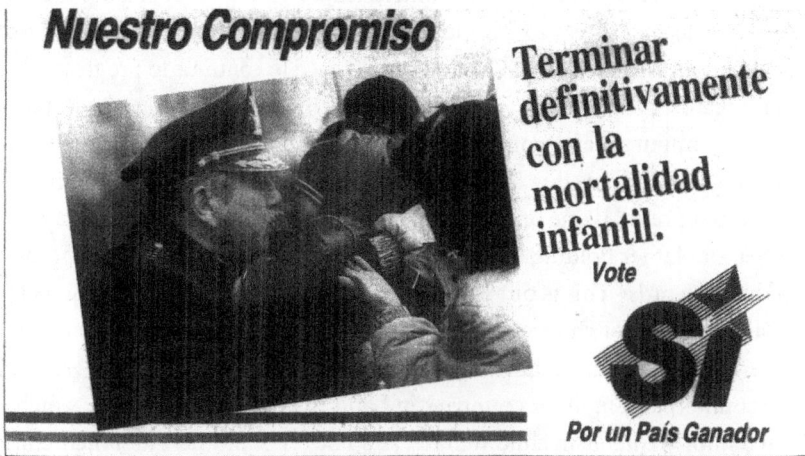

Fig. 7.9 "Our promise." (*El Mercurio*, 8 September 1988.)

to protecting both the Chilean family and its future. He is the wise patriarch at the head of Chile's national family.

These ads also played on the image of Pinochet as the stalwart defender of Chilean families. In general, Pinochet had tried to soften his image from that of a stern military commander to that of a concerned civilian politician. To do so, he had exchanged his military uniforms for suits and ties. As Sergio Bitar, a Concertación leader, argued in the *Fortín Mapocho*, an opposition newspaper, Pinochet's campaign was "trying to give the candidate Pinochet" a change of image from "'Prussian soldier,' tough, surly . . . to 'a caring grandfather,' affectionate to his grandchildren and friend of all Chileans."[39] While Pinochet's facial expressions and body language exude care and concern for the children in these ads, the military uniform serves as a subtle reminder of his position as head of the military. The use of children, therefore, allowed Pinochet to soften his military image by turning it toward the idea that he was a strong protector of Chilean children and families.

The benefits received by Chilean children and their families were also the theme of a spot that featured Joaquín Lavín. Lavín was a well-known figure because of his book *The Silent Revolution*, in which he praised Pinochet's neoliberal economic policies as having finally brought prosperity to Chile. In this ad, he focuses on showing how Chilean children were much better off than

39. *Fortín Mapocho*, 6 September 1988.

children in other Latin American countries, highlighting the rising number of children who had access to computers. Computers represented the modern technology and expertise that Chileans would need to continue to progress. The ad also features a number of interviews with children discussing the importance of computers and computer access for their future. These successes, according to Lavín, are due to Pinochet's "strength, generosity, and creativity." Lavín's spot precedes one on infant mortality, which features images of a new mother and father holding their baby in a modern, clean hospital, accompanied by the words "This is our promise." Another spot emphasized Pinochet's care and concern for children by asking the viewer, "Did you know?," and then answering by describing how Chilean children are taller and heavier than their counterparts in other countries in Latin America. These statistics highlighted improvements in child welfare, and images of mothers and their children being seen by women doctors accompanied the facts. Rounding out the portrayal of how families benefited from current policies is a spot featuring Pinochet talking directly to the viewer about his promises for the Chilean family. Thus Pinochet pledged to provide a home for Chileans in which to raise their children, education for those children, the opportunity for men to be business owners, and the idea that women deserved their own identities.

Pinochet, it seemed, was willing to promote new governmental programs and social spending in order to garner support. The target of the promised largesse, however, was not the touted individual of neoliberal policies, but once again the Chilean family. The campaign theme of "Chile, a Winning Country, a Promise to You, Your Family, and Your Children" captured the importance of the family in Pinochet's campaign. As the campaign put it, Pinochet would provide for Chilean families because with "SI, the nuclear family will be the base that sustains all of this great family that is the Chilean nation."[40] Indeed, Pinochet argued that if Chileans voted "thinking about the family, the children, the children of those children" as he, "Augusto Pinochet Ugarte, seventy-three years old, married, four children, twelve grandchildren, Chilean, and president" would, then a SI victory was assured.[41] Images of happy and prosperous Chilean families, a staple of government propaganda, were continually invoked to symbolize the past successes and future promise of Pinochet's continued rule.

The SI campaign legitimized Pinochet's rule by presenting him as the past, present, and future protector of both Chilean families and the Chilean nation.

40. *El Mercurio*, 2 October 1988, D8; 18 September 1988, D10.
41. *El Mercurio*, 2 October 1988, D24.

He and his government argued that a vote for the opposition was a vote to return to the chaos, violence, and economic crises that had threatened Chilean families during the Allende years. To further its image of Pinochet as the "good provider," the SI campaign repeatedly focused on the benefits of Pinochet's government (modernization, development, social peace). To portray his paternal concern and care, Pinochet highlighted the social programs directed specifically at poor Chilean families. These strategies depended on presenting an image of Pinochet as the Patriarchal Leader of the Chilean national family, and the government as a dedicated steward of the Familial State.

The NO Campaign: Rebuilding Democracy Through the Family

The NO campaign needed to confront directly both Pinochet's positive portrayal of the accomplishments of the military regime and his negative portrayal of a NO victory as a return to chaos, violence, and scarcity. The NO campaign argued that Pinochet's propaganda focused on a vision of either utopia or dystopia. Neither extreme, however, represented the reality of Chilean families or Chilean society. The actual experiences of many Chileans—a reality hidden by Pinochet—showed that families had not been taken care of or kept safe, but instead suffered from poverty, lack of health care and housing, disappearances, torture, and state violence. The NO campaign also turned to idealized understandings of familial unity to craft political arguments about the importance of respecting difference and dissent. They argued that citizens, like members of a family, were bound to disagree and argue; however, this did not mean dissenting members should be thrown out of the family. Instead, mutual respect and tolerance were in order. Finally, familial metaphors were employed to help bind the Chilean national community back together. The Concertación used the image of the nation as a family to reclaim the "Chileanness" of those who had been dubbed enemies of the military government, and it argued that only a change of government could protect all Chilean families.

THE FAMILY IN PAIN

In developing strategies for pursuing these political goals, the NO campaign frequently drew on the methods of a variety of activist groups that had invoked familial ideals in their critiques of Pinochet and his government. As explored in the previous chapter, many societal groups had used beliefs about the duties and responsibilities of the state to Chilean families in order to contest Pinochet's policies. The NO campaign referenced these familial critiques in discussing state-sponsored human rights violations, poverty, and exile. Probably the strongest invocation of how families had suffered under Pinochet was the television segment that featured a performance of the *cueca sola* by the Conjunto Folclórico, a division of the AFDD that had performed publicly throughout the 1980s. The spot begins with each member saying her name, her relationship to the disappeared, and the name of the disappeared. The women's statements are imposed one on top of the other so that it is hard to distinguish individual names. Their relationships to the disappeared, however—as mother, sister, wife—are clearly heard, highlighting that the familial relationships were more important than the individual cases. All the women are wearing white blouses and black skirts, invoking the black-and-white picture of the disappeared loved ones worn by AFDD members in their public protests.

After the introduction, the group plays and sings one of their *cuecas*. An older woman steps out, walks to the center of the room, and begins to dance alone, thus drawing attention to the absence of her missing partner. The *cueca sola* visually represents the question asked over and over by the family members of the disappeared, "Where are they?" Over the singing, a voice is heard saying, "This [the disappearances] can never again occur. No more disappeared."[42] The dancing of the *cueca sola* symbolically evoked the very real harm caused by Pinochet's policy of disappearing political opponents. The loved ones were gone and their mothers, sisters, and wives mourned their losses. By featuring the *cueca sola*, the NO campaign illustrated how Pinochet's repressive policies had hurt Chilean families.

The destruction of Chilean families under the military government was also addressed explicitly in additional spots that featured three prominent women who had lost loved ones to government repression. The first was a spot featuring Moy de Tohá, the widow of Allende's former minister of the interior José Tohá, who had died on 15 March 1974 under suspicious circumstances. The official cause of his death was suicide, a claim contested by both his widow and a subsequent official investigation.[43] Moy de Tohá talks about

---

42. In addition, the NO campaign also showed a spot featuring the rock star Sting, who had performed at an Amnesty International–sponsored concert in Mendoza, Argentina, to benefit and bring attention to the human rights groups of Chile and Argentina. Sting had written the song "They Dance Alone" to commemorate the fight of the AFDD. For a discussion of the concert, see AFDD, *Un camino de imágenes*, 95.

43. Ensalaco, *Chile Under Pinochet*, 25.

the suffering she and her family had endured under Pinochet and the lack of justice for her dead husband. The NO campaign also ran an interview with Sofía Prats, the daughter of Carlos Prats, the commander of the Chilean Army under Allende, who along with his wife had been killed by a car bomb in Argentina in 1975. Pinochet was widely believed to have ordered the assassination because Prats posed a threat to his control of the military.[44] Sofía Prats in her interview stresses how Pinochet's government had not investigated this horrendous crime, and she ends her appearance with the statement that "our family, our country needs truth and justice." The ad implicitly asked how Pinochet could provide for the general welfare if he refused to provide real Chilean families with truth and justice.

The final NO broadcast in this group featured an interview with Maria Maluenda, who was the mother of Ignacio Parada, a well-known communist activist. Appearing grave and dignified, she says, "This was our son, before they murdered him," while holding up a picture of Parada.[45] Her interview was the most direct of all the spots dealing with the human rights abuses, and it dramatically brought home to the viewer the pain and suffering of one real Chilean mother over the loss of her child. While Maria Maluenda was also a well-known partisan of the UP, the spot clearly highlighted her identity as a mother. These three women, grieving mothers and wives, each speaking about her particular losses, put a human face on the suffering that resulted from the actions of Pinochet and his government. Their testimonies both explicitly argued that it was Pinochet and his policies that had harmed Chilean families and challenged Pinochet's attempt to cast the opposition as a return to violence, chaos, and scarcity. Instead of the faceless "communists, foreign agitators, and terrorists" continually evoked in government propaganda, Chileans saw on television the actual family members of the victims of government repression. As the NO campaign argued, only by bringing back democracy could Chileans avoid future acts of state violence directed at their families.

Framing the human rights critiques through the testimonies or dances of wives and mothers brought to the fore the familial and emotional effects of these actions, rather than the political and legal condemnations that would likely invoke the ideological differences between the opposition and Pinochet. Those who had been disappeared were ordinary people, sons and daughters, wives and husbands, mothers and fathers, not terrorists. The disappeared left

44. Loveman, *Chile*, 275.
45. Hojman, "YES or NO to Pinochet," 183.

behind family members who claimed the right to speak out against the government and demand justice. The testimonies of members of Chilean families who had suffered stood in direct contrast to the SI campaign's positive images of familial prosperity and harmony. These spots also troubled the narrative of a NO victory meaning societal chaos and violence by showing the present suffering of families that did not know the fate of their loved ones.

The importance of the AFDD in constructing the human rights discourse as a critique against Pinochet can be clearly seen in the following print ad for the NO campaign (fig. 7.10). It features the upper body of a woman, with the black-and-white photo of a disappeared person pinned to her shirt. In not showing her face, the ad presents her as a symbol for the many women who had lost family members. The accompanying text stresses how the woman hopes that he or she returns, a clear reference to the disappeared family member. But the woman also hopes for a return to "the tranquility and the respect for human life" not just for herself, but also for all Chileans. The text continues, "It is up to us to make sure that the disappearances, the outrage, and the insensitivity never return. That never again will our families be the victims of the arbitrariness and terrorism of the state. It is time for change. We are all Chileans, we all have the right to life. No more disappeared."[46] Like the women of the Conjunto Folclórico dancing alone or the personal testimonies featured in the NO franja, the ad draws attention to the hypocrisy of a government that claimed to be the protector of Chilean families when in actuality it victimized Chilean families. The NO campaign drew on critiques based in familial beliefs that had been extensively deployed by societal groups such as the AFDD during its years of struggle against Pinochet. While the heavily censored television news did not often report on the actions of the human rights groups and their charges against the Pinochet government, the print media, including *Solidaridad* and *Apsi,* had regularly featured stories and interviews about the disappearances and reported on the actions of the AFDD and other groups.

The issue of exile was also understood through its impact on families. On 8 September, the third day of the franja, the NO campaign featured a long spot about Chilean exiles living in Sweden. The problem of exile was presented through the eyes of Pablo, whose parents had fled Chile when he was very young. Narrated by both Pablo and his father, the spot explains exile through the pain and confusion of this innocent victim. Pablo had been forced to grow up outside Chile, away from his extended family and country of origin. While

46. *Fortín Mapocho,* 27 September 1988, 5.

Fig. 7.10   "She hopes that he or she returns." (*Fortín Mapocho*, 27 September 1988.)

growing up, he was continually told stories about Chile. Now, at age twelve, he returns to a country that he doesn't know and does not resemble the country of his parents' stories. Pablo describes how he feels like a foreigner even though he is Chilean. Pablo's pain is brought home to the viewers through the image of a closed bathroom door and the sounds of crying. The spot ends by pointing out that thousands of Chilean families had to live in exile, and that they, like Pablo and his family, have experienced both the pain of leaving and the pain of returning.

Although subtle in its indictment of the present government, the spot highlighted the widespread use of political exile by Pinochet and exposed its cruel effects on Chilean families. As with the spots on other human rights abuses, to gain greater sympathy among viewers the discussion of political exile focused not on the politics of the people who were exiled but on the familial ruptures that resulted. Both the family that accompanied them abroad and family that remained in Chile suffered because of the political actions of Pinochet. Exile had divided Chilean families and hurt innocent Chilean children forced to grow up away from their homeland. This division also represented the symbolic division of the Chilean national family that resulted from the military government's policies. Pinochet had decided that those who opposed him were not "Chilean" and therefore sundered them from their homeland, splitting both actual families and the metaphoric national family. The NO campaign exposed the harm of these policies and promised to reunify what had been divided.

THE FAMILY IGNORED

The family was also used to represent the unjust reality of Pinochet's economic and social policies. Social movements protesting Pinochet had framed all sorts of issues—the housing deficit, high rates of mortgage default, high rates of unemployment and subemployment, problems of hunger and addiction—in terms of their effects on Chilean families. Images of Chilean families struggling with the effects of poverty visually contested both Pinochet's claims about the progress of Chile under his rule and the familial imagery of the SI campaign. Some of these images included a Chilean woman, her children, and her mother scrounging through the trash looking for things that could be sold, a family walking through the deserted dirt streets of a shantytown, and a family living in the cramped quarters of a poorly built shack. The NO campaign argued that for the past fifteen years, the military government had shown only its version of Chile—one filled with images of prosperous, happy nuclear families. These pictures, however, did not capture the reality of an increasing number of Chilean families who lived lives of misery and hopelessness. Their reality was not a part of official government propaganda and was often ignored by the military government.

This argument was central to the spots that discussed the increasing levels of poverty. One begins with the image of an impoverished Chilean family crowded around a TV watching a government propaganda commercial, which features its trademark images of happy, prosperous families. In the NO spot, the vision of prosperity being projected on the TV contrasts with the poverty of the "real" family, and the narrator describes a life of poverty for the families in the shantytowns on the edge of Santiago. The images behind the voice change to feature a communal kitchen. One of the women who runs the kitchen talks about how it feeds fifty children lunch and dinner during the week. She worries that the children often go hungry on the weekends because the majority of their fathers are out of work and cannot provide for their families. The spot ends with Dr. Eugenio Tironi, a well-known sociologist, promoting the need to improve the lives of poor Chilean families. He directly relates the high rate of poverty to the high rates of unemployment and the declining buying power of the minimum salary, which had fallen by 40 percent in the last ten years. Dr. Tironi makes clear that while social problems for Chilean families were escalating, the Pinochet government actually decreased social spending for education, health, and housing. The spot seeks to uncover the truth of Chilean families that had been occluded by Pinochet's propaganda. Voting NO, according to this spot, would mean increasing the levels of social spending and more equitably distributing the fruits of Chile's economic growth so that all Chilean families could prosper.

The NO franja also invoked the family to provide a human face for poverty caused by the unequal distribution of social benefits. One spot critiquing Pinochet's housing policies shows the unseen costs of the shining, modern area built in downtown Santiago. In order to build this development, poor families were relocated to even poorer neighborhoods on the outskirts of Santiago. The spot argues that in unfamiliar settings, the families struggle to survive. Instead of the two Chiles created by the military government, the NO spokesperson (again Dr. Tironi) promises that a vote for NO means modernity and development for all. Another spot portrays families living in government-built housing projects located on the outskirts of Santiago. Mothers holding their children explain to the viewer that they have neither electricity nor running water, and that the shantytowns are located far from sources of work. Another features the story of a young, pregnant mother who distributes the extra food supplements she receives from the government for her prenatal care to her other children, since the family does not have enough to eat. The viewer is left with the disturbing picture of hungry children and pregnant women living in poverty.

Finally, the NO campaign also used appeals to familial welfare to persuade Chilean women in particular about the need for change. The basic argument in these spots was that a NO vote would be better for the future of their family and children. This argument was most clearly presented in the propaganda that featured two well-known Chilean women, the writer Maria Cruz-Coke and Carmen Frei, the daughter of former president Eduardo Frei. Both women spoke from the belief that they knew what Chilean women needed and wanted. They presented themselves and all Chilean women through the familial roles of mothers and wives, arguing that Chilean women were most concerned about the welfare of their families. For Cruz-Coke, women's overriding concern was for "security and work for the family." She argued that, like herself, Chilean women and mothers wanted to make sure that their children and grandchildren could grow up in a country free from fear.

According to Carmen Frei, only a victory for NO would bring about this goal. Frei was featured on the second to last day of the franja, which probably reflected both her prestige and the worry that many NO strategists had about the women's vote. The NO campaign feared the possible effects of Pinochet's immense spending to obtain and maintain women's support, and opinion polls that showed that many women—particularly working-class women—were undecided.[47] Carmen Frei begins her spot by introducing herself and establishing her experiences as typifying those of Chilean women. She is married with three children and has dedicated her life to improving the lives of Chilean families. She then reminds the voters that her father had won his presidency with the overwhelming support of Chilean women, and that she understands the frustrations and the desire for change felt by many women. She contrasts her concern for Chilean women and families with the effects of the current government's policies. She attacks Pinochet by saying that "this government has said that it understands the problems of the Chilean family. On the contrary, I think that the regime is causing the disintegration of the Chilean family." She backs up her claim by listing the ways that the family was suffering, including how unemployment strained married couples' relationships and mothers were anguished over the lack of opportunities "for work and for education" available to their children. She empathizes with families who struggle daily to secure dignified housing and health care. She positions the military government as responsible for hate, violence, and the lack of options, and a NO vote as the first step toward a brighter future. According to Frei, "We [Chilean women] are tired of so much hate, so much violence. We want our children

---

47. Baldez, *Why Women Protest*, 171. The polls were accurate in predicting stronger support among women for Pinochet. Forty-seven percent of women voted for SI, while only 40 percent of men did (174).

to have opportunities. Today [our children] feel rejected by the country they belong to. We want to construct a future, a future for all, without deep divisions between Chileans. We want true reconciliation. For us, this is what NO represents. A future for us, for our family, for our children."

In the SI campaign, only Pinochet could protect Chilean families, and it was women—as mothers—who recognized the need for his continued presence. But Frei presented Pinochet as the real threat to the Chilean family, as a hypocrite, as a ruler out of touch with the realities of Chilean families. For her, a NO vote was the only way to provide a peaceful and unified future for the family. In both arguments, the Chilean family was under threat and women had to act as protectors of the family by voting for either SI or NO. The difference was over who actually threatened the family—the present government or the opposition. In her statement, Carmen Frei constructed the family as the ultimate victim of Pinochet's government. But she believed that women, acting from their deep concern for their family and their children, had the opportunity to bring about a better future for their families by supporting the NO vote.

Throughout the campaign, the creators of the NO campaign projected an overall vision of unity and presented the opposition as a viable alternative to Pinochet and the status quo. They needed to combat the government's characterization of the Concertación as a group of bickering politicians unable to govern Chile. The catchy and popular campaign slogan song ("Chile, la alegría ya viene") that was featured in all the NO's nightly franja helped to communicate this unity, as did the visual symbol of the rainbow, which captured the idea of unity through diversity. The NO campaign was particularly dedicated to promoting certain values—democracy, respect for human rights, justice, fairness, liberty, community, and better opportunities for all[48]—and feelings of "happiness, optimism, [and] hope."[49] As the campaign developed, it "established a radical contrast between its message and the daily manipulation of the news," which was still tightly controlled by the government.[50] The NO campaign's propaganda showed Chilean society how many families had suffered, either from human rights abuses committed by the military or from the implementation of its economic and social policies. Additionally, the Concertación employed familial metaphors to try to rebuild a sense of national belonging among a political community that had been divided into "true Chileans" and "enemies" by Pinochet. They turned to the metaphors, images, and symbols

48. Tironi, "Un rito de integración," 12.
49. Hirmas, "La franja," 110.
50. Valdéz, "Comisarios, jerarcas, y creativos," 96.

of the Familial Nation to again imagine Chile as an ideologically pluralistic society in which debate and dissent were respected. They argued that citizens, like members of a family, would disagree and argue; however, this did not mean dissenting members should be thrown out. Instead, mutual respect and tolerance were in order. Thus the NO campaign tried to project images of "reconciliation and social cohesion."[51] To do so, the NO's franja mixed its critiques of Pinochet with spots full of humor and music that reflected the daily lives of Chileans. As the campaign song noted, "without the dictatorship, happiness will come," and the NO campaign urged Chileans to vote for peace, liberty, and dignity, for the freedom to sing without fear.

For both sides, familial welfare was accepted as a criterion by which to judge the military government, and citizens were approached through their familial roles. But for the first time since the military coup, these competing visions of what was best for families could be openly discussed and judged. On 5 October, the Chilean populace voted 54 percent for NO and 43 percent for SI, giving NO a decisive victory. But the strong minority support for Pinochet reflected the strength of his supporters' belief that Pinochet and his government had protected and provided for their families, and that the continuation of Pinochet's rule actually ensured a better future for Chile. Of the people that cast their votes for Pinochet, 49 percent said that they had done so for reasons of order and tranquility, and 38 percent said they supported Pinochet because of the country's positive economic situation. Possibly reflecting changes at the international and national levels, only 16 percent stated that they supported Pinochet because of a commitment to anticommunism.[52] The lingering question over whether Pinochet would accept defeat was answered on 6 October when the government conceded the loss. Pinochet had not wanted to admit defeat and did so only after the three other members of the junta refused to agree to his requests to deploy the army in the streets of Santiago and grant him "extraordinary powers."[53] The Concertación and its supporters celebrated in the streets and for the moment everything seemed possible.

The Concertación in the 1989 Elections

The celebration was short-lived, however, as political elites and activists quickly turned their attention to the congressional and presidential elections triggered

51. Tironi, "Un rito de integración," 13.
52. Varas, "Crisis of Legitimacy," 76.
53. Loveman, *Chile*, 304.

by the NO victory. The time between the plebiscite and these elections, scheduled for December 1989, was filled with political wrangling between the military government and the opposition. Pinochet passed a slew of new laws to protect his political and economic legacy, while the Concertación attempted to soften the most antidemocratic features of the 1980 Constitution and Pinochet's new legislation. As the 14 December elections drew near, members of the Concertación employed "tact and toughness" to set a slate of candidates for each seat in the Chamber and the Senate.[54] As in the NO campaign, the Concertación surprised its critics with its ability to sustain and strengthen the coalition rather than succumbing to partisan bickering over how to divide political power.[55] The choice of Patricio Aylwin, a longtime leader and past president of the Christian Democratic Party, as presidential candidate epitomized the Concertación's emphasis on building unity and promoting societal reconciliation. Aylwin was "a leader whose conciliatory style had won wide respect and whose only notable flaws were a preference for baggy sweaters and a somewhat beatific facial expression."[56]

A unified and resolute Concertación faced a political opposition that had splintered under both the pressure of the loss of the plebiscite and profound differences in ideology. The Chilean right was now dominated by two parties: the National Renewal (Renovación Nacional, RN), led by the well-known conservative leader Sergio Onofre Jarpa, and the Independent Democratic Union (Unión Demócrata Independiente, UDI), a party founded on the idea of a protected democracy under strong executive control and neoliberal economic policies. UDI was led by Jamie Guzmán, the main intellectual force behind the 1980 Constitution. A fierce fight between traditional conservatives, dedicated regime supporters, and the new business elite ended with the nomination of Hernán Büchi, Pinochet's finance minister from 1985 to 1989. The presidential campaign for the right was complicated, however, by the participation of Francisco Javier Errázuriz, who ran a campaign for what he called the "centro-centro" (middle-middle), which he financed with his personal fortune. He promoted traditional conservative thought mixed with a healthy dose of populism designed to appeal especially to the poor.[57]

Given its victory in the plebiscite, the Concertación was heavily favored. In

54. Constable and Valenzuela, *Nation of Enemies*, 314.
55. Ibid., 313–14.
56. Ibid.
57. For descriptions of the 1989 campaign, see Oppenheim, *Politics in Chile*, 192–93; Loveman, *Chile*, 304–5; and Constable and Valenzuela, *Nation of Enemies*, 314–16.

the upcoming elections, it could depend on the campaign infrastructure established in the plebiscite that included a well-organized group of volunteers and local politicians that had worked to both register voters and secure a NO victory, as well as a group of organized and experienced political and media consultants. While Pinochet had been defeated, it was clear that the return to legitimate democratic governance was not a certainty. Pinochet still commanded almost unconditional support from certain sectors, including the military and much of the upper class. Aside from questions of legitimacy, the Concertación also needed a strong showing in order to elect both its presidential candidate as well as enough members to Congress to pass legislation. A top priority was to reform the protected authoritarian enclaves of the 1980 Constitution, such as the lack of civilian control of the military, and to do away with a group of senators that were appointed rather than elected. This task was made more difficult by a slate of electoral laws enacted by Pinochet that tilted the playing field toward the right.[58] In order to begin enacting its reforms, the Concertación needed not just to win a majority, but to win decisively.

Aylwin and the Concertación also saw the upcoming elections as a chance to help heal and reunite the body politic of Chile, a nation that had over the course of the last sixteen years been divided into a "nation of enemies."[59] The upcoming elections offered the possibility of strengthening both democratic practices and the moral legitimacy of democratic values. These values included the importance of human rights and the belief that public debate was the appropriate venue for conflict and contention. The Concertación was also morally committed to acknowledging the human rights abuses committed by the past regime and to addressing the "social debt" in terms of poverty and the dictatorship's lack of social spending. These issues and commitments helped bind together the disparate and sometimes contentious members of the Concertación. But debates over the specifics of balancing the need to pursue human rights abuses, address critical social issues, and also consolidate democratic governance represented important sources of ongoing conflict within the coalition.[60]

The issue of societal reconciliation was a central component of the Concertación's political project, and invocations of the family played a crucial role. Aylwin, in closing the NO campaign, had outlined the future project of the Concertación in the following words: "The victory of the NO will be a triumph of all Chileans . . . because it will be the start of a new era of national reconciliation

58. Loveman, *Chile*, 304.
59. The phrase is taken from the title of Constable and Valenzuela, *Nation of Enemies*.
60. See the discussion in Loveman and Lira, *Las ardientes cenizas*, 487–539.

instead of confrontation. We do not want vanquishers nor vanquished; in the new democracy there will be work for all."[61] Aylwin and the Concertación continued this emphasis on reconciliation in the presidential campaign. Invoking the family to metaphorically describe the national body, the Concertación sought to restore the political activists who had been exiled from Chile. In addition, familial metaphors were crucial in helping to restore the importance of debate and dissent within a democracy.

The first, and perhaps most important, use of the family was in the song and images used in the campaign's television propaganda. As in the NO campaign, the theme song was repeatedly played and easily recognized. On 14 November, the first day of the televised franja, the Concertación led off with their new theme song, "Somos mas" (We are more). The images that accompany the song feature all sorts of Chilean families, including extended families, nuclear families, and nontraditional families (e.g., a mother, daughter, and grandmother). The families are clearly from different geographic areas of Chile. The song ends with a picture of Aylwin smiling, accompanied by his wife and their children and grandchildren.

The use of familial imagery in the theme song is particularly striking and might be interpreted in a number of ways. Certainly, the great diversity of families depicted attempts to reflect the true diversity of Chile. Most viewers were meant to recognize themselves and their families in some of the depictions. In this way, the song attempted to create a feeling of similarity and community. Chileans were told through the theme song that they were all part of the greater national family, and thus they were bound together. This portrayal of Chilean sameness through real and imaginary family ties strengthened the general aim of the Concertación, which was to foster a sense of unity. Aylwin strengthened this vision of connection in the clip featuring his acceptance speech of the presidential nomination for the Concertación. At the end of the speech, he positioned himself as a lover of his family and his patria. Viewers relate to Aylwin through similar feelings of love toward their families and Chile. The spot ends with the promise that Aylwin can be the president of all Chileans. The familial imagery focused on what binds Chileans together, rather than what might divide them, such as political ideology or their view of Pinochet and the past.

Similar themes were also present in the song version of Aylwin's campaign slogan "Gana la gente" (The people win), also featured in the ads. The visual narrative for this song shows Chileans from all walks of life coming together

61. Quoted in ibid., 402.

to build a new home for Chile. The message is that if Chileans will unify and work together, then they can build a good home for their families and all of Chile. The ability of the home to represent the Chilean nation was made explicit in the remarks of Tito Fernández, a well-known folk singer. He stresses the unity of Chile through the metaphor of the home, opening his appearance by stating, "Welcome to our house, the new home we are building together," and ends by saying, "The great Chilean home is our home." The home, a physical place where families live and love together, is evoked metaphorically to strengthen the argument that the similarities between Chileans are more important than the differences.

The family was also employed to symbolically represent the Chilean nation. As Patricio Bañados (the respected journalist and NO spokesman) notes in another spot, the Chilean president "needs to be capable of guaranteeing the unity of the Chilean family," by which he means the metaphoric national family. Aylwin's rhetoric positioned himself as such a president. Indeed, Aylwin refers to Chile as the metaphoric mother of all Chileans in a spot on 6 December. In Aylwin's comments, the politicians are the fathers and the Chilean nation is the mother. The implicit argument being presented is that Aylwin is the inheritor of this tradition. Like previous great presidents, he too will rule wisely and in the best interests of the Chilean family. As the metaphoric father, he will work to build a better future for all Chileans. This paternal imagery was also adapted to appeal to specific groups. For example, a spot designed to appeal particularly to the youth features interviews with young people who had attended a Concertación rally. Talking to the camera, a young man in his car likened having Aylwin as president to having a cool father who still goes out and understands the concern of the youth. Aylwin, therefore, could be both the traditional father by upholding his responsibilities to the national family, as well as the hip father to a new generation of Chileans. His version of the Patriarchal Leader is based on a more consensual and democratic spirit than was Pinochet's. Aylwin would work with Chilean families, and not simply position himself as the seat of all political authority.

Aylwin and the Concertación had made "'reconciliation' the premise of their government," but how does reconciliation work in a coalition in which many groups demand both the truth about past events and justice for the victims and their families? As Brian Loveman and Elizabeth Lira point out, "Reconciliation with truth and justice is not possible without vanquished or accused."[62]

---

62. Loveman and Lira, *Las ardientes cenizas*, 485.

Familial discourses allowed the Concertación to allude to the human rights issue without addressing it directly. In the NO campaign, the human rights spot had featured the women of the Conjunto Folclórico dancing the *cueca sola*. In the presidential campaign, the spot featured a single middle-aged woman dressed in black and white. The image again called to mind the black-and-white pictures of the disappeared. The woman is shown walking alone in the desert under a clear blue sky, her long hair blowing in the breeze. The image manages to convey loneliness and peace, the desolation of the desert contrasting with the hope of the blue sky. The narrator of the spot says, "There are events that can only be spoken about with respect. The Chilean family suffers a very bitter pain. Perhaps for a father, a spouse, a brother, a daughter, a grandson, persons that we will remember forever. Today no one can hide them. In their memory we will salute all the men and women that in those years defended human rights with valor." The script draws on the cultural understanding of the human rights abuses fostered by the public acts and discourses of the AFDD. As mothers/daughters/wives/sisters, AFDD members had refused to keep silent about the disappearance of their family members, rejected the official denials, and demanded the truth. The ad also subtly reminds the viewer of the ongoing discoveries of secret grave sites in the northern areas of Chile. The spot claimed that the new democracy will not "hide" the bodies of the victims of military repression, but instead will work to find and bring to light the abuses of the past regime.

By referencing the pain suffered by the families and lauding their attempts to recover the truth and seek justice, the spot manages to critique the Pinochet government without focusing on the brutal facts and underlying political conflicts of the past. The spot does not say, for example, that the government of Pinochet disappeared a specific number of people; it does not feature scenes of violence against Chileans; it does not discuss the political commitments or actions of the victims. Instead, it focuses on the pain and the struggle of the Chilean families searching for their loved ones, which is a much less confrontational approach to human rights abuses. The viewer can feel sympathy for the woman and admiration for her courage without having to directly confront the truth that the military government detained, disappeared, and killed its own citizens. This more indirect critique fit well with the overall emphasis on the need to decrease feelings of fear, impotence, and uncertainty in the general populace. Immediately following the spot on human rights, the image shifts to an image of an extended family of parents, children, and grandchildren happily posing for a picture as the "Somos mas" theme plays in the background.

The lighter mood reinforced the campaign message that better times are coming for Chilean families. The abuses will be put in the past and all Chileans, as members of a national family, can reconcile with one another.

Conclusion

The December elections reaffirmed Chileans' support for the Concertación. Aylwin won 55 percent of the vote, Büchi 29 percent, and Errázuriz 15 percent. In the congressional elections, candidates for the Concertación won "72 out of the 120 Chamber of Deputies' seats and 22 out of 38 elective senatorial seats."[63] The elation felt by supporters of the Concertación was captured in the festivities surrounding the 11 March presidential inauguration, which culminated in a huge event in the National Stadium on 12 March. During the event, Aylwin acknowledged the human rights abuses committed in the National Stadium, which had served as a makeshift detention center in the months after the coup, by having members of the AFDD perform the *cueca sola*. The majority of the program, however, was dedicated to celebrating the triumph of democracy and the hope that it embodied for Chileans and their families.

As Chilean politics began the transition back to democratic rule, the government's responsibility to provide for Chilean families remained at the forefront of debates around political legitimacy. The importance of familial welfare as a criterion for judging whether a government deserved citizen support was clearly evident in both the SI and the NO campaigns. As in the elections of 1970 and 1973, and the societal mobilizations against Allende and Pinochet, Chileans were asked to judge both the past performance and the future promises of political leaders based on the effects of their policies on the welfare of Chilean families. Pinochet and his advisers emphasized their previous uses of the Familial State and the Patriarchal Leader to convince Chileans of the importance of a SI vote. Pinochet presented himself as a Patriarchal Leader who had both protected and provided for Chilean families. This portrayal was seen in propaganda that featured him as a valiant soldier who had saved Chilean families from communism and other ideologies that threatened traditional values. The SI campaign also focused on how Pinochet had provided for Chile's neediest families. Pinochet consistently argued that the Chilean family had benefited under his rule, by which he meant that his government had fulfilled its duties

---

63. Oppenheim, *Politics in Chile*, 183.

according to the beliefs of the Familial State. His policies had promoted not only order and stability but also better housing for families, good jobs for Chilean men, and women's peace and tranquility within the home. While Pinochet had embraced neoliberal economic policies, it was not the self-reliant individual that played a starring role in his propaganda, but once again the traditional Chilean family. Pinochet relied on familial uses developed over the course of his military dictatorship to justify his continued right to govern Chile.

For the first time since 11 September 1973, however, the opposition could freely confront Pinochet's claims and propose an alternative path. The opposition energetically contested Pinochet's uses of the family and portrayed an alternative vision of both the past and the future. As my analysis reveals, the NO campaign emphasized the myriad ways that Pinochet failed to live up to his promises to Chilean families. In responding to Pinochet's claims that he had provided a safe and secure environment for Chilean families, the opposition portrayed political repression (death, disappearances, and exile) as familial tragedies. The Concertación focused on the damage done to Chilean families as a way to strongly criticize Pinochet and his policies without appearing strident, demagogic, and conflictive. By employing long-standing beliefs about the duties of the Chilean state for familial welfare, the Concertación was able to discuss the issue of Pinochet's use of political violence without bringing up the political divisions and conflicts of the past. To contradict his claims about economic prosperity, modernization, and development, the opposition showed the dire reality of Chilean families living in the poblaciones. In other words, the Concertación directly attacked Pinochet's presentation of himself as a Patriarchal Leader and his government as fulfilling the requirements of the Familial State. In the 1989 elections, the Concertación also turned to invocations of the family to rebuild a sense of national community. It needed to include the political partisans whose "Chileanness" Pinochet had denied. The NO campaign turned to specific familial metaphors for the nation-state to relegitimize the practices and values of democratic governance.

While the SI and NO campaigns were bitterly divided over the question of Pinochet's legitimacy and legacy, their approaches also reflected a continuing consensus around the importance of the family as the foundation of Chilean society, the responsibility of the state to provide for the welfare of Chilean families, and the importance of familial roles in determining the relationships between citizens and the state.

CONCLUSION

The Political Is Personal

Throughout the preceding chapters, I have analyzed how the political is personal. While feminist scholarship has long exposed how people's personal lives are shaped by public, political action, this book illustrates how people's understandings of politics rely in part on their experiences, beliefs, and desires about the family. Our family lives are not simply shaped by politics; often we seek to understand our engagement in politics through familial beliefs. Specific beliefs about the family and its relationship to society often undergird our understandings of the role of the state and how we draw and redraw the imagined boundaries of our community. Familial beliefs influence both how we judge our leaders and governments and how those leaders position themselves as deserving of our support. We also turn to familial beliefs as citizens when we craft strategies to justify our political dissent and create public space for our ideas.

I examined Chilean politics through the familial lens of my four analytical categories: Familial State, Patriarchal Leader, Militant Families, and Familial Nation. These categories helped reveal the multiplicity of uses of the family and their importance to the struggles over political legitimacy that gripped Chile from the election of the socialist president Salvador Allende, through the military dictatorship of Augusto Pinochet, to the return to democracy under the Concertación. The chronological orientation of this study highlights the continuities in the use of the family by ideologically diverse political actors. It shows how no one sector of the political spectrum holds a monopoly on using the family as a political resource. Further, both societal and state actors turned to widely shared familial beliefs in crafting strategies for pursuing political goals. Thus political actors of all political orientations turned to familial ideology in conflicts over the political legitimacy of governments. Similarly, family is a powerful resource in the process of creating social mobilization and justifying dissent, especially in times of political repression. Many of Chile's most bitter political disputes took for granted a societal consensus around key ideals about the family and its relationship to the state.

To conclude, I will briefly speculate on the limitations of the political uses of family. Certainly, part of the political appeal of the family seems to be its malleability. In other words, a range of political actors can adapt the family to fit myriad purposes. Indeed, the family as a symbol or ideal is perhaps more flexible and adaptable than other types of political identities and institutions. But the full range of uses of family is not always equally available to all political actors or for all political goals. In general, it seems that political uses of family are affected by the degree of consensus or controversy over the definition of the ideal family, the historical development of political parties and their ideologies, and the personal characteristics of political actors. Finally, political contexts that limit the extent and scope of other forms of political discourse appear to be associated with increased use of family. Below, I briefly address how these factors constrain and enable the use of family in politics.

Constraining and Facilitating Factors

Creating and maintaining political communities, and justifying political leadership, are two of the most basic problems of politics. In attempting to create political systems that are deemed legitimate by their members, the family has proved particularly useful because it can be used to describe a wide range of political communities. Because familial beliefs continue to shape the everyday understandings of politics, those who engage in politics are often quite skilled in appealing to family for their own political purposes. They often adapt familial metaphors to changing understandings of politics, and likewise, changing ideas about the family can provide new metaphors for politics. Indeed, both recent history and political theory argue that changes in politics and changes in idealized understandings of the family are intertwined. For example, the historian Gordon Schochet notes that in Britain during the eighteenth century the growing dominance of the liberal idea of politics as a contract was accompanied by a shift toward the idea of marriage as a contract. And the political theorist Jacqueline Stevens traces how different forms of political society depend on the creation and regulation of specific forms of idealized families. Thus changes in dominant political beliefs might require changes in familial beliefs, and changes in families might influence changes in political beliefs. My analysis adds weight to a growing body of evidence that the familial and the political are intertwined. Familial metaphors remain a basic part of people's understanding of politics even as broader understandings of both politics and family change.[1]

The fundamental importance of familial beliefs to politics, and the fact that the family is widely used in a variety of countries by a wide range of political actors, does not mean it is without constraint. My analysis of twenty years of Chile's political struggles reveals that many factors can constrain or facilitate the ability of different people to employ familial beliefs. As with any discursive political resource, the extent to which citizens share particular understandings of the family influences its use. In Chile, during the time studied, there was a broad consensus that the state had specific responsibilities and duties toward the family (as opposed to individuals or other societal groups). Familial welfare was considered a public and collective good that the state was obligated to both protect and promote. How well governments or leaders performed those tasks, or might perform them if elected, represented a central criterion for judging their success and legitimacy.

This basic political agreement depended in part on a strong consensus regarding the ideal family type, the specific roles that individuals played in that family, and the duty of the state in promoting this ideal. At the time, the dominant ideal was the traditional, nuclear family, with the father firmly in charge. Whereas those on the Chilean left were more willing to acknowledge and support a greater variety of familial forms, the movement's leaders also strongly promoted a vision of the traditional family. Some revision of this ideal had also been incorporated into the programs of the Christian Democrats. While still upholding the normative power of the family as a married couple with children, Christian Democratic policies sometimes sought to equalize the power between a husband and wife within the family. But these initiatives remained at the margins of these respective parties and the general Chilean society during the time studied. This meant that political actors could rely on consensus around a nuclear family ideal in constructing political coalitions and promoting political projects.[2]

In addition, the ability of the family's welfare to serve as a criterion for judging the legitimacy of leaders and governments is also built on a broader consensus

1. Schochet, *Authoritarian Family*; Stevens, *Reproducing the State*. See also the extensive literature cited in chapter 1.

2. Rosemblatt also documents the importance of idealized ideas of men's and women's roles in the family as a basis for the political coalitions that held together the center-left Popular Front governments in the 1930s and 1940s. See her work in *Gendered Compromises*.

around the responsibility of the state for the family. For example, in the aftermath of the March of the Empty Pots and Pans, both the Christian Democrats and the National Party quickly incorporated the marchers' claims that Allende was antifamily. These claims against Allende (which were influenced by previous anticommunist campaigns) were then used to frame the electoral strategies of these parties in the 1973 congressional elections. This suggests that many members of the Christian Democratic and National parties believed that invoking governmental indifference to familial welfare helped them to create a powerful and persuasive argument against Allende. The use of the same arguments by Pinochet's authoritarian government in its attempts to justify its continued political control adds further weight to the importance of this consensus in shaping the uses of familial beliefs in Chile.

Widespread agreement around an image of the ideal family, or around the fundamental responsibility of the government for protecting the family, does not exist in all societies or at all times. Within the United States, current debates are questioning the belief that the ideal family consists of a married man and woman and their children. The current furor over permitting gays and lesbians to legally marry represents only the latest debate over what family is and should be in the United States.[3] Second wave feminists, especially radical and socialist feminists, previously challenged the traditional ideal by exposing the family as implicated in the unequal and oppressive treatment of women.[4] The debate around what constitutes an ideal family in the United States has limited the usefulness of this factor as a criterion for judging the government. For example, the Republican Party claimed to be protecting the family when it proposed the Federal Marriage Amendment in 2004, which proposed a constitutional amendment that defined marriage as between a man and a woman. This claim, however, did not draw on a generalized, societal consensus around either the definition of the family or the role of the government in protecting families. Instead, it revealed the lack of consensus around these issues. This failed legislation promoted conflict between those who believed strongly in the traditional family and those who wanted to recognize and support alternative families. Unlike Chilean political actors, who during the time studied

3. There is a growing literature in the United States that examines how state regulation of marriage has shaped the racial and gendered limitations of citizenship. See, for example, Yamin, "Nuptial Nation," and Novkov, *Racial Union*.

4. For the attack by radical feminism, see Firestone, *Dialectic of Sex*; for socialist feminism, see Jaggar, *Feminist Politics and Human Nature*, and Mitchell, *Woman's Estate*. For a critique of the way liberal theorists continue to ignore questions of equality, fairness, and justice within the family, see Okin, *Justice, Gender, and the Family*.

could easily invoke an ideal family, groups and individuals in the United States often must first work to build a consensus about the family and its proper relationship to the state. Further, the ongoing debates over the ideal family in the United States have created long-standing political conflicts and cleavages that might limit how the family can be used politically. Familial beliefs in this situation might serve to unite provisional coalitions or specific groups, but familial welfare seems less likely to be a basic criterion by which to judge the success of governments and political leaders.

A second set of factors that constrain the malleability of the family is the intersection between family and political ideology. Specifically, the past uses of the family by political parties, and the position of the family in the political thought of those parties, strongly influence the current beliefs about the relationship between family and politics. The Chilean case illustrates a broader distinction between the political left and the political right and how these groups can use the family. While both groups often claim to be acting to protect and to provide for families, they understand the meaning of "protect and provide" differently. In general, the political left focuses more on the material and economic security of the family. The political right, on the other hand, tends to frame its policies in terms of physical security and moral dangers. This characterization captures a general trend in the uses of the family. Because of these general tendencies, the left tends to invoke ideals of family and familial welfare to frame its commitment to promoting better material conditions for people. The right, on the other hand, is much more likely to talk about the need to protect the family from danger. For the right, the danger to the family is most often a physical threat (e.g., war, terrorism, crime) or an ideological threat (e.g., communism, feminism, secularism) to the "natural" family. But these general tendencies do not mean that the left does not also have deeply felt moral and ethical beliefs about the ideal form of family, or that the right abjures more material claims about familial welfare.

The historical development of familial discourses not only shapes their uses by political parties and activists but also influences public expectations of the government. For example, Chileans expected Allende and his socialist government to improve the material situation of working-class Chilean families. Allende's opponents incorporated this expectation into their criticisms, blaming the economic crisis on the president as a way of questioning his political legitimacy. The potential effectiveness of this attack can be seen in the response that it prompted. Allende argued that his economic policies were designed to provide materially for the family. The familial framing of the economic crisis promoted by the anti-Allende opposition, however, proved hard to combat. Even today, for many Chileans it is the lines and lack of consumer goods that symbolize the problems and failures of the Allende government.

The same dynamic can be seen in the attacks against Pinochet. Drawing on the political traditions of the right in Chile, Pinochet argued that his government was protecting the family from both physical and moral threats. While Pinochet also cast himself as providing for the material needs of Chilean families, his political position on the right meant that issues of physical safety and protection from moral threat would be given more weight in judging his success. This might be part of the explanation for why his government survived two economic crises that severely affected the material welfare of many Chilean families and fueled public protests. My analysis also highlights the centrality of the familial critiques of the opposition in convincing many Chileans that their families were no longer endangered either physically or spiritually by communism. Instead, after the activism of the AFDD and other opposition groups, it was Pinochet and his government that came to be seen by many Chileans as the greatest threat to their families' safety and welfare.

Thus the position of a government or leader on the ideological spectrum interacts with how the family serves as a criterion to judge success. While political ideology does not prohibit actors from going against the dominant tendencies of their political ideology (e.g., the right making arguments about material welfare and the left making claims to protect physical security), it appears that those claims are initially less persuasive. My analysis suggests that political actors need to invest more resources into promoting those claims that seem to contradict the general perception of their political positions. For example, in the United States, the Democratic Party might have a harder time selling itself as the protector of the moral values of families because it is going against current general perceptions about its focus on families' material welfare.[5]

The personal characteristics of political actors emerge as a third set of factors that can either enable or constrain the uses of family. In particular, presenting oneself as a good father or mother, or as pro-family, is easier for a candidate whose personal characteristics can be portrayed in terms that match current ideals. For male political actors, an individual's personal qualities and how closely they conform to societal ideals about what a father should look like can either facilitate or limit that person's invocations of paternal images. In

5. Lakoff in *Moral Politics* examines the difference between the Republican and Democratic parties in terms of the model types of families and familial authority in conservative and liberal ideology.

247247247

the Chilean case, most male political leaders, especially presidential candidates, attempted to present themselves as good fathers. Their personal characteristics were cast in ways that upheld the paternal ideal. Male candidates, if they could, highlighted their marriages, their children, and their ability to be good providers. Tomic, the Christian Democratic candidate in 1970, for example, explicitly used his status as the head of a traditional Catholic family to present himself as pro-family and capable of exercising power in a responsible manner.

Given the connections between paternal authority and political authority, those male political figures whose personal lives do not conform to this ideal are susceptible to critiques based on their (lack of) familial position. Personal characteristics, such as being too old, too young, divorced, single, homosexual, or childless, can become obstacles in presenting oneself as a leader in times and places where this ideal is strong. In the Chilean case, Jorge Alessandri was criticized as being antifamily because of his advanced age and his status as a bachelor. The most virulent attacks also implied that having never married meant that he was homosexual. These characteristics were presented as proof that Alessandri would not be able to be a good president because he could not "father" the Chilean nation. Male Chilean presidential candidates continue to use their familial roles in presenting arguments about their personal qualities and leadership potential.

A fourth factor is political stability. In times of political crisis, the Chilean case suggests that familial beliefs about politics often become an especially important resource for political actors. The impact of turbulent times can be seen across the different uses of the family. During a crisis, judging a government in terms of the family and its welfare seems to increase in potency. Thus, when anti-Allende women's groups framed their attacks against Allende in terms of threats to their families, they provided a clear reason for people's feelings of unease and worry (Allende's failure as president) and a clear response (protesting Allende and supporting the military). Pinochet invoked these feelings of fear and insecurity to justify his control of political power. Throughout his seventeen years in power, he attempted to maintain a sense of fear and crisis by constantly portraying the family as threatened and presenting himself as its protector. The brilliance of the NO campaign was to attack this sense of danger and threat by presenting a return to democracy as a return to happiness, security, and prosperity.

Finally, the family seems to play a greater role in political mobilization when access to the political realm is limited. Perhaps family-based claims and familial identities are harder for governments to control or repress because of the assumed fundamental role that families play in society. Groups and individuals who have traditionally been excluded from politics, and groups and individuals who live under repressive political systems, rely more heavily on the family as a tool to mobilize and to create a public space from which to criticize the state. The importance of family in defining politics helps explain the long-standing influence of maternalism in women's political participation. Because of the traditional exclusion of women from the political realm and the close connection between women and family, women are often uniquely positioned to use familial beliefs as a resource in mobilization.[6] This is true under more open, democratic systems and in the controlled spaces of authoritarian states. Women may have played such an important role in the Latin American democratization movements of the 1970s and 1980s because of their political experience in using their familial identities as mothers, grandmothers, wives, and sisters to mobilize and to justify their political actions. But if men's access to the political realm is denied or limited, they can also draw on the importance of their identities as fathers to justify political activism. During Pinochet's military dictatorship, poor men increasingly focused on their familial identities and roles in mobilizing and justifying political action. The family and familial identities might represent the last line of defense for citizen participation in the most repressive political regimes.

Closing Reflections: Chile Today

My interest in the political uses of family was initially sparked by the rival protests that followed Pinochet's return to Chile from London. On 10 December 2006, surrounded by his family, Augusto Pinochet died in Santiago's military hospital at the age of ninety-one. His death reignited the ongoing divisions within Chilean society over how to understand its political past. Perhaps for the last time, rival groups of protestors took to the streets to give voice and witness to competing versions of Pinochet's legacy. Four thousand mourners attended Pinochet's funeral with military honors at the Military Academy in Santiago, and perhaps as many as sixty thousand Chileans filed by his coffin to pay their last respects. In downtown Santiago, close to the Moneda, thousands more Chileans gathered to celebrate Pinochet's death, turning the streets

---

6. The importance of women's identities as mothers in Latin American women's movements is widely noted in the literature. See, for example, Alvarez, *Engendering Democracy*, and Bayard de Volo, *Mothers of Heroes*.

into a carnivalesque atmosphere with music and dancing.[7] Again, Pinochetistas and members of the AFDD presented their opposing views of Pinochet. He remained for many either their family's savior or destroyer. Pinochet's death failed to heal the divisions and conflicts that his rule engendered.

While the events surrounding Pinochet's death illustrate important continuities between the Chile of my study and the Chile of today, there have also been important changes. The election of Michelle Bachelet, Chile's first woman president, is perhaps the best symbol of these changes.[8] Bachelet embodies the antithesis of the traditional understandings of family that were dominant during the period of my study. The president from 2006 to 2010, she is known for joking about her "political sins." First, she is a single mother of three children. Her two oldest children are from her marriage to her former husband, and the youngest is from a long-term relationship with a man she never married. Second, she is agnostic. Third, she is a socialist. But these personal characteristics were not an impediment to her popularity. It is widely recognized that her candidacy and election were propelled by her support among Chileans who viewed her as approachable, down-to-earth, and concerned and knowledgeable about the struggles of everyday citizens.[9]

Bachelet's dramatic personal history also captured both the tragedies of Chile's past and the promise of its democratic future. She is the daughter of an air force general who died in military custody after being tortured. As a result of their own political involvements, Bachelet and her mother were also detained, held in a secret detention center, and tortured. But in 2004 Bachelet was appointed as Chile's first female defense minister, and she pledged to promote societal reconciliation and institutional change within the military. As a presidential candidate, her commitment to gender equality and deepening citizen participation also appealed to those who felt that the process of democratic consolidation had excluded many societal groups that had fought against the military dictatorship. Bachelet certainly does not fit within the Patriarchal Leader category, which was developed to analyze the uses of family

7. Daniel Schweimler, "Pinochet Funeral Reopens Wounds," BBC News, 13 December 2006, http://news.bbc.co.uk/2/hi/americas/6174673.stm; and "Tributes Paid at Pinochet Funeral," BBC News, 12 December 2006, http://news.bbc.co.uk/2/hi/americas/6171387.stm.

8. Many of these initial reflections are from research I conducted in Chile during Bachelet's election in December 2005 and January 2006, and from additional trips in November 2007, June, July, November, and December 2008, December 2009, and January 2010.

9. For recent analysis of Michelle Bachelet's election and presidency, see Thomas, "Michelle Bachelet's *Liderazgo Femenino*"; Thomas and Adams, "Breaking the Final Glass Ceiling"; Franceschet and Thomas, "Renegotiating Political Leadership"; and Ríos Tobar, "Feminist Politics in Contemporary Chile."

by the male political leaders that dominated Chilean politics in the 1970s, 1980s, and 1990s.

Does her presidency, however, mean that familial beliefs are becoming irrelevant to Chilean politics? While the particulars of some of the uses analyzed in this study have certainly changed, connections between the familial and the political still shape Chilean politics. For example, with more women entering politics, new definitions of political leadership less connected to men and masculinity are being advanced. Bachelet explicitly promoted a new definition of political leadership that could incorporate her more open, warm, and participatory leadership style, which she labeled "liderazgo femenino" (feminine leadership). Bachelet also strategically positioned her status as a single mother as a way to reach out to everyday Chilean women, many of whom are also single mothers and heads of households. Chileans saw Bachelet as a "woman's woman" who was pursuing the most masculine job in Chile not by taking on the traditional masculine leadership style, but by bringing in her own style of feminine leadership. She promoted her approach to leadership as a challenge to the usual style of Chilean politics and as a response to the anti-democratic and elitist politics of the parties in both the center-left Concertación and the rightist Alliance for Chile. As she promised after her victory, "We are going to have a new style in national politics, with more dialogue and participation."[10] In crafting a new feminine style of political leadership, however, Bachelet eschewed the most traditional definitions of motherhood; instead, she drew heavily on ideas associated with the women's movement in Chile that argued for the interconnected nature of democracy in both familial and political relations.

Michelle Bachelet's treatment of motherhood reveals that Chilean women now have a greater variety of cultural resources available to them and more flexibility in creating claims about their leadership strengths. The significance of Bachelet's campaign in this regard can perhaps be best seen through a brief comparison with Violeta Chamorro, president of Nicaragua from 1990 to 1997.[11] In pursuing her candidacy, Chamorro projected a political identity centered around her martyred husband, Pedro Joaquín Chamorro, and her family and

10. Quoted in Lydia Polgreen and Larry Rohter, "Where Political Clout Demands a Maternal Touch," *New York Times*, 22 January 2006, http://www.nytimes.com/2006/01/22/weekinreview/22roht .html?_r=1.

11. After Chamorro, Mireya Moscoso in Panama was elected in 1999. Since Bachelet's election, three other women have been elected president: Cristina Fernández de Kirchner in Argentina (2007), Laura Chinchilla in Costa Rica (2010), and Dilma Rousseff in Brazil (2010).

argued that it was her identity as a traditional Nicaraguan mother (apolitical, self-abnegating, subservient to the wishes of her husband) that provided her with the needed political skills. Her political leadership was based on the symbols of "wife, widow, mother, and Virgin,"[12] and she claimed that as a mother she had the leadership skills necessary to "reconcile the Nicaraguan people, torn by more than a decade of war."[13] Bachelet, on the other hand, used her experiences as a single mother and head of household not to justify her interests in politics, but as a basis for her greater understanding of the ordinary experiences of Chileans. Bachelet's personal history and political development would have made it impossible to embrace the traditional gender and family ideology used by Chamorro. Bachelet was not the wife, widow, or mother of any important male figures, and her political career was built on her activity first within the opposition to Pinochet and then through political appointment within the Concertación governments. Without the changes in the relationship between family and politics brought about by women's activism, Bachelet might not have had the cultural resources necessary to craft her version of "feminine leadership."

While Bachelet's successful challenge to traditional definitions of political leadership reflects an important change, it does not mean that the link between men's paternal roles and political leadership has disappeared. Bachelet's male opponents on the right, Sebastián Piñera and Joaquín Lavín, both crafted political appeals based on the connection between being a good father and being a good president. Following in the footsteps of political leaders such as Tomic and Allende, both Lavín and Piñera promoted their roles and responsibilities as fathers of traditional Chilean families to present their qualifications to govern. Their campaigns were replete with images of both candidates surrounded by their families (Lavín has nine children, Piñera four). Their wives appeared in television propaganda and campaign appearances testifying to their husbands' abilities to fulfill their duties as both fathers and presidents. The presentation of their families also allowed Lavín and Piñera to draw a stark contrast between their positions as fathers of traditional Chilean families and Bachelet's own status as a divorced single mother. Their presidential campaigns demonstrated the continuing importance of the category of Patriarchal Leader in election contests.

Whereas Bachelet challenged the definition of political leaders captured by

12. Kampwirth, "Mother of the Nicaraguans," 72.
13. Ibid., 67.

the category of Patriarchal Leader and sought to broaden definitions of political leadership, her government embraced the basic premise of the Familial State: that those in power had a fundamental duty to protect and provide for Chilean families. Even the political influence of free-market capitalism, with its emphasis on personal responsibility and individualism, has not managed to supplant beliefs that political leaders have responsibilities toward Chilean families. As president, Bachelet pursued a strong social welfare agenda. She continued the policies of the Concertación that have succeeded in reducing poverty levels in Chile from 38 percent in 1990, when the coalition took over from Pinochet, to 13.6 percent in 2006.[14] But Bachelet has more directly focused on women's positions, especially as mothers, and has pursued state policies that seek to increase gender equality. For example, in her far-reaching reform of Chile's pension system, not only did she increase the minimum pension to provide a more dignified life for the elderly, but she also targeted women's pensions by implementing a credit for mothers as a way to recognize their contributions to their family and society. Another priority for Bachelet's government was to provide access to child care to the poorest two-fifths of Chile's households in order both to allow poor women to work and to provide quality care to poor children. To fulfill this promise, Bachelet's government built an additional 3,500 child-care centers. Thus two signature reforms of her presidency have been policies aimed at safeguarding the welfare of Chilean mothers by protecting them from poverty in old age and by giving younger mothers more options. More generally, Bachelet has directed resources to programs aimed at providing more employment options for poor women and improving housing standards in the poblaciones.

While Bachelet's government experienced its fair share of challenges and failures, Bachelet left office on 11 March 2010 with 84 percent of Chileans approving the job she had done, and an incredible 96 percent seeing her as well liked and 92 percent seeing her as respected.[15] Her historically high approval ratings reflected her deft handling of the 2008 financial crisis. In the first two years of her presidency, Bachelet had faced intense criticism, often from within her own coalition, for her refusal to spend a growing reserve fund generated mostly by the high price of Chilean copper produced by the country's state-owned copper mines. Bachelet insisted on saving the money in case of future

14. Ríos Tobar, "Feminist Politics," 25.

15. Adimark, "Evaluación de gobierno post terromoto," March 2010, Santiago, Chile, http://www
.adimark.cl/es/estudios/index.asp?id=6 (accessed September 18, 2010). Adimark is a commercial polling company in Santiago.

need, which materialized in the form of the 2008 world recession sparked by the economic crisis in the United States. To mitigate its effects, Bachelet funneled state resources into social welfare programs designed to shield Chile's poor and working class from the effects of unemployment. Even a massive 8.8 earthquake two weeks before she was to leave office and a controversial government response did not diminish her popularity. Perhaps even more telling, all of the candidates in the 2010 presidential race, even the pro–free market billionaire Sebastian Piñera, who eventually won, pledged not only to support Bachelet's "red de protección social" (network of social protection) that had benefited poor families but also to extend many of her most popular programs to the middle class (Chilean law barred Bachelet from seeking a second consecutive term, a race she would have easily won).

Bachelet's election and presidency demonstrate that familial welfare continues to serve as one criterion for judging individual leaders and their governments. The ideal of the Familial State still influences politics even if neoliberal thought has helped change the role of the state in economic policies by increasing the societal emphasis on individualism and personal responsibility. It is clear that in her policies Bachelet embraced an inclusive understanding of Chilean families. Rather than idealizing the traditional nuclear family, many of her programs argued that all forms of families are valuable and should be recognized and supported by the state. Symbolically, Bachelet became the mother that governed and led the Chilean national family. As she argued in her presidential campaign, "Every family is a kingdom, in which the father rules but the mother governs."[16] Bachelet rejected the traditional authoritarian decision-making style associated with the idealized family and its associated, closed political society. Instead, a governing mother represents a new ideal that embraces multiple forms of families and can serve as a base for a more democratic and participatory model.

Bachelet's election thus demonstrates how particular uses of familial beliefs can change, while the importance of the generalized understandings captured by the categories in my analytical framework remains. Certainly, one of the greatest differences between Bachelet's Chile of 2006–10 and the period I studied is a greater willingness to challenge the idealization of the traditional family. For many Chileans, the traditional, patriarchal, nuclear family remains the ideal, but growing numbers are more willing to criticize the problems associated

---

16. This phrase is taken from one of the television spots produced by Bachelet for the second round of the presidential election. I conducted fieldwork in Chile during the campaign in December 2005 and January 2006.

with this ideal and to embrace alternative forms of family life, particularly the historically rooted and widespread family form that comprises women and their children. Both changes and continuities in familial beliefs, therefore, continue to be used as resources within Chilean politics.

My foray into the intersection of family and politics reveals the power of familial beliefs in defining and shaping politics and political struggles. Familial metaphors are used to imagine and maintain political communities, and familial welfare is often seen as a basic social good and thus the responsibility of the state. Familial welfare can be used as a criterion to judge the success or failure of a particular government or leader. Individual citizens continue to be drawn into politics because of their familial identities and to use these identities to claim the right to speak and participate. Familial beliefs, therefore, must be included in our attempts to understand politics. We need to study the ways in which the political is also familial.

BIBLIOGRAPHY

GOVERNMENT DOCUMENTS

Cámara de Diputados de Chile. *Sesiones regulares y irregulares.* Sesión 22, 2 March 1971.
———. *Sesiones regulares y irregulares.* Sesión 22a, 3 March 1971.
———. *Sesiones regulares y irregulares.* Sesión 36a, 11 May 1971.
———. *Sesiones regulares y irregulares.* Sesión 21, 30 November 1971.
———. *Sesiones regulares y irregulares.* Sesión 23a, 1 December 1971.
———. *Sesiones regulares y irregulares.* Sesión 24a, 3 December 1971.
CEMA-Chile. *Edición aniversario de fundación de CEMA-Chile.* Santiago: Editorial Antartica, 1987.
Gobierno de Chile, Junta Militar. *República de Chile, 1974: Primer año de la reconstrucción nacional.* Santiago: Editorial Nacional Gabriela Mistral, 1974.
Pinochet Ugarte, Augusto (Gen.). *Mensaje presidencial 11 septiembre 1973–11 septiembre 1974.* Santiago, 1974.
Secretaría Nacional de la Mujer. *Diez años de voluntariado, 1973–1983.* Santiago, 1983.
———. *Objectivos y programas.* Santiago, 1978.
———. *Valores patrios y valores familiares.* Santiago, 1982.
Senado de Chile. *Diario de sesiones del Senado.* Sesión 37a, Anexo de Documentos, Santiago, 1971.
———. *Diario de sesiones del Senado.* Sesión 74a, 7 September 1972.

NEWSPAPERS AND MAGAZINES

Amiga (Santiago)
Apsi (Santiago)
El Clarín (Santiago)
Fortín Mapocho (Santiago)
Mensaje (Santiago)
El Mercurio (Santiago)
La Nación (Santiago)
Qué Pasa (Santiago)
El Siglo (Santiago)
Solidaridad (Santiago)
La Tercera de la Hora (Santiago)
La Tribuna (Santiago)
Las Ultimas Notícias (Santiago)

PAMPHLETS, CONFERENCE PROCEEDINGS, AND MISCELLANEOUS PRIMARY SOURCES

AFDD. *Asi lo hemos vivido.* Fundación de Documentación y Archivo de la Vicaría de la Solidaridad, Santiago, 1983.

———. *Un camino de imágenes: 20 años de historia de la Agrupación de Familiares de Detenidos Desaparecidos de Chile.* Santiago: AFDD, 1987.

AFDD de Región V. *Report.* Fundación de Documentación y Archivo de la Vicaría de la Solidaridad, Santiago, n.d.

Campaña por el SI. *¿Por dónde ir?* Chile, n.d.

Comando nacional por el NO. *En base a informes de verificación diaria de publicidad en TV.* Santiago, 1988.

MOMUPO. *Inquietudes de la lucha . . .* May 1985.

———. *Inquietudes de la lucha . . .* July 1985.

———. *Inquietudes de la lucha . . .* August 1985.

———. *Inquietudes de la lucha . . .* September 1985.

Vicaría de la Solidaridad. *1985 Encuentro: Pobladores por una vida digna.* Fundación de Documentación y Archivo de la Vicaría de la Solidaridad, Santiago, 1985.

———. "Seminario de la familia popular y la vivienda." Working Paper, Fundación de Documentación y Archivo de la Vicaría de la Solidaridad, Santiago, January 1980.

SECONDARY SOURCES

Adams, Julia. *The Familial State: Ruling Families and Merchant Capitalism in Early Modern Europe.* Ithaca: Cornell University Press, 2005.

Agosín, Marjorie. *Scraps of Life: Chilean "Arpilleras": Chilean Women and the Pinochet Dictatorship.* Translated by Cola Franzen. Trenton, N.J.: Red Sea Press, 1989.

———. *Tapestries of Hope, Threads of Love: The "Arpillera" Movement in Chile, 1974–1994.* Albuquerque: University of New Mexico Press, 1996.

Allende, Isabel. *The House of the Spirits.* Translated by Magda Bogin. New York: Knopf, 1985.

Alvarez, Sonia E. *Engendering Democracy in Brazil: Women's Movements in Transition Politics.* Princeton: Princeton University Press, 1990.

Alvarez, Sonia E., Evelyn Dagnino, and Arturo Escobar, eds. *Cultures of Politics/Politics of Cultures: Re-Visioning Latin American Social Movements.* Boulder, Colo.: Westview Press, 1998.

Anderson, Benedict. *Imagined Communities: Reflections on the Origin and Spread of Nationalism.* New York: Verso, 1991.

Appelbaum, Nancy, Anne Macpherson, and Karin Rosemblatt, eds. *Race and Nation in Modern Latin America.* Chapel Hill: University of North Carolina Press, 2003.

Arriagada, Genaro. *Pinochet: The Politics of Power.* Translated by Nancy Morris, with the assistance of Vincent Ercolano and Kristen A. Whitney. Boston: Unwin Hyman, 1988.

Aylwin, Patricio Azócar. *El reencuentro de los demócratas: Del golpe al triunfo del NO.* Santiago: Ediciones B., 1998.

Baldez, Lisa. "Nonpartisanship as a Political Strategy: Women Left, Right, and Center in Chile." In *Radical Women in Latin America: Left and Right,* edited by Victoria

González and Karen Kampwirth, 273–98. University Park: Pennsylvania State University Press, 2001.

———. *Why Women Protest: Women's Movements in Chile.* Cambridge: Cambridge University Press, 2002.

Bayard de Volo, Lorraine. *Mothers of Heroes and Martyrs: Gender Identity Politics in Nicaragua, 1979–1999.* Baltimore: Johns Hopkins University Press, 2001.

Beck, Paul A., and M. Kent Jennings. "Family Traditions, Political Periods, and the Development of Partisan Orientations." *Journal of Politics* 53 (August 1991): 742–63.

Beetham, David. *The Legitimation of Power.* London: Macmillan, 1991.

Blofield, Merike. *The Politics of Moral Sin: Abortion and Divorce in Spain, Chile, and Argentina.* New York: Routledge, 2006.

Blofield, Merike, and Liesl Haas. "Defining a Democracy: Reforming the Laws on Women's Rights in Chile, 1990–2002." *Latin American Politics and Society* 47 (Autumn 2005): 35–68.

Brown, Wendy. "Finding the Man in the State." *Feminist Studies* 18 (Spring 1992): 7–34.

Bunster, Ximena. "Watch Out for the Little Nazi Man That All of Us Have Inside." *Women's Studies International Forum* 11 (Summer 1988): 485–91.

La campaña del no: Vista por sus creadores. Santiago: Ediciones Melquiades, 1989.

Chambers, Sarah C. *From Subjects to Citizens: Honor, Gender, and Politics in Arequipa, Peru, 1780–1854.* University Park: Pennsylvania State University Press, 1999.

Chambers, Sarah C., and Lisa Norling. "Choosing to Be a Subject: Loyalist Women in the Revolutionary Atlantic World." *Journal of Women's History* 20 (Spring 2008): 39–62.

Chaney, Elsa. "The Mobilization of Women in Allende's Chile." In *Women in Politics,* edited by Jane S. Jaquette, 267–80. New York: John Wiley, 1974.

———. *Supermadre: Women in Politics in Latin America.* Austin: University of Texas Press, 1979.

Chuchryk, Patricia. "Feminist Anti-authoritarian Politics: The Role of Women's Organizations in the Chilean Transition to Democracy." In *The Women's Movement in Latin America: Feminism and the Transition to Democracy,* edited by Jane S. Jaquette, 149–84. Boston: Unwin Hyman, 1989.

———. "From Dictatorship to Democracy in Chile: The Women's Movement in Chile." In *The Women's Movement in Latin America: Participation and Democracy,* edited by Jane S. Jaquette, 65–109. 2nd ed. Boulder, Colo.: Westview Press, 1994.

Clarke, James W. "Family Structure and Political Socialization Among Urban Black Children." *American Journal of Political Science* 17 (May 1973): 302–15.

Cockcroft, James, ed. *Salvador Allende Reader: Chile's Voice of Democracy.* New York: Ocean Press, 2000.

Collier, Simon. *Ideas and Politics of Chilean Independence, 1808–1833.* Cambridge: Cambridge University Press, 1967.

Collier, Simon, and William F. Sater. *A History of Chile, 1808–1994.* Cambridge: Cambridge University Press, 1996.

Collins, Joseph, and John Lear. *Chile's Free-Market Miracle: A Second Look.* Oakland: Food First, 1995.

Connell, R. W. "Political Socialization in the American Family: The Evidence Reexamined." *Public Opinion Quarterly* 36 (Autumn 1972): 323–33.

Constable, Pamela, and Arturo Valenzuela. *A Nation of Enemies: Chile Under Pinochet.* New York: Norton, 1991.

Crawford, Neta. "Understanding Discourse: A Method of Ethical Argument Analysis." *Qualitative Methods: Newsletter of the American Political Science Association Organized Section on Qualitative Methods* 2 (Spring 2004): 22–25.

Crummett, María de los Angeles. "El Poder Femenino: The Mobilization of Women Against Socialism in Chile." *Latin American Perspectives* 4 (Autumn 1977): 103–13.

Dandavati, Annie G. *The Women's Movement and the Transition to Democracy in Chile*. New York: Peter Lang, 1996.

Delsing, Riet. "La familia: El poder del discurso." In *Discurso, género, y poder: Discursos públicos: Chile, 1978–1993*, edited by Olga Grau, Riet Delsing, Eugenia Brito, and Alejandra Farías, 105–26. Santiago: LOM-ARCIS, 1997.

———. "Sobre mitos y relatos: El discurso chileno sobre la familia." In *Discurso, género, y poder: Discursos públicos: Chile, 1978–1993*, edited by Olga Grau, Riet Delsing, Eugenia Brito, and Alejandra Farías, 149–64. Santiago: LOM-ARCIS, 1997.

Di Palma, Giuseppe. *To Craft Democracies: An Essay on Democratic Transitions*. Berkeley: University of California Press, 1990.

Dore, Elizabeth, ed. *Gender Politics in Latin America: Debates in Theory and Practice*. New York: Monthly Review Press, 1997.

———. "The Holy Family: Imagined Households in Latin American History." In *Gender Politics in Latin America: Debates in Theory and Practice*, edited by Elizabeth Dore, 101–17. New York: Monthly Review Press, 1997.

———. "One Step Forward, Two Steps Back: Gender and the State in the Long Nineteenth Century." In *Hidden Histories of Gender and the State in Latin America*, edited by Elizabeth Dore and Maxine Molyneux, 3–32. Durham: Duke University Press, 2000.

———. "Property, Households, and Public Regulation of Domestic Life: Diriomo, Nicaragua." In *Hidden Histories of Gender and the State in Latin America*, edited by Elizabeth Dore and Maxine Molyneux, 147–71. Durham: Duke University Press, 2000.

Dore, Elizabeth, and Maxine Molyneux, eds. *Hidden Histories of Gender and the State in Latin America*. Durham: Duke University Press, 2000.

———. "Preface." In *Hidden Histories of Gender and the State in Latin America*, edited by Elizabeth Dore and Maxine Molyneux, ix–xiv. Durham: Duke University Press, 2000.

Drake, Paul W. *Socialism and Populism in Chile, 1932–1952*. Urbana: University of Illinois Press, 1978.

Drake, Paul W., and Ivan Jakšić, eds. *The Struggle for Democracy in Chile*. Lincoln: University of Nebraska Press, 1995.

Earle, Rebecca. "Rape and the Anxious Republic: Revolutionary Columbia, 1810–1830." In *Hidden Histories of Gender and the State in Latin America*, edited by Elizabeth Dore and Maxine Molyneux, 127–46. Durham: Duke University Press, 2000.

Elshtain, Jean Bethke. "Preface: Political Theory Rediscovers the Family." In *The Family in Political Thought*, edited by Jean Bethke Elshtain, 1–7. Amherst: University of Massachusetts Press, 1982.

Ensalaco, Mark. *Chile Under Pinochet: Recovering the Truth*. Philadelphia: University of Pennsylvania Press, 2000.

Fabj, Valeria. "Motherhood as Political Voice: The Rhetoric of the Mothers of Plaza de Mayo." *Communication Studies* 44 (Spring 1993): 1–18.

Farrell, Joseph P. *The National Unified School in Allende's Chile: The Role of Education in the Destruction of a Revolution*. Vancouver: University of British Columbia Press, 1986.

Felstiner, Mary Lowenthal. "Family Metaphors: The Language of an Independence Revolution." *Comparative Studies in Society and History* 25 (January 1983): 154–80.

———. "Kinship Politics in the Chilean Independence Movement." *Hispanic American Historical Review* 56 (February 1976): 58–80.

Firestone, Shulamith. *The Dialectic of Sex: The Case for Feminist Revolution*. New York: William Morrow, 1970.

Fischer, Kathleen B. *Political Ideology and Educational Reform in Chile, 1964–1976*. Los Angeles: UCLA Latin American Center, 1979.

Fliegelman, Jay. *Prodigals and Pilgrims: The American Revolution Against Patriarchal Authority, 1750–1800*. Cambridge: Cambridge University Press, 1982.

Franceschet, Susan. *Women and Politics in Chile*. Boulder, Colo.: Lynne Rienner, 2005.

Franceschet, Susan, and Gwynn Thomas. "Renegotiating Political Leadership: Bachelet's Rise to the Chilean Presidency." In *Cracking the Highest Glass Ceiling: A Global Comparison of Women's Campaigns for Executive Office*, edited by Rainbow Murray, 177–97. Santa Barbara, Calif.: Praeger, 2010.

Friedman, Elisabeth J. *Unfinished Transitions: Women and the Gendered Development of Democracy in Venezuela, 1936–1996*. University Park: Pennsylvania State University Press, 2000.

Frohman, Alicia, and Teresa Valdés. "Democracy in the Country and in the Home: The Women's Movement in Chile." Working Paper, Serie Estudios Sociales, FLACSO, Santiago, 1993.

Garreton, Manuel A. "Human Rights in Democratization Processes." In *Constructing Democracy: Human Rights, Citizenship, and Society in Lain America*, edited by Elizabeth Jelin and Eric Hershberg, 39–56. Boulder, Colo.: Westview Press, 1996.

Gaviola, Edda, Eliana Largo, and Sandra Palestro. *Una historia necesaria: Mujeres en Chile, 1973–1990*. Santiago: Aki and Aora, 1994.

Gill, Rosalind. "Discourse Analysis." In *Qualitative Researching with Text, Image, and Sound: A Practical Handbook*, edited by Martin W. Bauer and George Gaskell, 172–90. Thousand Oaks, Calif.: Sage, 2000.

Glaser, William A. "The Family and Voting Turnout." *Public Opinion Quarterly* 23 (Winter 1959–60): 563–70.

Gordon, Linda. *Pitied but Not Entitled: Single Mothers and the History of Welfare, 1890–1935*. New York: Free Press, 1994.

Grau, Olga, Riet Delsing, Eugenia Brito, and Alejandra Farías, eds. *Discurso, género, y poder: Discursos públicos: Chile, 1978–1993*. Santiago: LOM-ARCIS, 1997.

Guy, Donna J. "Parents Before the Tribunals: The Legal Construction of Patriarchy in Argentina." In *Hidden Histories of Gender and the State in Latin America*, edited by Elizabeth Dore and Maxine Molyneux, 172–93. Durham: Duke University Press, 2000.

Haney, Lynne, and Lisa Pollard. "Introduction: In a Family Way." In *Families of a New World: Gender, Politics, and State Development in a Global Context*, edited by Lisa Pollard and Lynne Haney, 1–14. New York: Routledge, 2003.

Hardy, Clarisa. *Organizarse para vivir: Pobreza urbana y organización popular*. Santiago: Programa de Economía del Trabajo, 1987.

Hardy, Cynthia, Bill Harley, and Nelson Phillips. "Discourse Analysis and Content Analysis:

Two Solitudes." *Qualitative Methods: Newsletter of the American Political Science Association Organized Section on Qualitative Methods* 2 (Spring 2004): 19–22.

Hill Collins, Patricia. "It's All in the Family: Intersections of Gender, Race, and Nation." *Hypatia* 13 (Summer 1998): 62–83.

Hirmas, María Eugenia. "La franja: Entre la alegría y el miedo." In *La política en pantalla*, edited by Diego Portales et al., 107–55. Santiago: ILET/CESOC, 1989.

Hite, Katherine. *When the Romance Ended: Leaders of the Chilean Left, 1968–1998*. New York: Columbia University Press, 2000.

Hojman, David E. "YES or NO to Pinochet: Television in the 1988 Chilean Plebiscite." *Studies in Latin American Popular Culture* 11 (1992): 171–94.

Hopf, Ted. "Discourse and Content Analysis: Some Fundamental Incompatibilities." *Qualitative Methods: Newsletter of the American Political Science Association Organized Section on Qualitative Methods* 2 (Spring 2004): 31–33.

Htun, Mala. *Sex and the State: Abortion, Divorce, and the Family Under Latin American Dictatorships and Democracies*. New York: Cambridge University Press, 2003.

Huneeus, Carlos. *The Pinochet Regime*. Translated by Lake Sagaris. Boulder, Colo.: Lynne Rienner, 2007.

Hunt, Lynn. *The Family Romance of the French Revolution*. Berkeley: University of California Press, 1993.

Hutchison, Elizabeth Quay. *Labors Appropriate to Their Sex: Gender, Labor, and Politics in Urban Chile, 1900–1930*. Durham: Duke University Press, 2001.

Jaggar, Alison. *Feminist Politics and Human Nature*. Lanham, Md.: Rowman and Littlefield, 1988.

Jaquette, Jane S., ed. *The Women's Movement in Latin America: Feminism and the Transition to Democracy*. Boston: Unwin Hyman, 1989.

———, ed. *The Women's Movement in Latin America: Participation and Democracy*. 2nd ed. Boulder, Colo.: Westview Press, 1994.

Jelin, Elizabeth, and Eric Hershberg, eds. *Constructing Democracy: Human Rights, Citizenship, and Society in Latin America*. Boulder, Colo.: Westview Press, 1996.

Jetter, Alexis, Annelise Orleck, and Diana Taylor, eds. *The Politics of Motherhood: Activist Voices from Left to Right*. Hanover: University Press of New England, 1997.

Joseph, Gilbert M., ed. *Reclaiming the Political in Latin American History: Essays from the North*. Durham: Duke University Press, 2001.

Joseph, Gilbert M., and Daniel Nugent, eds. *Everyday Forms of State Formation: Revolution and the Negotiation of Rule in Modern Mexico*. Durham: Duke University Press, 1994.

Kampwirth, Karen. "The Mother of the Nicaraguans: Doña Violeta and the UNO's Gender Agenda." *Latin American Perspectives* 23 (Winter 1996): 67–86.

Kann, Mark E. *The Gendering of American Politics: Founding Mothers, Founding Fathers, and Political Patriarchy*. Westport, Conn.: Praeger, 1999.

Kaplan, Caren, Norma Alarcón, and Minoo Moallem, eds. *Between Woman and Nation: Nationalisms, Transnational Feminisms, and the State*. Durham: Duke University Press, 1999.

Karl, Terry Lynn. "Dilemmas of Democratization in Latin America." *Comparative Politics* 23 (October 1990): 1–21.

Karl, Terry Lynn, and Philippe C. Schmitter. "Modes of Transition in Southern and Eastern Europe and South and Central America." *International Social Science Journal* 128 (May 1991): 269–84.

Kirkwood, Julieta. *Ser política en Chile: Las feministas y los partidos.* Santiago: FLACSO, 1986.
Klubock, Thomas Miller. *Contested Communities: Class, Gender, and Politics in Chile's El Teniente Copper Mine, 1904–1951.* Durham: Duke University Press, 1998.
Kornbluh, Felicia. "The New Literature on Gender and the Welfare State: The U.S. Case." *Feminist Studies* 22 (Spring 1996): 171–97.
Koven, Seth, and Sonya Michel, eds. *Mothers of a New World: Maternalist Politics and the Origins of the Welfare State.* New York: Routledge, 1993.
Kuznesof, Elizabeth, and Robert Oppenheimer. "The Family and Society in Nineteenth-Century Latin America: A Historiographical Introduction." *Journal of Family History* 10 (Fall 1985): 215–34.
Laffey, Mark, and Jutta Weldes. "Methodological Reflections on Discourse Analysis." *Qualitative Methods: Newsletter of the American Political Science Association Organized Section on Qualitative Methods* 2 (Spring 2004): 28–30.
Lakoff, George. *Moral Politics: What Conservatives Know That Liberals Don't.* Chicago: University of Chicago Press, 1996.
Landes, Joan B. *Women and the Public Sphere in the Age of the French Revolution.* Ithaca: Cornell University Press, 1988.
Lavrin, Asunción. *Women, Feminism, and Social Change in Argentina, Chile, and Uruguay, 1890–1940.* Lincoln: University of Nebraska Press, 1995.
Linz, Juan J., and Alfred Stepan, eds. *The Breakdown of Democratic Regimes.* Baltimore: Johns Hopkins University Press, 1978.
Lira, Luis Felipe. "Aspectos sociológicos y demográficos de la familia en Chile." In *Chile: Mujer y sociedad,* edited by Paz Covarrubias and Rolando Franco, 367–98. Santiago: UNICEF, 1978.
Lister, Ruth. *Citizenship: Feminist Perspectives.* New York: New York University Press, 1997.
Locke, John. *Two Treatises of Government.* Edited by Peter Laslett. Cambridge: Cambridge University Press, 1967.
Lomnitz, Larissa, and Ana Melnick. *Chile's Political Culture and Parties: An Anthropological Explanation.* Notre Dame: University of Notre Dame Press, 2000.
Loveman, Brian. *Chile: The Legacy of Hispanic Capitalism.* 3rd ed. New York: Oxford University Press, 2001.
———. *For la Patria: Politics and the Armed Forces in Latin America.* Wilmington, Del.: SR Books, 1999.
———. *Struggle in the Countryside: Politics and Rural Labor in Chile, 1919–1973.* Bloomington: Indiana University Press, 1976.
Loveman, Brian, and Elizabeth Lira. *Las ardientes cenizas del olvido: Vía chilena de reconciliación política, 1932–1994.* Santiago: LOM Ediciones, 2000.
Lowden, Pamela. *Moral Opposition to Authoritarian Rule in Chile, 1973–1990.* New York: St. Martin's Press, 1996.
Mallon, Florencia E. "*Barbudos,* Warriors, and *Rotos:* The MIR, Masculinity, and Power in the Chilean Agrarian Reform, 1965–74." In *Changing Men and Masculinity in Latin America,* edited by Matthew C. Guttman, 179–215. Durham: Duke University Press, 2003.
———. *Peasant and Nation: The Making of Postcolonial Mexico and Peru.* Berkeley: University of California Press, 1995.
Mattelart, Armand, and Michèle Mattelart. *La mujer chilena en una nueva sociedad: Un estudio exploratorio acerca de la situación e imagen de la mujer en Chile.* Santiago: Editorial del Pacífico, 1968.

Mattelart, Michele. "Chile: The Feminine Version of the Coup d'Etat." In *Sex and Class in Latin America: Women's Perspectives on Politics, Economics, and the Family in the Third World*, edited by June Nash and Helen Icken Safa, 279–301. New York: J. F. Bergin, 1980.

McClintock, Anne. *Imperial Leather: Race, Gender, and Sexuality in the Colonial Contest.* New York: Routledge, 1995.

Mitchell, Juliet. *Woman's Estate.* New York: Vintage, 1973.

Molyneux, Maxine. "Mobilization Without Emancipation: Women's Interests and the State in Nicaragua." *Feminist Studies* 11, no. 2 (1985): 227–54.

————. "Twentieth-Century State Formations in Latin America." In *Hidden Histories of Gender and the State in Latin America*, edited by Elizabeth Dore and Maxine Molyneux, 33–84. Durham: Duke University Press, 2000.

Montecino, Sonia. *Madres y Huachos: Alegorías del mestizaje chileno.* Santiago: Editorial Sudamericana, 1996.

Mooney, Jadwiga E. Pieper. *The Politics of Motherhood: Maternity and Women's Rights in Twentieth-Century Chile.* Pittsburgh: University of Pittsburgh Press, 2009.

Morandé, María Correa. *La guerra de las mujeres.* Santiago: Editorial Universidad Técnica del Estado, 1974.

Morse, Richard M. "Toward a Theory of Spanish American Government." *Journal of the History of Ideas* 15 (January 1954): 71–93.

Munck, Gerardo L., and Carol Skalnik Leff. "Modes of Transition and Democratization: South America and Eastern Europe in Comparative Perspective." *Comparative Politics* 29 (April 1997): 343–62.

Munizaga, Giselle. *El discurso público de Pinochet.* Buenos Aires: CESOC-CENECA, 1983.

Nash, June, and Helen Icken Safa, eds. *Sex and Class in Latin America: Women's Perspectives on Politics, Economics, and the Family in the Third World.* New York: J. F. Bergin, 1980.

Nicholson, Linda J. *Gender and History: The Limits of Social Theory in the Age of Family.* New York: Columbia University Press, 1986.

Novkov, Julie. *Racial Union: Law, Intimacy, and the White State in Alabama, 1865–1954.* Ann Arbor: University of Michigan Press, 2008.

O'Donnell, Guillermo, and Philippe C. Schmitter. *Transitions from Authoritarian Rule: Tentative Conclusions About Uncertain Democracies.* Baltimore: Johns Hopkins University Press, 1986.

O'Donnell, Guillermo, Philippe C. Schmitter, and Laurence Whitehead, eds. *Transitions from Authoritarian Rule: Prospects for Democracy.* Baltimore: Johns Hopkins University Press, 1986.

Okin, Susan Moller. *Justice, Gender, and the Family.* New York: Basic Books, 1989.

Oppenheim, Lois Hecht. *Politics in Chile: Democracy, Authoritarianism, and the Search for Development.* Boulder, Colo.: Westview Press, 1999.

Orloff, Ann Shola. "Markets Not States? The Weakness of State Social Provisions for Breadwinning Men in the United States." In *Families of a New World: Gender, Politics, and State Development in a Global Context*, edited by Lynn Haney and Lisa Pollard, 217–44. New York: Routledge, 2003.

Oxhorn, Philip. *Organizing Civil Society: The Popular Sectors and the Struggle for Democracy in Chile.* University Park: Pennsylvania State University Press, 1995.

Paley, Julia. *Marketing Democracy: Power and Social Movements in Post-dictatorship Chile.* Berkeley: University of California Press, 2001.

Pateman, Carole. *The Disorder of Women: Democracy, Feminism, and Political Theory*. Stanford: Stanford University Press, 1989.

———. *The Sexual Contract*. Stanford: Stanford University Press, 1988.

Pateman, Carole, and Elisabeth Grosz, eds. *Feminist Challenges: Social and Political Theory*. Boston: Northeastern University Press, 1986.

Pinochet, Augusto. *Política, politiquería, y demagogia*. Santiago: Editorial Renacimiento, 1983.

Power, Margaret. *Right-Wing Women in Chile: Feminine Power and the Struggle Against Allende, 1964–1973*. University Park: Pennsylvania State University Press, 2002.

Przeworski, Adam. "Some Problems in the Study of the Transition to Democracy." In *Transitions from Authoritarian Rule: Prospects for Democracy*, edited by Guillermo O'Donnell, Philippe Schmitter, and Laurence Whitehead, 47–63. Baltimore: Johns Hopkins University Press, 1986.

Puryear, Jeffrey M. *Thinking Politics: Intellectuals and Democracy in Chile, 1973–1988*. Baltimore: Johns Hopkins University Press, 1994.

Radcliffe, Sarah A., and Sallie Westwood, eds. *"ViVa": Women and Popular Protest in Latin America*. New York: Routledge, 1993.

Remmer, Karen L. *Military Rule in Latin America*. Boston: Unwin Hyman, 1989.

Richards, Patricia. *"Pobladoras," "Indígenas," and the State: Conflicts over Women's Rights in Chile*. New Brunswick: Rutgers University Press, 2004.

Ríos Tobar, Marcela. "Feminist Politics in Contemporary Chile: From the Democratic Transition to Bachelet." In *Feminist Agendas and Democracy in Latin America*, edited by Jane S. Jaquette, 21–44. Durham: Duke University Press, 2009.

Rosemblatt, Karin Alejandra. "Domesticating Men: State Building and Class Compromise in Popular-Front Chile." In *Hidden Histories of Gender and the State in Latin America*, edited by Elizabeth Dore and Maxine Molyneux, 262–90. Durham: Duke University Press, 2000.

———. *Gendered Compromises: Political Cultures and the State in Chile, 1920–1950*. Chapel Hill: University of North Carolina Press, 2000.

———. "What We Can Reclaim of the Old Values of the Past: Sexual Morality and Politics in Twentieth-Century Chile." *Comparative Studies in Society and History* 43 (January 2001): 149–80.

Salazar, Gabriel, and Julio Pinto. *Historia contemporánea de Chile*. Vol. 1, *Estado, legitimidad, ciudadanía*. Santiago: LOM Ediciones, 1999.

Schatzberg, Michael G. *Political Legitimacy in Middle Africa: Father, Family, Food*. Bloomington: Indiana University Press, 2001.

Schild, Verónica. "New Subjects of Rights? Women's Movements and the Construction of Citizenship in 'New Democracies.'" In *Cultures of Politics/Politics of Cultures: Re-Visioning Latin American Social Movements*, edited by Sonia E. Alvarez, Evelyn Dagnino, and Arturo Escobar, 93–117. Boulder, Colo.: Westview Press, 1998.

Schirmer, Jennifer. "The Seeking of Truth and the Gendering of Consciousness: The CoMadres of El Salvador and the CONAVIGUA Widows of Guatemala." In *"ViVa": Women and Popular Protest in Latin America*, edited by Sarah A. Radcliffe and Sallie Westwood, 30–64. New York: Routledge, 1993.

Schneider, Cathy Lisa. *Shantytown Protest in Pinochet's Chile*. Philadelphia: Temple University Press, 1995.

Schochet, Gordon J. *The Authoritarian Family and Political Attitudes in Seventeenth-Century England: Patriarchalism in Political Thought*. New Brunswick, N.J.: Transaction Books, 1988.

Scott, Joan Wallach. "Gender: A Useful Category of Historical Analysis." *American Historical Review* 91 (December 1986): 1053–75.

Shanley, Mary Lyndon. "Marriage Contract and Social Contract in Seventeenth-Century English Political Thought." In *The Family in Political Thought*, edited by Jean Bethke Elshtain, 80–95. Amherst: University of Massachusetts Press, 1982.

Shayne, Julie D. *The Revolution Question: Feminisms in El Salvador, Chile, and Cuba*. New Brunswick: Rutgers University Press, 2004.

Sigmund, Paul E. *The Overthrow of Allende and the Politics of Chile, 1964–1976*. Pittsburgh: University of Pittsburgh Press, 1977.

Skocpol, Theda. *Protecting Soldiers and Mothers: The Political Origins of Social Policy in the United States*. Cambridge: Harvard University Press, 1992.

Smith, Brian H. *The Church and Politics in Chile: Challenges to Modern Catholicism*. Princeton: Princeton University Press, 1982.

Stallings, Barbara. *Class Conflict and Economic Development in Chile, 1958–1973*. Stanford: Stanford University Press, 1978.

Stallings, Barbara, and Andy Zimbalist. "The Political Economy of the Unidad Popular." *Latin American Perspectives* 2 (Spring 1975): 69–88.

Steinmetz, George. "Introduction: Culture and the State." In *State/Culture: State Formation After the Cultural Turn*, edited by George Steinmetz, 1–49. Ithaca: Cornell University Press, 1999.

Stern, Steve J. *Battling for Hearts and Minds: Memory Struggle in Pinochet's Chile, 1973–1988*. Durham: Duke University Press, 2006.

———. *Remembering Pinochet's Chile: On the Eve of London, 1998*. Durham: Duke University Press, 2004.

———. *The Secret History of Gender: Women, Men, and Power in Late Colonial Mexico*. Chapel Hill: University of North Carolina Press, 1995.

Stevens, Jacqueline. *Reproducing the State*. Princeton: Princeton University Press, 1999.

Strach, Patricia. *All in the Family: The Private Roots of American Public Policy*. Stanford: Stanford University Press, 2007.

Strauss, Anselm L., and Juliet Corbin. *Basics of Qualitative Research: Grounded Theory Procedures and Techniques*. Thousand Oaks, Calif.: Sage, 1990.

Taylor, Diana. *Disappearing Acts: Spectacles of Gender and Nationalism in Argentina's "Dirty War."* Durham: Duke University Press, 1997.

———. "Making a Spectacle: The Mothers of the Plaza de Mayo." In *The Politics of Motherhood: Activist Voices from Left to Right*, edited by Alexis Jetter, Annelise Orleck, and Diana Taylor, 182–97. Hanover: University Press of New England, 1997.

Thomas, Gwynn. "Michelle Bachelet's *Liderazgo Femenino* (Feminine Leadership): Gender and Redefining Political Leadership in Chile's 2005 Presidential Campaign." *International Feminist Journal of Politics* 13 (March 2011): 63–82.

———. "The Ties That Bind: The Familial Roots of Political Legitimacy." In *Feminists Contest Politics and Philosophy*, edited by Lisa N. Gurley, Claudia Leeb, and Anna Aloisia Moser, 155–74. New York: P.I.E.–Peter Lang, 2005.

Thomas, Gwynn, and Melinda Adams. "Breaking the Final Glass Ceiling: The Influence of Gender in the Elections of Ellen Johnson-Sirleaf and Michelle Bachelet." *Journal of Women, Politics, and Policy* 31 (April 2010): 105–31.

Tinsman, Heidi. *Partners in Conflict: The Politics of Gender, Sexuality, and Labor in the Chilean Agrarian Reform, 1950–1973*. Durham: Duke University Press, 2002.

Tironi, Eugenio. "Un rito de integración." In *La campaña del NO: Vista por sus creadores*, 11–15. Santiago: Ediciones Melquiades, 1989.

Valdés, Teresa, and Marisa Weinstein. *Mujeres que sueñan: Las organizaciones de pobladoras en Chile, 1973–1989*. Santiago: FLACSO, 1989.

Valdéz, Juan Gabriel. "Comisarios, jerarcas, y creativos." In *La campaña del NO: Vista por sus creadores*, 95–101. Santiago: Ediciones Melquiades, 1989.

Valenzuela, Arturo. *The Breakdown of Democratic Regimes: Chile*. Baltimore: Johns Hopkins University Press, 1978.

———. "The Military in Power: The Consolidation of One-Man Rule." In *The Struggle For Democracy in Chile, 1982–1990*, edited by Paul W. Drake and Ivan Jakšić, 21–72. Lincoln: University of Nebraska Press, 1995.

Valenzuela, María Elena. *La mujer en el Chile militar: Todas ibamos a ser reínas*. Santiago: Ediciones Chile América-CESOC-ACHIP, 1987.

Valenzuela, María Elena, and María Teresa Marshall. *La mujer y el gobierno militar*. Santiago: FLACSO-ACHIP, 1986.

Valenzuela, Samuel J., and Arturo Valenzuela. *Military Rule in Chile: Dictatorship and Oppositions*. Baltimore: Johns Hopkins University Press, 1986.

Varas, Augusto. "The Crisis of Legitimacy of Military Rule in the 1980s." In *The Struggle for Democracy in Chile, 1982–1990*, edited by Paul W. Drake and Ivan Jakšić, 73–97. Lincoln: University of Nebraska Press, 1995.

Verdery, Katherine. "From Parent-State to Family Patriarchs: Gender and Nation in Contemporary Eastern Europe." *East European Politics and Societies* 8 (Spring 1990): 225–55.

Yamin, Priscilla. "Nuptial Nation: Marriage and the Politics of Civic Membership in the United States." Ph.D. diss., New School for Social Research, 2005.

Yuval-Davis, Nira. *Gender and Nation*. Thousand Oaks, Calif.: Sage, 1997.

INDEX

abortion and birth control, 79–80, 199
Acción Mujeres de Chile, 62, 64, 68, 71, 72
Adams, Julia, 16 n. 27
AFDD (Agrupación de Familiares de
  Detenidos Desaparecidos), 1, 172–81, 224,
  226, 237, 238
Agosín, Marjorie, 177
agricultural reforms, 43, 60, 61, 93, 94, 165
Agrupación de Familiares de Detenidos
  Desaparecidos. *See* AFDD
Alessandri, Jorge
  1958 presidential run of, 59, 63
  1970 presidential run (*see also under* anti-
    communist scare campaigns): attacks by
    opponents during, 62, 72–73, 84, 88–89,
    247; family beliefs in, 62, 63–64, 65–68;
    mothers, portrayal as protector of, and
    65–66; platform for, 61; social class and,
    71, 74, 88–89; vote tally for, 90
Alessandri, Silvia, 99, 102
"Alessangre," 73
Allende, Salvador
  1958 presidential run of, 59, 63
  1964 presidential run of, 60, 63, 71–72, 90
  1970 presidential run of: appeals to women
    in, 63, 85–87; family beliefs in, 62–63,
    84–90; platform for, 60–61, 132
  agricultural reform under, 43 n. 46, 61 n. 8,
    93, 94
  as champion of working class, 84, 89–90, 129
  class conflict and, 7–8, 71, 74, 97–98, 107, 132–33
  confirmation as president of, 92–93
  early achievements as president of, 93–94
  economic crisis under, 105–6, 111, 113–20,
    245–46
  elite opposition to, 61 n. 8, 111
  fall of, explanations for 7–8, 245–46
  family beliefs and the political legitimacy of
    (*see also under* Familial Nation; Familial
    State; Militant Families; Patriarchal

Leader): analytical categories and, 14,
  16–18; methods of examination of, 23–24;
  during 1970 presidential election, 63,
  84–90; during 1973 congressional election,
  111–31, 244, 245; during presidency, 91–92,
  95, 97–98, 104–5, 110, 136–37
governance by executive order and, 94
housing programs of, 155, 182–83, 187 n. 49
as ladies' man, 6 n. 5
March of the Empty Pots and Pans, UP
  response after, and, 106–11
military coup against, pressure for, 131,
  134–36, 142–44
Ministry of the Family proposal of, 29,
  50–51, 52, 53
Mothers' Centers (CEMA-Chile) and, 149
political attacks on, 68–71, 244 (*see also*
  anticommunist scare campaigns)
as protector of families, 84, 89
reforms of: economic, 93, 94, 106; educational, 131–35
United States actions against, 72 n. 28, 111
  (*see also* CIA)
on women, 49
women's rights and roles and, 49, 86–87,
  109–110 n. 66
Alvarez, Sonia, 17 n. 28
Amiga, 146, 152, 155–57
analytical framework for familial beliefs, 12–19
anticommunist scare campaigns, 65 n. 16
  of 1964, 71–72
  of 1970, 62, 64, 68–72
  of 1973, 113, 120 (*see also* CODE)
  and March of the Empty Pots and Pans, 98
antifascist anti-Alessandri campaigns, 72–73
Apsi, 178, 189–90, 191, 192, 226
Aylwin, Patricio, 233, 234–36

Bachelet, Michelle, 28, 249–53
Badiola, Sergio, 147

www.ingramcontent.com/pod-product-compliance
Lightning Source LLC
Chambersburg PA
CBHW021854020426
42334CB00013B/326